Building powerful and robust websites with Drupal 6

Build your own professional blog, forum, portal or community website with Drupal 6

David Mercer

PUBLISHING

BIRMINGHAM - MUMBAI

Building powerful and robust websites with Drupal 6

First published: March 2008

Production Reference: 1190308

Published by Packt Publishing Ltd.
32 Lincoln Road
Olton
Birmingham, B27 6PA, UK.

ISBN 978-1-847192-97-4

www.packtpub.com

Cover Image by Vinayak Chittar (vinayak.chittar@gmail.com)

Credits

Author

David Mercer

Reviewer

Larry Garfield

Development Editor

Rashmi Phadnis

Technical Editors

Usha Iyer

Ajay Shanker

Editorial Team Leader

Mithil Kulkarni

Project Manager

Abhijeet Deobhakta

Project Coordinator

Abhijeet Deobhakta

Indexer

Hemangini Bari

Proofreader

Cathy Cumberlidge

Chris Smith

Production Coordinator

Shantanu Zagade

Cover Work

Shantanu Zagade

About the Author

David Mercer was born in August 1976 in Harare, Zimbabwe. Having always had a strong interest in science, he came into regular contact with computers at university where he graduated cum laude with majors in applied math and math (although he minored in computer science).

As a programmer and professional writer who has been writing both code and books for about nine years; he has worked on a number of well known titles, in various capacities, on a wide variety of topics. His books have sold tens of thousands of copies and have been translated into over six different languages to date.

David finds that the challenges arising from the dichotomous relationship between the science (and art) of software programming and the art (and science) of writing is what keeps his interest in producing books piqued. He will no doubt continue to write professionally in the future.

David balances his time between programming, reviewing, writing, and contributing to interesting Web-based projects such as RankTracer and LinkDoozer. When he isn't working (which isn't that often) he enjoys playing guitar (generally on stage and unrehearsed) and getting involved in outdoor activities ranging from touch rugby and golf to water skiing and snowboarding.

Visit www.ranktracer.com or find him on www.linkdoozer.com where he is generally lurking.

It is necessary to first thank my girlfriend, Bronagh. Without her gentle yet persistent encouragement this may well have turned into a Drupal 10 title. The editorial team (and Louay) at Packt, along with Larry Garfield who did a sterling review job, put in many long hours and I thank them for their efforts too. In addition, my ever supportive family were always at hand to provide a change of pace and scenery that enabled me to work with greater effort throughout.

Finally, I would like to thank my readers. The success of the first edition of this book has made it possible (and necessary) to sit down and write this book. I hope it does its job well.

About the Reviewer

Larry Garfield holds both a bachelors and masters degree in Computer Science from DePaul University, where he was a co-founder of the school's Linux Users Group. He has been writing PHP since 1999 and is a Zend Certified Engineer. He has been active in the Drupal community for over two years, working on the Drupal core, various contributed modules, and user support, and was recently named as a member of the Drupal Association Board of Directors. In mid-2007 he founded and co-organized the GoPHP5 Project to help the PHP community fully transition to modern PHP 5 environments.

Larry is currently a programmer and technical architect for Palantir.net, a Drupal-based website consulting firm in Chicago, USA that works primarily with higher education and cultural institutions such as museums. Prior to that, he freelanced for Chicago-area businesses and political campaigns. Larry also worked for three years as an IT journalist covering handhelds and mobile phones.

I'd like to extend my sincere thanks to the entire Drupal community. Even after more than two years, I am still in awe of how strong, supportive, and vibrant this community continues to be. It is a privilege to be a part of it. I'd also like to thank my colleagues at Palantir.net for putting up with my continual Drupal evangelism.

Table of Contents

Preface

The Internet is arguably one of the most profound achievements in human history. It has become so pervasive in our lives that we hardly even notice it—except when it happens to be unavailable! It's one of those things that make you sit back and wonder how people got along without it in the *old days*. Without the ability to surf the Internet to order groceries, do our banking, book flights and make travel arrangements, meet friends, meet partners, download music and videos, study, run businesses, trade shares, run campaigns, express views, share ideas, learn about other people… where would we be?

Fundamentally, in a world of so many people, where the sheer vastness of our societies is a hindrance to communication, the Internet has stepped up to the plate and brought everyone that little bit closer together. Utilizing a stunning array of technologies, spread out over the entire globe, the Internet has simply dropped the barriers of time and geographical distance to turn the entire world into a local community center.

Lately, the all-encompassing focus of commerce on the Internet has begun to shift. Millions upon millions of people are waking up to the possibility of sharing their lives and experiences with others through the medium of blogs and social media. Others simply want an online presence to show off their work, art, or music. Still others have important causes and need the Internet to disseminate information or provide a meeting point for like-minded people. Whatever the demands, the Internet has to find a way to efficiently meet these needs or face being superseded by something else in the future.

What the Internet needs is something that makes it easy for people to do whatever it is they want without having to pour intellectual resources into understanding the technologies on which the Internet is based. What the Internet has got is precisely this—Drupal!

Drupal is what you need to use to build anything from a static homepage, to a fully-fledged, customizable, and interactive website in several languages, with tens of thousands of users all over the world. Assuming you fall somewhere between these two extremes, this book is what you need to guide you on your way.

Building powerful and robust websites with Drupal 6 will help cut down your learning time by providing precisely the information you need when you need it. It will help to reduce the trial and error associated with learning Drupal and provide practical, methodical and efficient processes and content to help you become a knowledgeable and competent website creator and administrator.

What This Book Covers

Chapter 1 introduces you to the world of Drupal and looks at where Drupal comes from, where it's going, and what it can offer you. Because it is important to understand the nature of the tasks that lie ahead, it also discusses how to plan and build your website. Finally, we scrutinize the Drupal community and learn how to make the most of Drupal as an organized, living entity and not just a piece of software.

Chapter 2 deals with how to get everything you need up and running on a development machine and also briefly looks at how all the requisite technologies gel together to produce your working Drupal site. Once everything is up and running, and after looking over some of the more common installation problems, the chapter presents a short tour of Drupal in order to give you an idea of what to expect.

Chapter 3 sees us adding functionality to the newly created site. The focus of this chapter is really on modules and how they can be added and enabled, and also how to obtain modules that are not part of the standard distribution. This chapter ends off with a discussion on how to control blocks and menus.

Chapter 4 looks at the most general settings that all Drupal administrators need to contend with. Everything from determining your site's name to dealing with the cache or file system settings gets treated here before we look at more focused and complex issues in the chapters to come.

Chapter 5 concerns itself with the topic of access control. Drupal has a sophisticated role-based access control system that is fundamentally important for controlling how users access your site. This chapter will give you the information required to implement proper access controls.

Chapter 6 gets to the heart of the matter by beginning the book's coverage on content. Working with content, what content types are available, administering content, and even a discourse on some of the more common content-related modules serve as a basis for moving to more advanced content-related matters that follow in the next chapter.

Chapter 7 gives you the edge when it comes to creating engaging and dynamic content. While this chapter doesn't require you to be an expert in HTML, PHP, and CSS, it does introduce you to the basics and shows how, with a little knowledge, extremely powerful and professional custom content can be created.

Chapter 8 gives you a run down of how attractive interfaces are created in Drupal through the use of themes. As well as discussing briefly some of the considerations that must be taken into account when planning your website and ends off by looking at how to make important modifications to your chosen theme.

Chapter 9 really adds the icing on the cake by looking at a host of more advanced topics. From implementing openID functionality, to working with Actions and Triggers or providing enhanced language support, all the way through to building dynamic content using jQuery and Javascript, you will find something to enhance your website and add that something special.

Chapter 10 takes a pragmatic look at the types of tasks you will need to be proficient in to successfully run and maintain a Drupal site. Whether it's setting up cron jobs or making backups of your database, everything you need to do throughout the course of running your newly created website will be covered here.

Appendix A deals with the all-important topic of deployment. Because all major work should be done on a copy of your website on a development machine, this appendix presents a sound process for taking the finished product and making it available for public consumption on your host site.

What You Need for This Book

You need to have the following:

- PHP, Apache and MySQL (Apache2triad or XAMPP)
- Drupal 6

Who is This Book for

This book is for people with little to now experience in website design, people who are not familiar with PHP, MySQL or HTML, and above all people with little to no experience in using Drupal. Intermediate Drupal users may also find this book helpful because of its broad, practical coverage of all the Drupal fundamentals.

Conventions

In this book, you will find a number of styles of text that distinguish between different kinds of information. Here are some examples of these styles, and an explanation of their meaning.

There are three styles for code. Code words in text are shown as follows: "We can include other contexts through the use of the `include` directive."

A block of code will be set as follows:

```
#header {
   background: #193547;
   border: 1px solid #aaa;
   border-bottom: none;

}
```

When we wish to draw your attention to a particular part of a code block, the relevant lines or items will be made bold:

```
#header {
   background: #FF0000;
   border: 1px solid #aaa;
   border-bottom: none;
}
```

New terms and **important words** are introduced in a bold-type font. Words that you see on the screen, in menus or dialog boxes for example, appear in our text like this: "clicking the **Next** button moves you to the next screen".

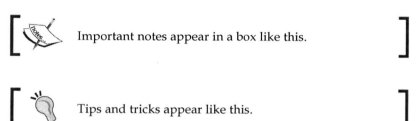

Important notes appear in a box like this.

Tips and tricks appear like this.

Reader Feedback

Feedback from our readers is always welcome. Let us know what you think about this book, what you liked or may have disliked. Reader feedback is important for us to develop titles that you really get the most out of.

To send us general feedback, simply drop an email to feedback@packtpub.com, making sure to mention the book title in the subject of your message.

If there is a book that you need and would like to see us publish, please send us a note in the **SUGGEST A TITLE** form on www.packtpub.com or email suggest@packtpub.com.

If there is a topic that you have expertise in and you are interested in either writing or contributing to a book, see our author guide on www.packtpub.com/authors.

Customer Support

Now that you are the proud owner of a Packt book, we have a number of things to help you to get the most from your purchase.

Errata

Although we have taken every care to ensure the accuracy of our contents, mistakes do happen. If you find a mistake in one of our books—maybe a mistake in text or code—we would be grateful if you would report this to us. By doing this you can save other readers from frustration, and help to improve subsequent versions of this book. If you find any errata, report them by visiting http://www.packtpub.com/support, selecting your book, clicking on the **Submit Errata** link, and entering the details of your errata. Once your errata are verified, your submission will be accepted and the errata added to the list of existing errata. The existing errata can be viewed by selecting your title from http://www.packtpub.com/support.

Questions

You can contact us at questions@packtpub.com if you are having a problem with some aspect of the book, and we will do our best to address it.

Introduction to Drupal

1

Up until quite recently, the most important thing a newcomer to the Web could do in order to prepare for building a website was to buy a book on how to learn programming in any one of the major web-centric languages like PHP or Perl. The not inconsiderable task of learning the niceties of the chosen language to a respectable degree would then consume a fair chunk of time and patience. Once our hapless newcomer had sufficient mastery of the fundamentals, applying that knowledge to program efficiently and reliably, with the tenacity to stick with a job until the site was developed, could arguably be described as a Herculean accomplishment.

This state of affairs is, and quite rightly should be, entirely unacceptable to someone like yourself! It's like forcing lawyers to learn the intricacies of architecture, construction, and masonry simply because they require a courtroom in which to work. It should be quite apparent that separating the technical task of *developing the software* for a website from the *function* of that website is a very sensible thing to do, the main reason being that it allows people to focus on what they are good at without them having to devote time and energy to becoming good software developers too.

It's not surprising then, that in recent years the open-source community has been hard at work pulling the programming world out of the software dark ages by providing us with flexible frameworks for building web-based enterprises. These frameworks free website creators from the intellectual burden of learning software development ideas and concepts, allowing them instead to focus more on goal/business-oriented configuration and customization tasks.

Drupal is one such result of the software-development evolution, and this book seeks to provide you with the fundamental information needed in order to use it effectively. Because this book focuses more on beginner-level aspects of administering Drupal, you will be pleased to know that there will be little to no coding involved—you're not required to learn how to develop Drupal modules from scratch, for example. That's not to say this book will be elementary; on the contrary, the knowledge gained here will enable you to tackle problems beyond the scope of this material with confidence.

Before we begin building anything that resembles a website, I'm sure you have plenty of questions about the how, what, where, and why of Drupal. Consequently, this chapter will not only provide a backdrop for the rest of the book, but will also serve as an introduction to the technology as a whole, incorporating a discussion on the following:

- Drupal—an overview
- How Drupal came to be
- What Drupal has to offer
- Uses of Drupal
- Building a Drupal site
- The Drupal community
- The Drupal license

Let's begin…

Drupal—An Overview

Drupal is an **Open-Source Content Management System**. If you are new to both computing and Drupal, then this probably doesn't clear things up very much. First of all:

> The term **open-source** describes software whose source code is made available, most often subject to certain conditions, for use or modification by users or other developers as they deem fit.

The specific conditions under which Drupal is made available will be scrutinized more closely in the section *The Drupal License*, later in this chapter.

Above and beyond that, what open source means for someone who intends to make use of Drupal, is that there is no obligatory payment required for this unquestionably valuable software. You also join a large community (also to be discussed later in this chapter) of Drupal users, developers, and administrators who subscribe to the open-source philosophy—in other words, someone out there will probably be willing to spend time helping you out should you get stuck.

That's a pretty good deal for those who are still not convinced about open-source technologies as a whole—not only do we not have develop the entire site ourselves, but we also get to take advantage of the collective wisdom of thousands of other people.

Is there anything else we can say about open source? Sure; with an active community like the one associated with Drupal, development advances rapidly and flexibly because any problems can be spotted early and dealt with effectively. This means that you can expect a high level of stability, security, and performance from Drupal websites.

OK, but what is the Content Management System (CMS) part all about?

 A content management system is software that facilitates the creation, organization, manipulation, and removal of information in the form of images, documents, scripts, plain text (or anything else for that matter).

If you have a need to organize and display fairly large amounts of information, especially when it is likely that content will be created or delivered from a variety of different sources, then a content management system is undoubtedly what you need.

That's basically all you have to know. Drupal provides a free platform, along with its attendant community, for satisfying a wide variety of content-management requirements. Precisely, what type of things one can achieve is the subject of the section entitled *What Drupal Has to Offer* later in this chapter. For now though, let's turn back the hands of time and take a look at how we ended up with Drupal as we know it today.

How Drupal Came to Be

As with so many modern success stories, this one started in a dorm room with a couple of students needing to achieve a specific goal. In this case, Dries Buytaert and Hans Snijder of the University of Antwerp wished to share an ADSL modem connection to the Internet. They managed this via the use of a wireless bridge, but soon after, Dries decided to work on a news site, which would in addition to the simple connection the students already shared, allow them to share news and other information.

Over time the site grew and changed as Dries expanded the application and experimented with new things. However, it was only some time later in 2001 when it was decided to release the code to the public in the hope this would encourage development from other people that Drupal became open-source software. It's clear that releasing the source to the public was the right choice, because today Drupal has a well organized, thriving community of people ranging from contributors, adminsitrators, a security team, and a global presence, to plenty of users who make invaluable additions to the Drupal project on a regular basis through bug reports and suggestions.

In only a few years, Dries and others have taken a small inter-dorm-room application and turned it into a technology that is contributing to the way in which the global society communicates through the Web. This is embodied in their brief mission statement that reads:

> *By building on relevant standards and open-source technologies, Drupal supports and enhances the potential of the Internet as a medium where diverse and geographically separated individuals and groups can collectively produce, discuss, and share information and ideas. With a central interest in and focus on communities and collaboration, Drupal's flexibility allows the collaborative production of online information systems and communities.*

Ultimately, where Drupal is going and how it came to be are also driven by the philosophies that guide those responsible for developing this technology. As you will see throughout the course of this book, it is fair to say that the Drupal community has so far succeeded in meeting its lofty targets.

What Drupal Has to Offer

As users of technology and software, we should never be lax in what we demand from the technologies that serve us. It is fitting, therefore, at this stage, to discuss what we expect from Drupal in order to ensure that it will satisfy our needs.

There are three different aspects of Drupal we need to consider when looking at whether it is a *good* technology to use in general. Will it be:

- **Reliable and robust**: Are there a lot of bugs in the code? Will it affect my site if I have to forever add patches or obtain updates for faulty code?

- **Efficient**: Does the code use my server's resources wisely? Am I likely to run into concurrency problems, or speed issues early on?

- **Flexible**: If I change my mind about what I want from my site, will I be able to implement those changes without redoing everything from scratch?

While Drupal will always be a work in progress, it can be taken for granted that the source code used to build your website has been meticulously crafted, and well designed. In fact, the previously listed points are taken so seriously by the developers of Drupal that they are written into their set of principles that are available at http://drupal.org/node/21945.

While it won't influence us much for the moment, it is worth noting the following:

 A great advantage of Drupal is that the code itself is very well written, which makes modifying it easy. This means that as you attempt more advanced tasks, the very way in which Drupal is written will lend an advantage over other platforms.

The next thing we need to consider is what Drupal is like for us, as administrators, to use. Naturally, things should be as easy as possible, so that we don't spend time bogged down with problems or complicated settings, or worse yet, have to modify the source code on a regular basis. Ideally, we want a system that is:

- **Easy to set up and run**: Can I start creating a site with the minimum of fuss? Do I have to learn about other technologies before I am able to use Drupal?

- **Intuitive to work with**: Once I have begun finding my way around, will it be easy to learn new things? If I am not a particularly technical person, will I struggle to administer my site?

- **Flexible and easy to extend**: I know I can make a basic site, but I really want to create a unique and sophisticated, ground-breaking site—can it be done with Drupal?

Again, these are precisely the attributes that Drupal is known for. If you have other questions about Drupal that are not specifically mentioned here then try to relate them to the bullet points. If you still struggle, try looking through the Drupal forums.

Finally, and perhaps in some respects most importantly, it is important to consider whether or not Drupal creates a good environment for site users. Obviously, a technology that is well designed and easy to administer would still not be very helpful if, for example, its use is prohibitively complex. The best way to find out what type of environment Drupal can provide is to go ahead and check out the Drupal home page at `http://drupal.org`—since it is built with Drupal and is a good example of what one can do.

It's a good idea to register an account if you have a moment or two. It's not absolutely necessary, but believe me, it will be of great benefit in the long run. Perhaps treat your registration process as a quick and easy way to see a bit of the site.

It stands to reason that if the main site that is developed in Drupal is easy to use, then you in turn will be able to create an easy-to-use site for your users.

Uses of Drupal

Any enterprise that requires a fair amount of working with content is a likely candidate for Drupal, but, because of its extensibility and flexibility, you are really not very limited in any sense. The following list shows the most common uses at present and comes from the case studies page (http://drupal.org/cases) on the Drupal site:

Community Portal Sites: If you want a news website where the stories are provided by the audience, Drupal suits your needs well. Incoming stories are automatically voted upon by the audience and the best stories bubble up to the homepage. Bad stories and comments are automatically hidden after enough negative votes.

News Publishing: Drupal is great for newspapers and other news organizations.

Aficionado Sites: Drupal flourishes when it powers a portal website where one person shares their expertise and enthusiasm for a topic.

Intranet/Corporate Web Sites: Companies maintain their internal and external web sites in Drupal. Drupal works well for these uses because of its flexible permissions system, and its easy web-based publishing. No longer do you have to wait for a webmaster to get the word out about your latest project.

Resource Directories: If you want a central directory for a given topic, Drupal suits your needs well. Users can register and suggest new resources, while editors can screen their submissions.

International Sites: When you begin using Drupal, you join a large international community of users and developers. Thanks to the localization features within Drupal, there are many Drupal sites implemented in a wide range of languages.

Education: Drupal can be used for creating dynamic learning communities to supplement the face-to-face classroom or as a platform for distance education classes. Academic professional organizations benefit from its interactive features, and the ability to provide public content, member-only resources, and member subscription management.

Art, Music, Multimedia: When it comes to community art sites, Drupal is a great match. No other platform provides the rock solid foundation that is needed to make multimedia-rich websites that allow users to share, distribute, and discuss their work with others. As time goes on, Drupal will only develop stronger support for audio, video, images, and playlist content for use in multimedia applications.

Social networking sites: Drupal has many of common the features used in social networking sites. You can build a collection of social networking applications for your site or use Drupal as a white label social networking service.

Drupal can be thought of as the Internet's Jack-of-all-trades — it excels in many areas, but at heart it is a generalist. So while you can use Drupal for a great number of things, perhaps limit its use to those things that complement its design — like those mentioned in the previous list.

Building a Drupal Site

Unlike building a house, development of a website takes place on a *copy* of the site instead of the real site. This means that while the site is being built, it is not available for the public to view and use on the Internet. With a bit of thought, this should make sense. Any potential community member who comes across a site under construction would probably become frustrated with bits and pieces that don't yet work, error messages, untidy presentation, or any other thing that could scare people away at the drop of a hat.

Some readers may well be wondering what to do with their domain in the meantime, assuming one has already been purchased. The best solution is to put up what is known as a **placeholder page** that delivers a simple message to the effect that this is the right site, the development is in progress on the working site, and that potential members should visit again in the near future.

It is a good idea to install Drupal on your host site at the start of the process to ensure that the platform you are using on the live site will meet your needs (i.e. does it have PHP5, is the database suitable, can you use clean URLs, and so on). Drupal has the option to be switched to offline status in order to prevent people from making use of it — this effectively turns the site into a *placeholder page*.

Appendix A on *Deployment* outlines the process of moving a fully functional website onto a live web domain. The process for doing the whole site and a single page is more or less the same, but naturally, moving a single page is a lot less involved.

Planning Your Site

It is important that as the creator of a new site you spend some time gathering information on the needs of the community you intend to serve. Doing this now will help in the long run because having a thorough understanding of a site's requirements allows you to develop it with specific goals in mind. This in turn enables a more focused and coordinated approach to the site's development.

It's tempting to dive straight into building your site, but spending some time planning everything now will save you time in the long run!

One of the best ways to determine what you will need is to build a list of tasks that the site must be able to perform. Effectively, after creating a list of the various requirements, the site's administrator (most probably yourself) should have a clear enough idea to go ahead and begin working. Unfortunately, it is often hard to predict exactly what is needed by simply sitting down and writing, so a good way to start is by looking at similar sites. Go ahead and take note of everything that is useful and desirable on other sites and add this to the list.

If you get stuck, or run out of ideas, it's helpful to try a little thought exercise as follows. Split yourself into two people:

- The community member who knows what his or her needs are
- The Drupal administrator who needs to find out what to build

Use the administrator persona to question the community member about what has to be done. Approaching the problem from two perspectives often helps mimic real-world situations where software developers try to find out exactly what their clients need by asking probing questions before they start working on a project.

Try and get to a stage where you feel comfortable with at least 80% of what is required from your site, from there it is probably more efficient to go ahead and begin building, rather than waste time scraping out more information. As Drupal is extensible and flexible, it is quite easy to modify it at a later stage.

Here is a list of some of the most important topics you will need to decide on:

- The type of site—is it a forum, or a blog, or something else entirely?
- The way you are going to run the site—stats, logging, or performance issues
- The security, roles, and permissions involved
- The need for integration—syndication, aggregation, or alerts

Apart from your site's functionality, start thinking about how the site should look. Obviously, an attractive and unique interface for users to work with is your ultimate goal in this respect. The use of themes to create a visually appealing site is a fairly important topic that we discuss later in the book in Chapter 8, but please do give some thought to this aspect of your site early on, regardless.

Not only do you want to design an interface that looks pretty, but it also needs to be intuitive and easy to use. This is very important as studies have shown that users will often base their opinion of a site on how easy it is to use and not always on other criteria that you might think important, such as speed. People often *believe* that a slower running site is faster if they manage to accomplish their tasks on it more easily.

By observing similar sites and anticipating the needs of potential users, you can develop a specification for your own site. Having a site outline or specification to work towards is valuable in itself as an exercise.

Analyzing the Proposed Solution

Once there is a specification to work with, we know *what* is needed. It is time to look at *how* to deliver it. To do this, we really need to go back over all the points listed and find out *what is involved* in getting each one done. Knowing what lies ahead is the best way to handle problems preemptively!

The three main areas of concern that we need to deal with are discussed next...

Feasibility

Having a wish-list is a great way to decide on what you want, but that doesn't mean it is feasible. In order to be feasible, the criteria should not involve an inordinate amount of effort relative to the benefits it will return. For example, if the site specification calls for a feature that requires a hundred hours of brutal, frustrating programming, then it is probably not in your interests to waste time doing it if it is not going to affect your community significantly.

Ultimately, it may be better to look for a cheap and elegant alternative, either amongst the plethora of contributions (also called contribs), or from third-party software providers. One of the old programming mantras, *There's more than one way to do it!*, holds true here.

Phone a Friend

Look at the requirements very carefully. Are you sure you can actually provide everything that is required? If not, spend some time looking over this book and the Drupal site to see if you can learn anything new. If you are absolutely stuck, then get on the forums and lists and ask for help.

Critical versus Desirable Criteria

In order to determine the priority of tasks during your site's development phase, it is a good idea to divide all requirements into two categories — those that are fundamentally necessary to the success of the website, such as finding a service provider, and those that are not, such as deciding on whether to make hyperlink color dark blue or light blue.

There are a couple of reasons for this:

- Doing so will help you allocate time and resources to certain tasks while putting others on a backburner.

- You are aware of those features that do not necessarily need to be included at all in the event that time is short.

In both these cases, it is important to know what has to be finished and what can perhaps be left out or left for another day. With your plans laid out and ready to implement, it is important to recognize that you are not alone and that Drupal and its community will prove to be a most useful companion in the coming days, weeks, and months.

The Drupal Community

Drupal has coherent and in-depth support structures that are fairly easy to learn your way around. There are a host of categories ranging from information, polls, forums, and news to support, which can be found at the home page: `http://drupal.org`.

It is strongly recommended that you regularly make use of `drupal.org` and constantly use different elements and sections in order to become proficient at extracting the information and software you require—especially because the Drupal site will change from time to time!

All the information contained in the site is well organized, and easy to access from the main navigation bar at the top of the page, as shown here:

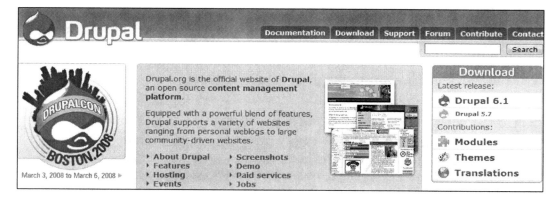

Each and every tab in the navigation bar has a host of its own links and pages, although there are some categories that contain inter-related topics. At any rate, let's go through each one quickly to see what they have to offer.

Documentation

This section is a great repository of information, catering for a wide variety of different needs. The content is gathered into five main sections, as shown here:

Getting Started	About Drupal
• Projects and Features	• Welcome
• Before You Start	• Drupal.org FAQ
• Drupal 5	• Is Drupal right for you?
• Drupal 4.7 and earlier	• Books about Drupal
• Core Modules	• Support and professional services
• Troubleshooting FAQ	• Donating to the project
	• Mailing lists
	• Marketing Resources

Customization - Tutorials, Snippets and HowTo

• Tutorials	• Theme Snippets
• HowTo	• Videos and slides
• Snippets	• Contributed modules

Theme Developers' Guide

• Theming overview	• Using Theme Override Functions
• Regions in themes	• Using Theme Override Functions For Forms
• PHPTemplate theme engine	• Theme screenshot guidelines
• Contributed themes	• Theme HowTos
• Making a theme customizable	• Other theme engines
• Troubleshoot your theme	• Adding your theme to Drupal.org
• Updating your themes	

Developing for Drupal

• Contributing to Development	• Usability research
• Coding standards	• Join forces with others
• Writing secure code	• Install profile developer's guide
• CVS	• Module developer's guide
• Patches	• Translator's guide
• Drupal's APIs	• Updating your modules
• HowTo: Benchmark Drupal code	• Drupal test suite
• Setting up a development environment	• Migrating from other software

Each of these categories contains a series of links to informative pages (that in turn, often contain links to other pages) that do a good job of explaining their respective topics. It's worth pointing out that a block appears on the left-hand side of these pages, containing links to related topics under the same category heading in order to help you navigate through the information with ease. The following screenshot shows the **Is Drupal right for you?** page:

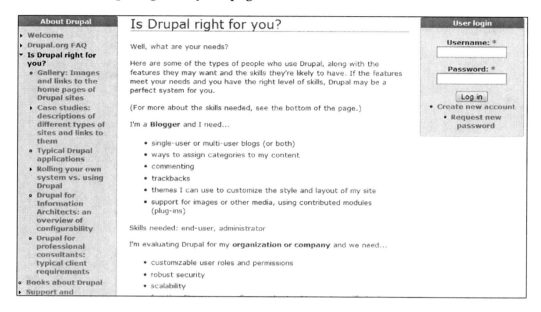

You are urged to look through at least the first section before moving onto the following chapter in order to learn as much about Drupal as possible. It is also a good idea to use these handbooks in tandem with this book, so that you can complement the practical advice and experience you gain here with reference-type material presented on the site.

Download

We will be visiting this section again in the following chapter when we begin to set up everything in preparation for site development. However, there are a few interesting points to note before we get there. The first is that you need to be quite careful about the Drupal version—or indeed modules and themes—you download, because each successive version makes changes and improvements on previous versions, and also sometimes messes up compatibility with other features.

If you decide to add a module (by this I mean that at some stage you *will* want to add a module), then viewing the projects page at `http://drupal.org/project`, or by clicking the **Downloads** tab, gives the following page.

Project types

- **Drupal project**

  Get started by downloading the official Drupal core files. These official releases come bundled with a variety of modules and themes to give you a good starting point to help build your site. Drupal core includes basic community features like blogging, forums, and contact forms, and can be easily extended by downloading other contributed modules and themes.

- **Installation profiles**

  Installation profiles are a feature in Drupal core that was added in the 5.x series. The Drupal installer allows you to specify an installation profile which defines which modules should be enabled, and can customize the new installation after they have been installed. This will allow customized "distributions" that enable and configure a set of modules that work together for a specific kind of site (Drupal for bloggers, Drupal for musicians, Drupal for developers, and so on).

- **Modules**

  Modules are plugins for Drupal that extend its core functionality. Only use matching versions of modules with Drupal. Modules released for Drupal 5.x will not work for Drupal 6.x. These contributed modules are not part of any official release and may not be optimized or work correctly.

- **Themes**

  Themes allow you to change the look and feel of your Drupal site. These contributed themes are not part of any official release and may not work correctly. Only use matching versions of themes with Drupal. Themes released for Drupal 5.x will not work for Drupal 6.x. Many of these themes can also be previewed on the third party site **the Theme Garden**

- **Theme engines**

You can see from the notes presented on this page, if you happen to need a module that was developed for Drupal 5.x, and you are using version 6.x, then you are shortly going to experience no small amount of frustration—this is especially valid at this time given that 6.x is brand new, and hence many modules have yet to be updated.

Problems like this can occur because modules are developed separately from the core, which means that it is up to the individual module developer to keep up to date with any changes coming from the main development team.

Naturally, not everyone will keep their modules up to date in a timely manner, because often these developers are not getting paid and are under no obligation to do the work at all. They are simply providing us with the best code they can deliver when they can deliver it.

In terms of how to use the download pages, it is worth noting that there are four main links given in each downloadable item's box (for example, click on the **Themes** link to view a list of downloadable themes). These are: **Download**, **Release notes**, **Find out more**, and **Bugs and feature requests**. The first option is pretty self explanatory, but you should always take a look at the **Find out more** option before downloading anything, to ensure that you are getting precisely what you want.

For example, the **Find out more** page for the **Acidfree** project contains information on history of **Updates**, and plenty of material on **Releases, Resources, Support**, and **Development**—all pretty useful if you are not sure what **Acidfree** does to begin with.

That aside, the point of this section is that you should try to *think carefully* about what you want before downloading everything. In the next chapter, we will put words into practice and make use of this section to obtain a copy of Drupal.

Support

The **Support** section can be regarded as a kind of catch-all page, and actually contains a number of links to the various other community pages, many of which can also be opened by using their tabs in the main navigation bar. For example, you can navigate to the **Drupal handbook** (to be discussed shortly) from the **Online documentation** section to find out some basic information on Drupal, as shown here:

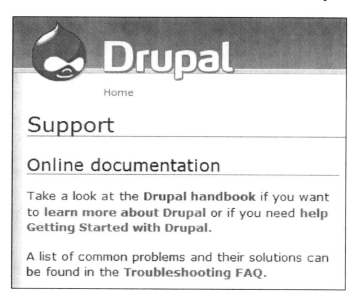

Briefly, in this section:

- Documentation and help facilities are provided in the **Online documentation** section, and include help on some common problems as well as installation and general information.

- Links to security advisories and announcements as well as the option to subscribe to the security announcement mailing list or RSS feed are provided under the **Security** section.

- Links to the forums, in case you need help, are provided under the **Forums and Support** section, as well as archives and a **Tips for posting to the Drupal forums link.**

- If you are not an English language speaker, or your community predominantly speaks some other language, then it is worthwhile checking out some of the other language sites under the **Other languages** section, which includes German, French, Spanish, and Afrikaans.

- Links to a number of professional services related to Drupal, including hosting and consulting, are provided under the **Professional services and hosting** section.

- Bug reports can be sent in by visiting the **Bug reports** section. Please be aware that you should always check whether or not a bug has been reported before submitting a report. Any submission incurs a cost in terms of man-hours because someone has to look over it, and the time wastage can be substantial if everyone keeps reporting the same bug over and over again.

- The **Feature requests** section gives you the opportunity to look over what other people would like to see incorporated into Drupal as shown here:

Of course, you can also submit your own requests.

- There is also an interesting option to obtain support over an **IRC channel**. IRC, or Internet Relay Chat, allows for real-time, typed discussions over the Internet. Joining a group like this is obviously a great advantage in that it immediately gives you access to many other Drupal people.

- There is a support **Mailing list** section that you can join, a **Developer support** section, and a forum to raise issues about the actual Drupal website under the **Drupal.org problems** section.

- Other sections include **Books about Drupal** and, following in the ever popular social bookmarking trend, a **Tags** section has been added too. There is a **Web watch** section as well.

If in doubt as to where to go, the **Support** page is probably the best place to start. More often than not though, you will have a fairly good idea of what you need, and should be able to go straight there.

Forum

The forums are probably the single greatest problem-solving resource and information-based asset. Unlike the other types of information on the site (with the exception of the Freenode Drupal IRC), which are largely static, written answers or guides, the forums provide you with an interactive environment in which to learn. Of course, they also provide you with a medium for sharing whatever you have learned as well.

At the time of writing, there were in excess of 200,000 support-related posts alone. This should give you a good idea of how widely used these forums are. The following screenshot shows the **Forum** home page as well as the first few forum categories. From the large number of posts, you can tell that this is already a fairly large repository of knowledge, and hopefully you will take the time to add to it yourself.

Forums

- Login to post a new forum topic.

Forum	Topics	Posts	Last post
General Important: no support questions here!			
News and announcements For news and announcements to the Drupal community at large.	1173	12498	29 min 16 sec ago by slimandslam
General discussion For less technical discussions about the Drupal project. Not for support questions!	13216	55470	17 min 1 sec ago by sepeck
Drupal showcase Showcase your site to others, maybe share a little about it - modules, theme, why you used Drupal.	2948	14187	47 min 24 sec ago by elsterama
Events For events, conferences and other Drupal happenings.	251	1357	5 days 44 min ago by saneangel
Usability feedback For interface guidelines, mockups, and usability feedback.	792	3756	1 day 1 hour ago by secgeek
Support Try **searching the forums** first or a specific project's **bug reports**. Remember all support on this site is on a volunteer basis, so please visit the **forum tips** for posting hints.			
Pre installation questions Is Drupal a viable solution for my website?	2676	11060	1 hour 9 min ago by Steven_NC
Installation problems For problems with installing a new Drupal site.	8017	33679	37 min 41 sec ago by Slaven
Upgrade problems For problems with upgrading an existing Drupal site.	2157	8581	1 hour 37 min ago by jared.lenover
Post installation Drupal is up and running but how do I ...?	46451	168578	13 min 19 sec ago by ilabs
Converting to Drupal Need help migrating your site to Drupal?	927	3671	4 hours 36 min ago by rernst
Hosting companies For questions about commercial Drupal hosting.	559	4348	1 hour 10 min ago by crucialx

Looking at the entire page, there are three main forum categories—**General**, **Support**, and **Development**—that in turn have a number of subcategories to make navigating the structure fairly easy. Notice too that there is a block on the right-hand side of the page containing a list of the most recent posts. As well as this, you can also use the search tool, shown at the top right-hand side of the page or at `http://drupal.org/search/node`, to search for relevant information or users.

Finally, assuming you are a registered (and logged-on) Drupal user, you can also post new topics to the forum using the link given under the page's main heading, as shown here:

Forums

- **Post new forum topic.**

Before posting off hundreds of questions and salutations, please be aware that there is a certain etiquette to using these forums, and it should be followed at all times. Look at the following page before you begin writing any posts to the site:

`http://drupal.org/forum-posting`

A quick summary is as follows:

- Search the forums for your intended topic and use those posts instead of creating redundant information.
- Make forum post titles informative and meaningful.
- Submit a good amount of system-specific information in your support queries—for example, mention the Drupal version along with the database and database version.
- Bear in mind that not everyone using the forum is a native English speaker; so some posts may be construed as rude or abrupt when that is not the intention.
- Remain polite and reasonable—even if you are frustrated over a particular problem.
- Donate some time to responding to and helping other posters.
- If you would like, enable your contact tab so that people can offer support via email. Do this by editing your contact information as shown here:

☑ Personal contact form
Allow other users to contact you by e-mail via **your personal contact form**. Note that while your e-mail address is not made public to other members of the community, privileged users such as site administrators are able to contact you even if you choose not to enable this feature.

Some of you may have noticed the link entitled **Recent posts** on the right-hand side of the page. Clicking on this link brings up a list of the topics that have recently been active, as shown here:

Recent posts

| | All recent posts | | My recent posts | | |

Type	Post	Author	Replies	Last updated
Issue	Duplicate entry errors in search indexer new	Gábor Hojtsy	34 34 new	8 sec ago
Issue	Can't specify content type at import new	rubinsta	11 10 new	17 sec ago
Issue	Getting everytime somebody login errors! new	softtouch	0	25 sec ago
Forum topic	IMCE - no "browse server" button new	stevekerouac	1 1 new	30 sec ago
Issue	Link to referring nodes appear only after manual update of reffering node new	Zbyna	0	1 min 7 sec ago
Issue	How does this work? new	spatz4000	2 2 new	2 min 2 sec ago
Forum topic	ASPO International (Peak Oil org.) goes Drupal new	Samuel Lampa	7 7 new	2 min 28 sec ago
Issue	Doesn't work for me or bug ? new	chazz	0	3 min 9 sec ago
Issue	I can not log in ... new	Drunkensailor	5 5 new	3 min 54 sec ago
Project	Codes new	Pasqualle	0	4 min 26 sec ago

If you would prefer to view the discussions that you personally have contributed to, then click the **My recent posts** tab instead.

Contribute

At first glance, you might be forgiven for thinking that there is very little to contribute to the Drupal community while you are still learning the software. As this is not entirely true, it is worthwhile seeing what there is available to us:

Contribute

View | Revisions

Thank you for your interest in contributing to the Drupal project! Contributors are Drupal's most valuable asset, and are the sole force behind improvements to the platform and the community itself. Please check out our projects **mission** statement and **principles** so you can direct your efforts effectively and in line with the communities goals.

There are several areas in which you can provide assistance:

User support

Even the most gifted Drupal developers were new once, and chances are someone has helped you at some point along the way. No matter what your skill level, you can give back by sharing what you know with other users who need support. It's a nice thing to do, and who knows? You might learn something, too!

Find out how to help with user support.

Donations

Would like to help out but don't have the time? Want to say "thank you" to the folks who have put work into making Drupal what it is? Want to ensure that Drupal's infrastructure stays healthy and strong? A great way to do this is to provide donations.

Donate now or find out how to help with donations.

Documentation

Whether you're interested in providing fine-grained API documentation, writing step-by-step tutorials for the handbook, or producing multimedia

Development

Drupal thrives on developer contributions, in the form of both contributed modules and functionality to core. Helping out in development helps the

For starters, the easiest way to support Drupal is by making donations—I can all but hear the sighs and groans, but bear in mind what you are getting is absolutely free. You can also help market Drupal by writing reviews, or incorporating the Druplicon onto your site, and so on. There is also always a need for people to help test, translate, support, and document Drupal.

Finally, once you have gained some experience and feel confident enough, look towards helping with Drupal development. Whatever you choose to do, any information or help you require in order to become pro-active within the community is readily available under the **Contribute** section.

Contact

The **Contact** page allows you to send an email off to the Drupal team, and you need to remember that no technical support queries will be addressed here—*you must use the support forum for that.* Select the most pertinent category from the drop-down list provided and away you go. An example is shown here:

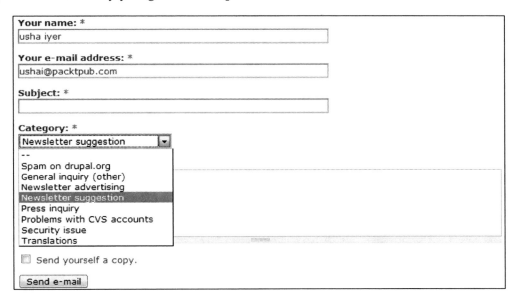

That about wraps it up for our coverage of the Drupal community. You should feel fairly confident that you can use the site efficiently, and find help if needs be. Before we continue onto the next chapter, though, there is one more important issue we need to discuss ...

The Drupal License

Naturally, you should want to inform yourself of any and all legalities and responsibilities you have when it comes to using software developed by others. To this end, you will find that when you download a copy of Drupal, it will contain a license file for your perusal—it is actually required as part of the license that this copy be included.

If you're like me, then you find it challenging to remain awake when faced with the prospect of reading through licenses and other legal documents. So, instead of subjecting you to a verbatim recount of the entire license, I will instead give you the paraphrased version that is intended to provide you with the *essence* of what the license is getting at as it applies to Drupal.

Please bear in mind that what I say here is in no way a legal document. You **must** read the whole license yourself if you wish to follow the letter of the law.

As odd as it may sound, one of the fundamental reasons for using the GNU GPL (General Public License) is to protect and help you — the people who use the software. The GPL is fundamentally different from the licenses of proprietary software, which by and large are designed to protect the rights of the corporate entities that developed and created the software.

Incidentally, the GPL is not tied specifically to Drupal; rather Drupal makes use of the GPL, which is a kind of generic license for distributing open-source software. You can check out the GNU homepage for more information on this movement, in general: http://www.gnu.org/home.html.

The way things work is that the software is copyrighted, and then licensed, for everyone to use freely. This might strike you as a little odd at first because what is the point of copyrighting something if you are simply going to let anyone else make use of it? The reason for this is that copyrighting and licensing the software gives the developer the power to obligate people who use that software to afford everyone they hand it out to (with or without modifications) the same rights that are vested in the original software.

What this means is that, effectively, anyone who makes use of this software cannot create proprietary software from it. So, if you decide to build upon and improve Drupal in order to sell it on as your own product, then you will be bound by the same terms and will have to release the source code to anyone who asks for it.

Remember though, the aim of the GPL is not to take credit for your own work by forcing you to release it under the GPL. If you have developed identifiable programs or code that are wholly your own and are independent from the original source code provided, then the GPL does not apply to your work.

A summary of some of the main points in the license is as follows:

- You are free to copy the software covered by the GPL, as well as distribute these copies however you see fit. The most important thing is not to remove the licensing.

- You can hack around with the source code and create whatever type of derived product you want. Again, you must pass on the same license (as you received it) with the original code, only this time you must make it very clear what changes you introduced.

- You mustn't break the terms of the GPL at any stage, or you will find your current license to use the software terminated.

- You aren't forced to accept the conditions of the license. (You can tell this from the fact that you don't have to sign anything.) However, if you don't accept the terms of the license, you can't make use of the software.

- If you do decide to redistribute the software yourself, then you can't add restrictions or modify the license in any way. You also aren't required to ensure that the parties you distribute the software to comply with it.

- If you are compelled by a court ruling (or any other legal proceeding) to enforce conditions that do not meet the requirements of the GPL, then you must not distribute the software at all.

- Keep an eye on the version of the license that is distributed with the software. If there is one present then you must use that version (in some instances of the GPL, a later one is also suitable, but never an earlier one).

- There is no warranty on this software, and no one who modifies or distributes the software in terms of the GPL is responsible for anything—especially damages or failure to operate and so on.

At the end of the day, the only time you do need to worry about the niceties of the GPL is when you decide to set up a business installing, configuring, and customizing Drupal websites for money, or modifying, and redistributing the original source code.

Summary

This chapter has served as an introduction to the world of Drupal as well as backdrop for the rest of the book. Several important things were discussed here, which will play an important role in the future as you develop your skills and knowledge.

Without a doubt, one of the most important aspects of becoming a successful Drupal administrator is being able to make efficient use of the community. By now, you should have registered on the Drupal site and taken at least a cursory glance at much of it. As time goes by, you will hopefully develop relationships with other members and eventually become a great asset for the community at large.

I hope you found that researching and deciding on what your site requires was not too tedious. Remember that any background work put in now will pay off later.

With the introductory material out of the way, it is time to get down to business, and the next chapter will see us setting up the development environment as well as obtaining and installing the latest version of Drupal.

2
Setting Up The Development Environment

It is widely accepted that during the process of building your website, you should not make it available for people to use over the Internet. Making a site *live*, while still in the process of making changes and breaking and fixing things, means that it is possible for people to find the site, attempt to use it, and form an exceedingly bad opinion of your web development skills. In the worst case, malicious users might gain access to sensitive information due to improperly implemented security settings, among other things.

Rather than allowing the public access to a work-in-progress, it is far better to set up a PHP-enabled web server on your home or office PC—or some other platform if available. This server, along with PHP and the database, can then be used to design and build everything before deploying the final product to the live site.

This chapter, therefore, will ensure that you have a development environment correctly and efficiently setup in order to begin working on Drupal directly in the chapters that follow.

Specifically, the following important topics are covered:

- A brief introduction to the technologies involved
- Obtaining and installing Apache, MySQL, and PHP
- Obtaining and installing Drupal
- Troubleshooting common problems
- A short tour of Drupal

Installation and setup for Apache, MySQL, and PHP will only be covered for Windows because the process for setting up a LAMP (Linux, Apache, MySQL, PHP) stack is very well documented and should be quite easy.

Before we begin, however, there is one crucial bit of advice to be given:

 Ensure that you have access to a good, preferably broadband Internet connection, as you will be downloading a fair amount of software.

If you already have a development environment setup and running, feel free to skip the first few sections and move directly to the section titled *Obtaining and Installing Drupal*. Alternatively, if you already have Drupal working but wish to learn how to upgrade to a newer version, then go to the section titled *Upgrading Drupal* in Appendix A.

It should also be noted that because Drupal has been developed with flexibility in mind, it is possible to use it off IIS as an alternative web server, as well as utilize PostgreSQL as an alternative database because support for these are actively being developed. By far and away, however, the most popular combination is Apache, MySQL, and PHP, so this is what is covered here.

The Drupal Environment

I know most of you will be eager to get going at the moment, and might well prefer to dive straight into making modifications to your Drupal site. Before we do so, we can take a few moments to read over this section to gain an appreciation of how everything is put together behind the scenes.

Having a basic knowledge of how the various technologies co-operate in order to produce a working Drupal site will help immeasurably in the long run.

Take a look at each of the individual underlying technologies we will be using:

- **PHP**: PHP, or PHP Hypertext Preprocessor, is the language in which Drupal is written. PHP is widely used on the Internet for a multitude of different projects and is renowned for its ease of use. The current version of PHP is PHP5, which is what we will use in this book.

  It is strongly recommended that you use PHP5 from now on because support for PHP4 will soon be discontinued and Drupal 7 will no longer run on anything less than PHP5!

  The good news is that we will not have to delve deeply into programming code in order to build a site—Drupal handles most, if not all, of the complex programming issues.

- **Apache**: This is the web server we will use to serve web pages during the development phase. Apache is the most popular web server on the Internet, with millions of live sites using it every day. In fact, as the Apache website says: *It is more widely used than all the other web servers combined.*

- **MySQL**: This is the database software that we will use to store all the information required to keep the website running. Everything from customer details to product information and a host of other things will be stored in the MySQL database.

  You *must* make use of MySQL 4.1 or a later version in order to work with Drupal 6.

  Keeping with the trend of popularity, MySQL is also the world's most popular bit of database software with over six million active installations worldwide.

Now, since we don't want to waste too much time downloading and installing all the different pieces of software we need individually, we are going to use a package installation, which provides us with everything we need with only one installation. The package we will use for the purposes of this book is called **Apache2Triad**.

 Apache2Triad is not the only package that is available. You might also wish to try out the ever popular XAMPP distribution that is available at `http://www.apachefriends.org/en/xampp.html`.

Now that we know *what* we are using, it is important to take a quick look at *how* it is used. The following diagram shows a simplified view of how everything works, with the shaded section denoting the package containing the Apache web server, PHP interpreter, and MySQL database, with Drupal installed on the system:

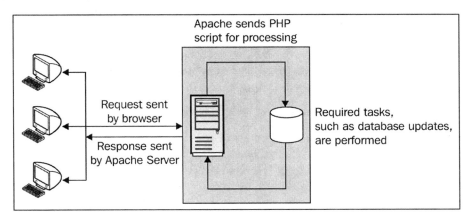

So, whenever a user does anything with your Drupal site (hopefully like contributing meaningfully), here's what happens:

1. The relevant information is sent off to the server in the form of an HTTP (HyperText Transfer Protocol) request.

2. The server receives the HTTP request and says, Ah! This is a PHP page that has been requested. I need to send it off for processing by the PHP engine. The PHP page then gets processed and executed appropriately, and any actions that are required as a result of the user's request are performed.

3. Once that is done, an appropriate response is returned by the server to the user's browser, and the cycle continues.

There are quite a few methods of providing dynamic web content that don't rely on PHP server requests. Instead, processing can be done on the browser itself (features like this are often loosely termed *Web 2.0*) but what you have been shown here is fundamentally how everything works, even if there are exceptions to the rule.

Obtaining and Installing PHP, Apache, and MySQL

As mentioned in the previous section, we are going to make use of a package installation in order to simplify the task of creating a workable development environment. You will notice that most software installation is really about learning a single process and repeating it for whatever software you need. More often than not, you will:

1. Go to the software producer's site.

2. Find the download page and download the appropriate package.

3. Unpack the software or run the executable file, depending on the method of installation.

4. Install and configure the software – most often you will be guided through the process in one way or another.

5. Test your setup.

That sounds easy enough; so head on over to `http://apache2triad.net/`, which is the homepage for the Apache2Triad project, and click the **Downloads** link in the left-hand box towards the bottom of the screen. (Feel free to browse around to learn more about this useful enterprise.) This will take you to the downloads page on the SourceForge site at: `http://sourceforge.net/project/showfiles.php?group_id=93507`.

Select the desired package—for the purposes of this book, release package 1.5.4 was used because it incorporates PHP5. At the time of writing, this was the most appropriate release, but you should feel free to use a later version, if there is one, as this will not affect the installation procedure.

Once **Download** is clicked for a package you will be presented with a list of download options. Release package 1.5.4 has only one option, as shown in the following screenshot:

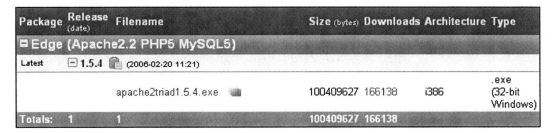

Package	Release (date)	Filename	Size (bytes)	Downloads	Architecture	Type
□ Edge (Apache2.2 PHP5 MySQL5)						
Latest	□ 1.5.4 📄 (2006-02-20 11:21)					
		apache2triad1.5.4.exe	100409627	166138	i386	.exe (32-bit Windows)
Totals: 1	1		100409627	166138		

This is the package we will download and install. Click the package name .exe file, and select a mirror site from which to download. Depending on your PC's security settings, you may be given the following message:

Click **Save File** to continue. At this point, you may take a break for a cup of coffee or tea if you have a slow connection as it may take a while—the download is in excess of 95 Meg.

Apache2Triad comes with a number of useful applications in addition to the core technologies needed for Drupal However, if this download is too large, then consider downloading XAMPP instead. XAMPP has lighter distributions of about 35 Meg available and will allow you to make use of Drupal easily.

At some stage during the setup process, the installer will ask you to confirm several settings and you are free to make changes as and when prompted. Take note that you will be asked to enter a password. Please ensure that you use something that is memorable and secure. Use eight characters or more and preferably some numerical digits.

 Remember your password as it is needed in order to run the initialization tasks a little later in the setup process – don't forget it!

Once everything has been done, you should receive a success message and the option to reboot. Save and close whatever important documents are open before clicking **OK**. Once the machine has restarted, you should have a whole list of new and exciting options to explore from the **Apache2Triad** option under **All Programs** in the **Start** menu. For example, the following options are made available with the 1.5.4 distribution:

There is quite a lot more than what we really need for our immediate purposes, but just to ensure that everything is going according to plan, click **open site root** in the **Apache2Triad** menu to open the following web page:

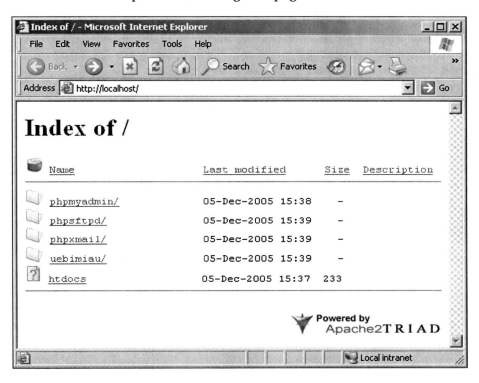

This confirms that everything is up and running as expected. Pretty easy so far! One thing to make note of in the previous screenshot is the final link called **htdocs**. Traditionally in Apache servers, htdocs is known as the *root* folder, and all the web pages that are to be made available must be placed inside htdocs. If something is not in htdocs, then it is not possible to browse it.

From this we know that we will have to locate the actual folder called htdocs on the file system in order to know where to put Drupal once it is downloaded. Assuming that you have gone with the default setup, you will find htdocs in the following directory (on Windows machines) along with everything else that was installed and created during setup: C:\apache2triad\.

It is worthwhile taking a look at what has been provided as part of the Apache2Triad installation because some of the facilities made available to you could well be most useful as time goes by. You will also find that many hosting packages on live sites offer pretty much the same functionality.

Of particular interest and use to us Drupal people is phpMyAdmin, which is a complete database management tool for MySQL. It can make life a lot easier whenever it is necessary to deal with data directly.

 If you are struggling to log onto phpMyAdmin or any other part of the site, then try using **root** as the username and whatever password you set during the setup process.

At this point, we now have a platform from which to begin building the Drupal site. Of course, we still need Drupal.

Obtaining and Installing Drupal

Chapter 1 has already looked over the downloads page on the Drupal site; so there isn't too much to present us with problems at this point. Head on over to `http://drupal.org/download` and click the Drupal version number you wish to download — generally, *the latest stable release* is suitable. Click **Download** to grab the latest copy and save it to your `C:` drive, or your `My Documents` folder (or wherever you want).

 Drupal bugfix versions are represented by an additional digit after the main release version (i.e. 6.1, 6.2, and so on). Bugfix versions should be used over the initial release for obvious reasons!

Now, the Drupal download is different from the Apache2Triad installer in that we will install Drupal ourselves; it doesn't come with its own installer `.exe` file. Instead we are asked if we would like to **Save** (or **Open**) a `.tar.gz` file. In the event that your PC doesn't recognize `.gz` files (this is for Windows users), then download a zip program like 7-zip (`http://www.7-zip.org`).

Once you are able, open and decompress the downloaded `tar.gz` file, then extract it to the `htdocs` folder of your Apache2Triad installation. To make life easier, perhaps rename the extracted folder to something more memorable and shorter than its default name, for example, I have simply called mine `drupal`, as shown in the following screenshot.

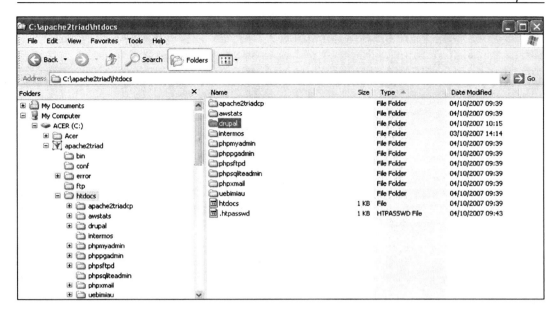

With that done, open up a browser and navigate to http://localhost/**drupal**. Remember to exchange the bolded section for the actual name of your folder in the htdocs directory. You should be presented with the first page of the installation dialog, which looks like the following screenshot:

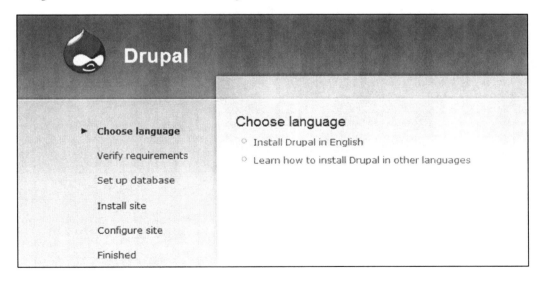

For the purposes of this book we will deal with English, but that's not to say we will neglect coverage of other languages and Drupal's growing support for the international community. Chapter 9 will discuss this in more detail.

Go ahead and click **Install Drupal in English** in order to begin the process. The first batch of settings you are required to specify relate to the database that Drupal will use to power the site. Initially, the database does not yet exist, so let's create it quickly before continuing.

Open up a new browser and navigate to http://localhost/phpmyadmin and enter the name of the database you would like to use for the site. Give the database either the same name as your site, or, if that is not a suitable choice for one reason or another (perhaps your name has special characters or is too long), give it a sensible nickname, as shown in the following screenshot:

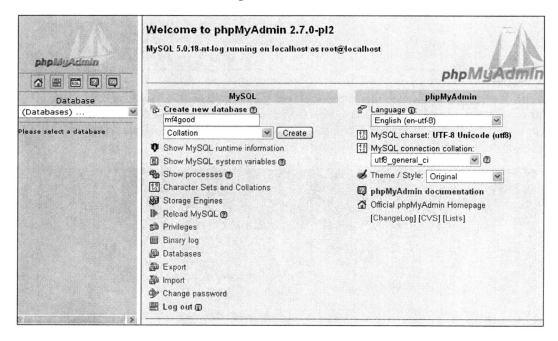

In this instance you can see that I have specified a database name of mf4good, which is an abbreviation of the full name of the demo site. Clicking **Create** brings up the following page and confirms that the new database now exists (although it still possesses 0 tables, as shown in the left hand frame).

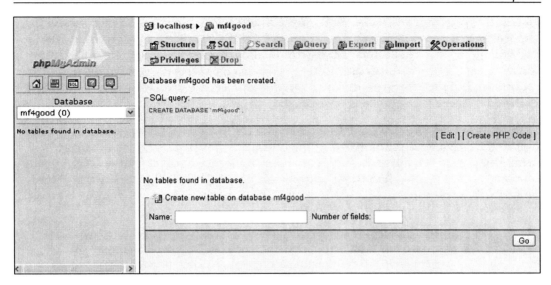

We can now continue with the Drupal installation. The database settings page looks something like the following screenshot:

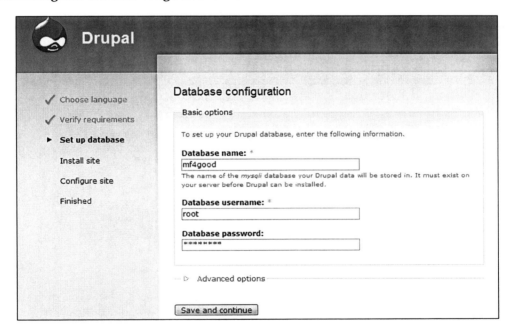

Notice that I have referenced the database just created, specified the user as root, and provided the password I supplied upon setup of Apache2Triad (since this is the only user that currently exists in our pristine environment).

Generally speaking, and for a number of reasons, it is not a good practice to use the superuser to access your database. The superuser (most often called `root`) is the one created by Apache2Triad upon setup to allow complete control over the entire environment, and this superuser has permissions far in excess of what we actually require in order to use Drupal. However, in this case, we can be slightly lazy and not bother to create other database users for now.

Since we are using our own personal machine for testing and development, we can ignore the **Advanced options** link at the bottom of this page because the default settings are appropriate as-is. If you are using a database server that does not reside on your own machine, then these settings can be used to specify the host, port and table prefix as required.

 A table prefix is prepended to the front of each table name in the database to prevent one installation from overwriting the tables of another. This can happen if, for example, another package using the same database has table names in common with Drupal's.

The following page allows us to specify some general administrative and configuration parameters. The first part deals with the site name and email address:

Configure site

All necessary changes to *./sites/default* and *./sites/default/settings.php* have been made. They have been set to read-only for security.

To configure your website, please provide the following information.

Site information

Site name: *

Market Force for Good

Site e-mail address: *

dave@marketforce4good.org

The *From* address in automated e-mails sent during registration and new password requests, and other notifications. (Use an address ending in your site's domain to help prevent this e-mail being flagged as spam.)

To begin with, you most likely won't have email setup on your current domain but this is not really a problem because you can enter any valid email to which you have access here. This will become important when the live site begins emailing people though.

The settings, as shown in the following screenshot, are very important because they control the administrator's (User 1) login information:

Ensure that you can remember whatever information is provided here because these settings specify the administrator's details. Forgetting them could mean a real struggle to get back into the site (it's not impossible provided you have root access to the database and can access all the information directly from PHPMyAdmin). The email address used here should be one that is convenient and active, and does not necessarily have to be a part of your new site's domain—anything will do.

The administrator account (User 1) is all powerful and has complete control over Drupal! Never use this account for everyday use of the site. Instead, create new users with specific access permissions to perform day-to-day tasks. More information on how to implement proper access control can be found in Chapter 5

Quickly decide on a couple of server settings, and one in particular is quite important, as shown in the following figure:

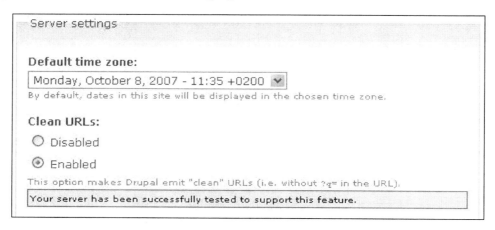

Clean URLs make your site easier to index for search engines, and have a whole host of benefits and knock on effects. Assuming you are using the latest version of Apache2Triad, this option should be available. If it isn't, then don't panic because it may be available on the live site. At this point, it may be prudent to try and install a copy of Drupal onto the live site to check this out because if it is not available, then there are steps you can take to rectify the problem. More information on this can be found in Appendix A, in the section entitled *Configure the Site*.

Finally you can select the option, to automatically update your Drupal distribution using Drupal's powerful new update module:

Update notifications:

☑ Check for updates automatically

With this option enabled, Drupal will notify you when new releases are available. This will significantly enhance your site's security and is **highly recommended**. This requires your site to periodically send anonymous information on its installed components to drupal.org. For more information please see the update notification information.

With that, hopefully you are presented with a clean bill of health, as shown in the following screenshot:

Drupal installation complete

Congratulations, Drupal has been successfully installed.

You may now visit your new site.

It's also quite possible that there are some rather alarming warnings or errors written in red at this point and the most common of these are dealt with shortly in the following section, entitled *Troubleshooting Common Problems.*

Everything else henceforth is configuration and customization, and if you have not experienced any errors or difficulties so far, please feel free to skip this next section.

Troubleshooting Common Problems

In this section, we will take a look at two of the problems most likely to occur during the setup process. We will also take a look at how they manifest themselves and how to solve them quickly. It should be noted that at this early stage, there are not many things that can go wrong as the installation routine is fairly well used. This is good news because it is likely that any errors are the result of typos or something quite simple, which should be easy to rectify.

Unfortunately, we can't hope to cover absolutely everything in this section; so we will also outline a brief process that can be used to solve *any problem*, and not just the ones involved with installation. Having a sound process to follow is immeasurably more valuable than being shown solutions to each and every problem.

If, while setting up the database, you received a message like the one shown in the following screenshot:

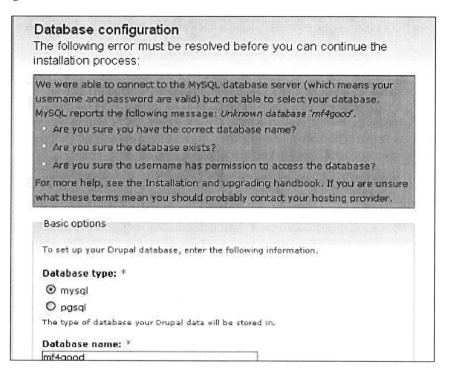

It is likely that you have made a typo in the **Database name** field, or have not correctly created a new database for Drupal to use. Check that you have not made a typo and that you have created a database with the desired name by revisiting http://localhost/phpmyadmin.

You might also have come across this rather ugly looking message towards the end of the installation process, as shown in the following screenshot:

> # Drupal installation complete
>
> • warning: mail(): SMTP server response: 550 Relay denied in C:\apache2triad\htdocs\drupal\includes\mail.inc on line 191.
> • Unable to send e-mail. Please contact the site admin, if the problem persists.
>
> Congratulations, Drupal has been successfully installed.
>
> Please review the messages above before continuing on to your new site.

This error occurs when Drupal attempts to send an email to confirm that the site has been set up, but finds that it is unable to do so. This problem is not critical because it doesn't prevent Drupal from completing its installation, but obviously, you would like the system to be able to send emails because they are useful for testing (and, of course, if you forget your password). The problem here is related to the environment itself and is not specifically a Drupal one.

PHP has reported to Drupal that it is not able to send out the email because it cannot find a suitable SMTP server. This is a common problem on Windows installations because unless an SMTP server is specified, there is no way PHP can decide for itself. To rectify this, open up the `php.ini` file located in `C:\windows` and search for the `[mail function]` entries. Modify it to match an SMTP server that you have access to (for example, if you use Outlook, you can find the address of an SMTP server from viewing your account server settings):

```
[mail function]
; For Win32 only.
SMTP = mail.mysmtpserver.com
smtp_port = 25
```

Once you have made the relevant changes, save the file and then restart the Apache server so that it can pick up the new settings.

 Restart the Apache server by opening up the **Apache2TriadManager** from the start menu and clicking the red icon next to **Apache2**. Once the server has stopped, simply click the icon again to restart.

But what if something else has gone wrong? Two more common problems are:

- *Clean URLs* — if in any doubt, don't enable these, because this can cause great problems after deployment to the live site if the live site does not support them by default.

- *Permission issues* — the `settings.php` file in **sites/default** makes use of certain properties of PHP and it is possible that there are conflicts here. Follow the instructions provided in the comments of this file if you suspect the problem lies here:

To see what PHP settings are possible, including whether they can be set at runtime (ie., when `ini_set()` *occurs), read the PHP documentation at* `http://www.php.net/manual/en/ini.php#ini.list` *and take a look at the* `.htaccess` *file to see which non-runtime settings are used there. Settings defined here should not be duplicated there so as to avoid conflict issues.*

Further than this, the types of problems that can occur are not easily isolated; so we have outlined *how* to go about solving them. The following list of points highlight a process that can be used to troubleshoot any problems:

1. Scrutinize any error messages you get and attempt to solve the problem yourself.

2. Visit the Drupal forums and search for similar problems.

3. Look through the troubleshooting FAQ at `http://drupal.org/node/199`.

4. View the bug list (`http://drupal.org/project/issues`) to see if your problem is a reported bug.

5. If you can't find bugs, similar posts, or problems, then try posting a focused and informative query on the forums and ask someone in the community to lend a hand.

6. To supplement this, get on Google and try using relevant keywords to locate a similar problem, hopefully with a solution presented.

For now though, you should be ready to continue with the final few tasks in the setup process, which will be performed in the following section.

Drupal's Post-Installation Status

It's worth noting before we continue further that it is often beneficial to have several development sites in order to play around with different things without mucking up other work. The process outlined so far in this chapter can be repeated as many times as you like to set up as many development sites as you like—simply create a new database (or, alternatively, provide any new Drupal installation with a table prefix in the **Advanced options** section) and add the Drupal files to the `htdocs` directory (ensuring they have a unique name) before browsing the new folder and repeating the installation process.

Whatever you decide, the next step is to click on the **your new site** link to bring up the default administration page (refer to the following figure):

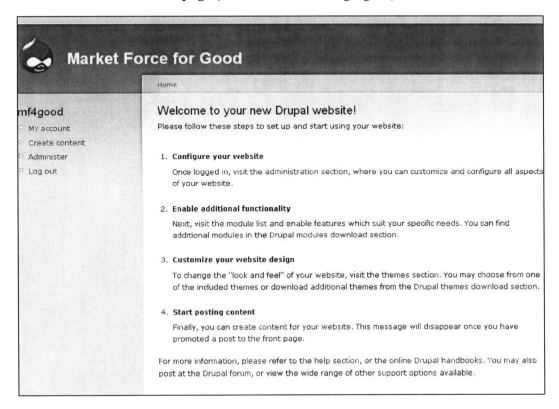

Quite conveniently, we have everything we need to do laid out in four simple steps and this is more or less the route we will follow in order to get everything up and running too.

Bear in mind that this page will be replaced once you start adding content and modifying the site; it is only a temporary placeholder. The first port of call is the **administration section,** so click there. At this point it is quite likely that there will be another one of those red error messages urging you to check the status report. If that is the case, then go ahead and do so – you will no doubt be presented with something that looks similar to the following screenshot (hopefully with less red involved):

Drupal	6.0
✓ Access to update.php	Protected
✓ Configuration file	Protected
⚠ Cron maintenance tasks	Never run
Cron has not run. For more information, see the online handbook entry for configuring cron jobs. You can run cron manually.	
✓ Database updates	Up to date
✓ Drupal core update status	Up to date
✗ File system	Not writable
The directory *sites/default/files* does not exist. You may need to set the correct directory at the file system settings page or change the current directory's permissions so that it is writable.	
✓ GD library	bundled (2.0.28 compatible)
✓ MySQL database	5.0.18
✓ PHP	5.1.2
✓ PHP memory limit	
✓ PHP register globals	Disabled
✓ Unicode library	PHP Mbstring Extension
✓ Update notifications	Enabled
✓ Web server	Apache/2.2.0 (Win32) PHP/5.1.2

This page displays information about the fundamentals of the Drupal installation. Anything showing in red or yellow needs attention. At the moment, the **Cron maintenance tasks** seems to be in trouble, but with a close inspection of the reasons for the error, you will see that the problem is not that difficult to solve – the cron has not been run.

 Cron tasks are automated chores that Drupal needs to perform regularly in order to make sure that everything continues to run smoothly. We discuss cron jobs in more detail in Chapter 10, so don't worry if you are not familiar with them at the moment.

To deal with the cron error, click on the **run cron manually** link. This executes the cron script and we are one down with one to go.

During development, it is a good practice to periodically run the cron so that Drupal can perform its internal maintenance tasks.

Next, click on the **file system settings page** link. This will bring up the following dialog that allows you to specify where and how files should be uploaded to and from during the course of the site's normal operation:

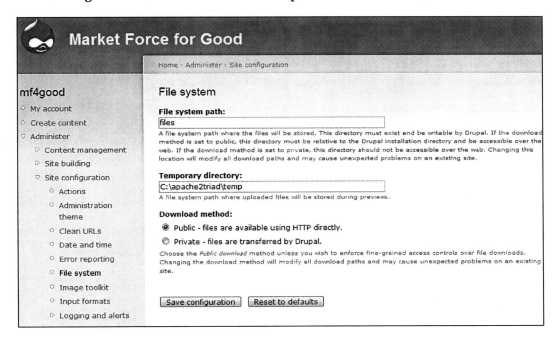

Unless you specifically know whether or not the site will require public or private downloads, don't worry about any of these settings for now—`files` are discussed in more depth in Chapter 4. Choose the **Public** download method and click on the **Save configuration** button before going back to the server status report (click on **Reports** and then **Status Report** in the main menu) to confirm that the installation now has a clean bill of health.

Before we move ahead to the customization and configuration topics of Chapter 3, it is important that we glance over Drupal to get a feel of how everything is organized.

Administrator's Overview

The homepage as it stands (you get back to it by clicking **Home** in the breadcrumb or the Drupal icon) is more or less a task oriented overview of some of the more important features of Drupal's **administer** menu shown on the left of the screen.

Since the **administration section** is where the business of building and running a Drupal site occurs, let's take a look at what that page provides and how it is organized. Clicking on this link (or **Administer** in the main menu) brings up the admin page as shown by the following screenshot:

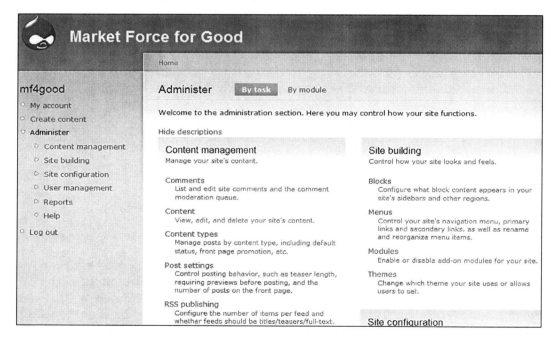

The admin page can be viewed either **By task** as shown here or **By module**. Either way, whatever you view here can be found in the **Administer** menu on the left-hand side.

At the moment, viewing the admin section **By task** is probably more intuitive but at a later stage you might find that having direct access to specific modules is more efficient, and in this case, the **By module** view will probably be more suitable.

Administration is broken up into five main categories that cover all the aspects of running the site.

Content Management: Fundamentally, content management is the most important aspect of any large site because it directly determines how easy or hard it is for users to access the information they are looking for. This section gives a broad and fine grained control over what content the site can present, how it is organized, how it is created and disseminated as well as who can comment on it and when.

User Management: One of the largest factors in determining the success of a site is who becomes part of its community. The term **who** in this case is used very loosely, because you will find that any content related site is a target for malicious users, bots and spammers, and how you control the use of a site leads directly to how appealing the target audience will find it.

Reports: Think of reports as your eyes and ears on the ground. They play an invaluable role in keeping you informed of what is happening behind the scenes. They help to keep you aware of important system updates, potential dangers or malicious use of a site, and much more.

Site Building: Divided into four main sections, this category powers the development of the site's functionality and features, and allows you to determine how that functionality is presented. Modifications to this section, especially to the **Modules**, can impact all other parts of the site and you will find that changes here require revisits to the other main categories because new modules invariably mean new site features. More on **Modules** in Chapter 3.

Site Configuration: This category contains a grab bag of features that can be used to alter the way in which a site deals with a variety of different issues ranging from performance and logging, to images, triggers, and maintenance.

The price one pays for having a powerful and flexible system like Drupal is that it comes with, necessarily, a huge amount of options and parameters that need to be understood and implemented. Spending time learning and experimenting with these is one of the things that will take you from novice to pro. Ultimately, I'm sure you will agree that the organization of this array of features within Drupal makes it quite intuitive.

Right now, it's time to a have a quick bit of fun before we get to the more serious matter of building a site in the next chapter.

Creating a Basic Drupal Page

Let's make some modifications to the site via the admin page to confirm that everything is working normally, and to highlight how easy it is to implement very powerful features at the click of a button. We'll run through a few quick steps to get some interesting new features along with some new content on the site, and then view it all as any visitor to the site would.

Go ahead and follow these steps:

- Click on **Modules** under the **Site Building** category of the admin page. This will bring up a long list of modules that are available.

- Select **Search**, **Poll** and **Blog**, then scroll to the bottom of the page and click on **Save configuration**.

- Click on **Create content** in the main menu and then select the **Poll** option.

- Fill out an arbitrary question with some options, as shown in the following screenshot, and then click **Save** (don't worry about any of the other options available for now):

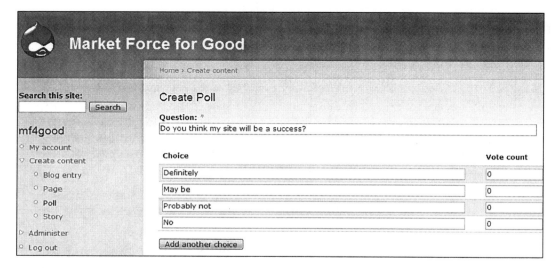

- Click on **Create content** again, but this time select the **Blog entry** option.

- Fill out the fields available with any info, and click the **Save** button (again, don't worry about any other settings or options for now).

- Return to the admin page and select the **Blocks** option under **Site Building**.

- Scroll down the page and make changes to the table shown in the following screenshot by dragging and dropping **blocks** to the desired **region**:

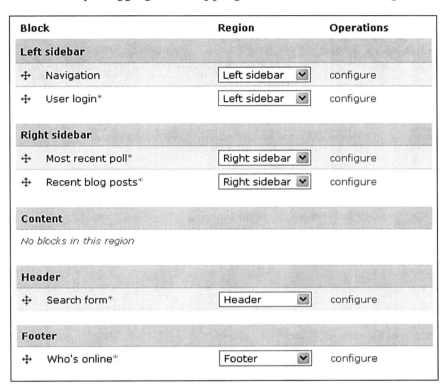

- In particular, notice that the **Most recent poll** has the **Right sidebar** region selected, as does **Recent blog posts**. The **Search form** has the **Header** region specified and **Who's online** is given the **Footer** region.

  For convenience's sake, make sure you set **User login**. If you don't specify a **region** for this **block**, it will not show up when you log out and you have to manually navigate to `http://localhost/drupal/user/login` to get back into the admin section.

  For now, don't worry too much about taking this all in, we will cover it in detail at a later stage—this exercise is simply going to give us our first look at a basic Drupal web page and its layout.

- Once these changes are made, click **Save blocks** and then **Home**.

The site should now look something like the following screenshot (minus the numbering):

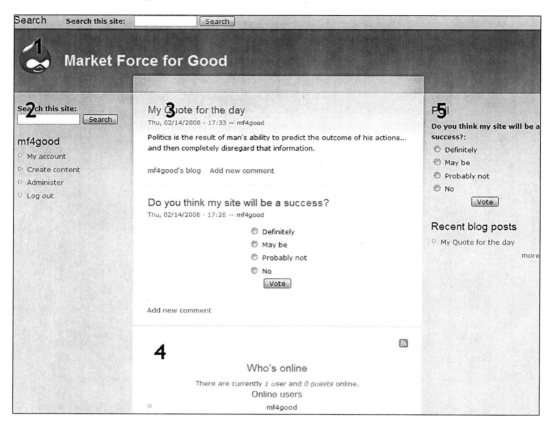

There are several main areas of interest numbered in this screenshot and we should look over them here in order to get a feel for what to expect in the chapters to come. Bear in mind that Drupal really doesn't impose many limitations on where and what you can place on any part of a web page, so the following explanation is really only a guide:

1. The page header contains your site's logo and slogan, among other things. It also provides a link to the landing or home page. Recall that we specified the search block to appear in the header region and you can now see it above the logo.

2. (& 5) Left and right sidebars are predefined regions that contain blocks. Blocks are effectively containers of information, or navigational links (or pretty much anything else you care to think of). Notice too that we now have blocks on the right-hand side (**Most recent polls** and **Recent blog posts**) because we set some of them to appear in the right sidebar earlier on. We told Drupal to display the **User login** in the left sidebar, but this is not visible because, of course, the screenshot was taken after login.

3. Content is generally displayed in this region of a site and the method of display is customizable and selective as we will see in due course. Since we did not specifically tell Drupal otherwise when we created some content, what we created is displayed automatically—we could have told it not to make the post visible here at all if we liked; we will talk about how to control content in more detail in Chapter 6.

4. The footer often contains information that is not immediately the most important on a page but is still relevant and useful. In this case we asked Drupal to display who is online here, but equally we might want to add a copyright notice or terms of use and so on.

This section has touched upon the power and elegance of Drupal by adding impressive features at the touch of a button and with little to no experience and certainly no programming skills required. However, it is quite possible that you don't want anything like what we have just seen. Perhaps you only want a single sidebar, or none at all. Maybe you want advertising across the top of the page or content displayed in drop-shadowed boxes? Whatever it is, the coming chapters will see to it that you are equipped with the requisite information to implement your goals.

Summary

This chapter covered the installation of PHP, MySQL, and Apache in a package called Apache2Triad—although XAMPP is also recommended. As a result, the foundation from which to build a live site in the coming days and weeks has been laid. Having taken the time to set up a working development environment, you can be assured that any needless time wastage has been prevented.

With the facilities provided by Apache, PHP, and MySQL installed on a test machine, we turned our attention to obtaining and installing Drupal itself—hopefully, you found that quite easy with the much improved installation features of Drupal 6!

Finally, we became acquainted with Drupal itself by adding new modules, posting some content to the site, and specifying where this content could be displayed on a typical page. In doing so, we were able to briefly discuss the anatomy of a basic Drupal page.

If you have gotten this far, then congratulations, you are ready to begin developing a new site! It's time to get your hands dirty…

3

Basic Functionality

I am sure you are more than keen to begin working on the layout and functionality of the site. That's not to say we are going to discuss the type of layout that involves themes just yet, because there is plenty of work to be done deciding what goes where before we look at things like fonts, colors, and images. While we aren't working with anything as exciting as new images or flashy graphics, much of what we cover in this section is a matter of taste, and you can get fairly creative.

Drupal is a modular system. Its functionality is held in modules that integrate into the main *workflow* at various points, altering the way other parts operate or even adding new features entirely. In order to build a fully functional website, we use modules that either come as part of the standard Drupal download (known as the *core*) or are provided by the good people of the Drupal community.

The terms *module* and *functionality*, with respect to Drupal, are synonymous, from the point of view that modules provide functionality. Hence, the discussion of Drupal functionality is really a discussion about modules.

Adding a new module is one thing, but presenting its functionality is also important and this requires us to look at menus and blocks as an integral part of our discussion on functionality. Accordingly, in this chapter, we are going to take a close look at:

- Adding modules
- Third-party modules
- Configuring modules
- Working with blocks
- Menus, primary and secondary links

Be aware that we won't be discussing some of the content-related modules in too much depth because these will be covered in great detail in Chapters 6 and 7. While the focus of this chapter is on getting the basics up and running, we will also look at how to include other modules from the Drupal site in order to demonstrate its power and flexibility. This will also reveal the considerable advantage of having an entire development community at hand to help out.

Adding Modules

It is by enabling certain modules that you will be able to achieve a diverse, and more importantly, functional site. As there are plenty of modules available, I can't hope to bore you with the all the ins and outs of every single one. Instead, we will enable and briefly work with some of the more interesting and useful ones.

If there is a module required by your site that is not covered here, simply follow the same method of enabling and testing that is discussed throughout this chapter, and apply it to that specific module. You will be up and running in no time at all!

Before we begin discussing each individual module, head on over to the **Modules** section under **Site Building** in the **Administer** menu item, and decide which ones to enable initially, based on your site's forecasted needs. Bear in mind that it is very easy to come back at a later stage and add or remove modules—this is part of the beauty and power of a system like Drupal.

For the purposes of this chapter, we will need the following modules:

- **Forum**
- **Comment**
- **Search**

Once you have made a selection, click **Save configuration**. At this point, it is possible that Drupal presents something like the following query:

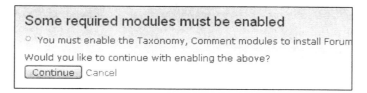

This tells us that the **Forum** module has *dependencies*. In other words, it cannot do its job without the facilities provided by the other modules listed. Many modules are interdependent and Drupal gives clues as to what relies on what on the modules page. For example, **Forum** displays the following:

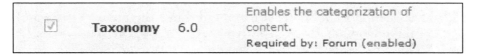

In this instance, it is telling us that it depends on two other modules, both of which are enabled.

Looking at **Taxonomy** as shown by the following screenshot:

☑	**Taxonomy**	6.0	Enables the categorization of content.
			Required by: Forum (enabled)

The converse is displayed, insofar as it tells us that while **Taxonomy** itself has no dependencies, it is required by **Forum**. Note too that Drupal prevents us from disabling any module that is required by another enabled module, by disabling the checkbox next to the module's name. Disabling the **Taxonomy** module in this case requires us first to disable all modules that depend on it first—in this case, **Forum**.

For at least a few of these modules, we will have to put in some serious thought before they are actually implemented on the site. In particular, **Forum** needs to be discussed in some depth, but before we do that, let's take a look at what else is available, courtesy of the Drupal community.

Third-Party Modules

One of the greatest things about Drupal is that the community contributions can promote and increase the diversity and features of any given project because they lower the development burden for website builders like you and me. This is an exceptionally valuable property of most, if not all, open-source projects.

What this means is that we can take a leisurely scroll over a variety of modules that have been made by someone, improved on by someone else, or changed into something else, and pick and choose the best. The converse of this is, of course, that any of your own developments can be made available to everyone else to use.

There are certain issues associated with using contributed modules such as the one we are going to incorporate into the demo site here. It is important to understand that people are providing useful software without enforcing payment. Please take it upon yourself to drop the developers a line every now and then to thank them for any functionality they have spent time and effort on.

Contributions (or more succinctly, *contribs*) like any software, are subject to bugs or errors, so make sure you backup everything, database included, before implementing any changes.

For more information on properly backing up a site, see Chapter 10. Remember, if something breaks your code, then it is your responsibility, and not the contributor's.

Downloading Modules

The Drupal website houses a list of contributions that are available to add under the **Modules** tab of the **Downloads** page (http://drupal.org/project/modules). At the top of the **Modules** page there is a selection of Drupal versions from which you can choose the appropriate one, and then browse the modules by category, name or date, as shown in the following screenshot:

Modules

Browse by category	Browse by name	Browse by date

Filter by Drupal Core compatibility: [6.x ▾] [Filter]

Modules are plugins for Drupal that extend its core functionality. Only use matching versions of modules with Drupal. Modules released for Drupal 5.x will not work for Drupal 6.x. These contributed modules are not part of any official release and may not be optimized or work correctly.

Obtaining the correct version is very important because a module developed for the 5.x family will almost certainly not work with the latest 6.x family. Unfortunately, the upgrading of contributions is not necessarily done at the same time as the core development; so it may be that there are some modules only built for older versions of Drupal—hopefully by the time you read this, most modules, if not all, will have been made compatible with 6.x.

For the purpose of demonstration, we will obtain a copy of a contribution that will save any site administrator a lot of time. The **DHTML Menu** module provides dynamic menu structures that do not require a page refresh in order to navigate a given menu. It can be found under the **Content Display** category.

 You need to be logged into the site in order to be able to apply a version filter.

Once you have found it, select the correct version, click **Download**, and save the zipped file. It may be more expedient to create a directory, say drupal_downloads, to save these files to. That's all there is to downloading modules.

Before we move on, it's a good idea to take a look over the list of all modules available to see what is achievable with Drupal. For example, did you know that you can use Drupal as an e-commerce website, complete with products or services and a shopping cart? Payment facilities such as PayPal, or credit cards and pretty much anything else that a fully-fledged online store would need are readily implementable—or will be, once the **E-Commerce** module has been upgraded to work with 6.x.

Learning just what can be achieved with Drupal modules now can really cut down the amount of time spent developing or looking for solutions to problems later on.

Installing Modules

Each module can be different depending on how it needs to alter the system in order to function. The best way to learn about how to install modules is simply to go ahead and do it. Since we have already downloaded one, let's continue and install it.

Open up the `.gz` file saved on your machine (refer to the previous section). Depending on the module in question it will have anywhere from one file to tens of files. The first thing to do is open up the `readme` file as this will, more than likely, have some detailed information on what to expect from the module, and how it functions.

Assuming you have the right module for the job, the next task is to create a `modules` folder in `sites/all` or `sites/default` that will house all the contributed modules and *keep them separate from the core modules in the* `modules` *folder*—Drupal will automatically pick up any modules added to this new folder.

With that done, extract the contents to the new `modules` folder:

Navigate to **Modules** under **Site Building** in the **Administer** menu section to see the results:

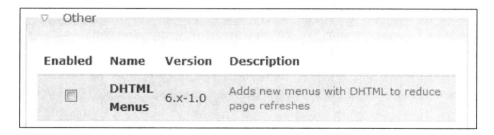

With some contributions performing their own database modifications behind the scenes, it is now easier to install a module (than it used to be), but it is also easier to shoot yourself in the foot. This is because the changes take place without your direct control. Admittedly, these changes, more often than not, are fairly harmless, but be cautious and make backups regardless.

That's pretty much all there is to do, but we still need to ensure that we can make use of this module from the administrator's point of view.

Enable the module and click **Save configuration**. Take note of the message highlighted in green as this will inform you of any updates and changes that are available, as shown in the following screenshot:

> ○ DHTML menu has been installed. If you wish, you may immediately enable it for the main navigation menu or adjust your block settings in detail.
>
> ○ The configuration options have been saved.

Note that in order to notify you of any important upgrades for modules and themes, Drupal requires the cron script to run. Once the cron has run, Drupal will recommend that you view the **Available updates** page (under **Reports** in **Administer**) to check on the status of each of the installed modules.

More on updates in a moment, first we still need to test out the module and put it to work, so navigate to the **Blocks** section of **Site building**. There will now be additional menu options, as shown in the following screenshot:

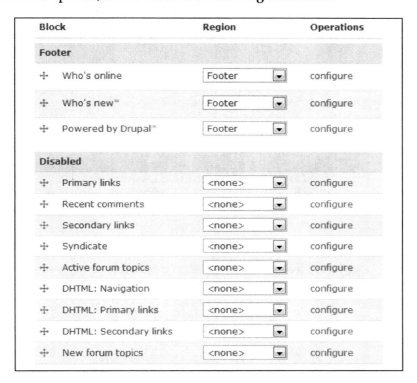

This specific module automatically creates a new DHTML menu for any menu that exists on the system and prefixes that menu name with **DHTML:**. In order to see the new menu in action, drag and drop the **DHTML: Navigation** block to the bottom of the **Left sidebar** region and then click **Save blocks**.

You should find now that there are two navigation menus in the left sidebar, with the bottom one being far more efficient in that it navigates without having the page refresh every time something is clicked. Play around with the new menu until you are satisfied it works correctly, then remove the old menu by dragging and dropping it to the **Disabled** region of the **Blocks** page.

The **DHTML Menu** module is a good example of how easy it can be to add some really nice features to a Drupal site. The problem for us is that this module is too easy to use—it doesn't really have much in the way of configuration parameters (although, it does have one or two) for us to make use of, so it hasn't really forced us to learn much more than how to download and install something.

Configuring Modules

Obviously, the nature of the setup for one module can differ wildly from the next. This is because modules can provide nearly any type of functionality imaginable, ranging from a simple poll to a search engine, or whatever. Accordingly, there are a host of different settings associated with each one.

The inherent broadness of function associated with modules means that the configuration and use of each one can also vary greatly. Because of this, it can be quite confusing at first to find out where to go in order to administer or make use of any changes implemented by a module.

Luckily, we can go back to the main administration page and view all the administrative tasks by clicking on **By module**. Navigating to this section will now present the configuration options associated with each module, including the latest one, the **DHTML Menu**:

Clicking on the **DHTML Menu** option brings up the following dialog that can be used to control the appearance and how certain menu items behave and are displayed. For example, you may have noticed that the **Administer** menu item appears twice in the DHTML navigation—remove this by deleting admin from the text area provided. Doing so means you have to double-click on **Administer** in order to open up its page.

DHTML Menu

☑ jQuery slide effect

Menu slides when it opens and closes.

Duplicated menu items:

admin

You can specify a list of menu items that should be displayed twice: Once as a parent item that expands and collapses the sub-menu and again as its own child item, which points directly to the page (the parent items still links on double-click). Enter one internal path (like "admin") on each line. To specify a custom link text, put it after the path, separated by a space.

[Save configuration]   [Reset to defaults]

With the **jQuery slide effect** setting saved, the menu now slides gracefully when it opens and closes.

The second option, **Replace navigation block,** presented in the **By module** view of **DHTML Menus** allows you to automatically replace any current menu items with their DHTML menu counterparts – this can save a bit of time dragging and dropping menus around the **Blocks** page.

Changes made to other modules can have a whole spectrum of different effects as we will see shortly and not all of them are implemented quite as easily as this one.

Forum

Go along to the **Forum** section under the **By module** view to begin working with it:

Forum

Enables threaded discussions about general topics.

○ Configure permissions

○ Forums

○ Get help

The first option, **Configure permissions**, is without doubt very important but we will discuss this particular issue later on when we deal with users, roles and permissions in Chapter 5. The final option, **Get help**, provides a nice summary of what the module in question does, how it works, and a bit about how to make use of it—along with links to any pertinent help on the Drupal site.

This leaves us with the **Forums** option in the middle that, when clicked, presents the following page for configuring the site's forums:

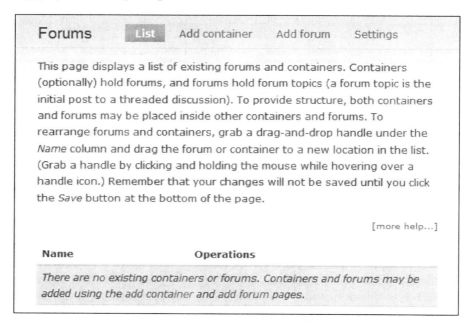

How to organize a **forum** really depends on how broad the scope of the discussion topics are going to be, how many people will be using the forums, and the nature of the topics up for discussion. What you are aiming for is an intuitive, logical, easy-to-use structure that will facilitate and encourage discussion by allowing users to easily find information, as opposed to frustrating them with a poor structure that effectively hides topics—this is a general problem and not one that is unique to Drupal.

Let's take a look at how to go about organizing an example wildlife and conservation forum. A good idea is to draw out the structure beforehand so that you can see how everything relates, and make changes before creating or deleting forums. For example, it may seem logical to split up forums depending on location, so that people in the US go straight to the North American forums and people in Africa go straight to the African forums.

Unfortunately, this has several drawbacks because there would be a lot of repeated topics for each continent (since wildlife issues are the same the world over). Even worse, if someone living in the States was concerned about canned lion hunting in South Africa, where would they go to discuss this, Africa or North America? It seems that partitioning forums based on location, in this instance, is probably not a good idea.

The best way to do it is by issue. People want to discuss issues or topics, so they naturally look for content based on these criteria. When looked at in this light, the meaning of the **add containers** tab becomes clear, because now we can organize forum topics based on their common issues.

In Drupal, a *container* holds a grouping of forums, so adding a container based on common issues for a number of forums is a very logical way to break up forums into intuitive chunks. For example, one of the major areas of concern for wildlife today is the topic of conservation. This in turn has many facets, all of which would no doubt be of interest to a concerned audience. The environment is also an issue that should be discussed, and everyone is interested in research these days. These all seem like viable containers because they logically encapsulate the bulk of what people using this site will discuss.

Moving ahead on this line of thought, each of the potential containers has distinct sub-categories that users would intuitively understand as topics for debate—we'll see the actual structure I came up with in a moment.

Once you have a nice structure jotted down on paper, it is time to actually implement the forums on the site. Let's set about this by creating the containers first. Click **Add container** to bring up a page to specify the name of the container, a brief description, the parent, and a weight.

Since you should have already decided on a structure, it is easy to see which container or forum has which parent. The top-level container should obviously leave the parent as **<root>**. You can set the weight of the container or forum if you would like them to be presented in an order other than alphabetical—the smaller the weight, the closer to the top of the pile it will appear.

Keep adding containers and forums, along with helpful descriptions until the entire structure is complete. The following screenshot shows an example structure for the putative wildlife and conservation forum. (There are, no doubt, more topics that could be added or changed, but this suffices for the moment.)

Name	Operations
✛ Carbon Emission	edit container
✛ Global Warming	edit forum
✛ Conservation	edit container
✛ Commercial Fishing	edit forum
✛ Commercial Hunting	edit forum
✛ Initiatives	edit forum
✛ Legislation	edit forum
✛ Environment	edit container
✛ Human Population Management	edit forum
✛ Pollution	edit forum

There are a few things to note here. First of all, there is some overlap in terms of how categories mesh on a conceptual level. For example, **Global Warming** should logically appear under **Pollution**, so why does it have its own forum? The answer is that you need to think about which issues are likely to be most important. As **Carbon Emissions** are currently a huge talking point, it warrants a promotion to its own forum even though it is conceptually a subcategory of pollution.

Secondly, I have only added a single parent layer of containers, with forums appearing under them. It is possible to add containers and forums within other containers and forums, and so on, but in the interests of making it easy to find topics, try keeping a flat structure instead of creating a deep navigation structure wherever possible. It is easier for people to search a list than to navigate a deep hierarchy.

Finally, there are some generic configuration options that warrant some attention. Most of the defaults are pretty sensible, but you may wish to click the **Settings** tab, and decide on such things as how many posts to display in one go and in which order:

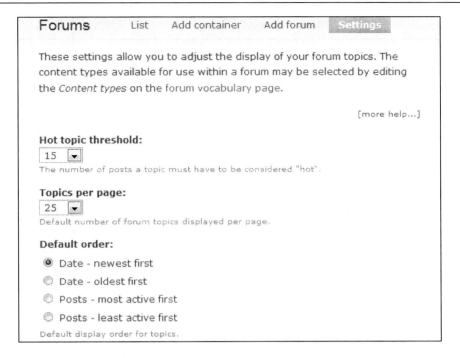

Once you are done, click **Save configuration** and the forum is more or less ready to go. Before we continue with configuring the other enabled modules, here's a quick peek at how a registered user would view the forum that has been set up so far:

Forum	Topics	Posts	Last post
Carbon Emissions			
✉ Global Warming	0	0	n/a
Conservation			
✉ Commercial Fishing	0	0	n/a
✉ Commercial Hunting	0	0	n/a
✉ Initiatives	0	0	n/a
✉ Legislation	0	0	n/a
Environment			
✉ Human Population Management	0	0	n/a
✉ Pollution	0	0	n/a

Forums
Post new Forum topic

Not bad for a few minutes work! The best thing about this forum is that it is easily modified to adapt to how the community makes use of it—adding, renaming or removing containers and forums is very easy. Just be careful not to continuously modify your forums because this can make it difficult to use and frustrating for members.

In reality, you should play around with each and every module, and ensure that it is working to your satisfaction. We don't have space to do so here, so it is left to you to post some comments and replies and get a feel of how things work.

Comments

As the **Comment** module is needed by the **Forum** module, it's a good idea to look at it here. A comment, as the name implies, allows users to remark about content they find on the site—as simple as that. How to figure out who can comment, and on what, is the subject of Chapter 5 on *Users, Roles, and Permissions*.

You can find **Comment** under the **By module** view in the **Administer** menu—alternatively, go through **Content management** and then **Comments**. Ignoring the permission configuration for the moment, clicking on **Comments** brings up a list of all the comments on your site. The following screenshot shows the **Comments** page once a few comments have been added to the site:

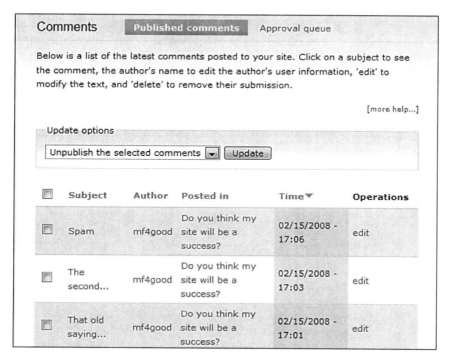

Drupal provides a fairly comprehensive interface for working with comments. There are a few **Update options** available in the drop-down list that delete or unpublish comments. If you never want to see a particular comment again on your site, then **Delete the selected comments** is the way to go. If you only want to prevent the comment from being displayed, without being removed entirely, then **Unpublish the selected comments** is the correct update option to use.

Assuming you have decided to unpublish a comment for some reason or other, you will have to look for it under the **approval queue** tab (towards the top of the page) instead of the main page. The approval queue allows you to search through and edit posts that have landed up here for whatever reason—it may be that they have been unpublished, or it may be that you have decided to force all comments into the **approval queue** for moderation. However, the comments may land up here, there are two update options available again, this time you can either delete the comment or publish it.

There are a number of other important categories associated with comments, namely **Default comment settings** or **Default display mode**. As of Drupal 6, these options are attached to each specific content type in order to provide fine grain control over how to view and post comments for individual types. Accordingly we must visit each different content type (in the **Content types** page under **Content management**) in order to make the appropriate comment settings.

Select the **edit** option next to a content type you wish to work with (for example, **Blog entry**) and then scroll down the page to the **Comment settings** section, browse through the available options and make any changes you would like before clicking **Save content type**.

For example, the **Default display mode** was changed to **Threaded list – collapsed** in order to bunch related comments together without displaying the body for each comment. The **Default display order** was also changed to **Date – oldest first** so that comments can be viewed as a conversation from the top of the page downwards.

Using these settings, comments on a page now look something like the following figure:

First comment by mf4good
Second comment by mf4good
    Reply to the second comment by mf4good

Now, earlier comments appear towards the top of the pile, with replies to those comments posted underneath and indented. Of course, this may not be to your liking, and these comments might just be easily displayed, as in the following screenshot:

Reply to the second comment   Thu, 02/28/2008 - 20:43 — mf4good

I disagree strenuously...

delete edit reply

Second comment   Thu, 02/28/2008 - 20:42 — mf4good

This is the second comment added to the post.

delete edit reply

First comment   Thu, 02/28/2008 - 20:42 — mf4good

This is the first comment added to this post

delete edit reply

It shouldn't be too hard to work out what changes were made in order to get the comments looking like this, so it is left as an exercise. Deciding the best method to display comments is really up to you, and any decisions made should take into account how comments are used on the site. You might find that it is better to allow users to decide for themselves and it is possible to give them control over the display of comments by selecting a different **Comment controls** option.

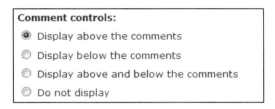

In this case, display controls are now shown before any comments on the site and a user can make up their own mind about how to view comments on the site.

The remaining sections provide a few options on how users actually create their comments. Once again, you should really take into account the type of site being built. For example, it might seem sensible to force users to preview their comments, but a bunch of regular community users who post very frequently will find this tedious.

Assuming you are going to allow anonymous users to post comments, decide whether they are to leave contact information with their posts. From the point of view of keeping up the standard of posts, it is probably a good idea to have postings from anonymous viewers sent to the **approval queue** so that you don't become a victim of spam attacks or cheap advertising—although, we will look at other methods of combating spam in Chapter 5.

Incidentally, if you would like to preview how one can decide whether comments must be approved or whether they can be displayed immediately, select **Configure permissions** under **Comment** in the **By module** view of the **Administer** menu. The default configuration parameters are displayed (along with those for each other module), as shown in the following screenshot:

Permission	anonymous user	authenticated user
access comments	☐	☑
administer comments	☐	☐
post comments	☐	☑
post comments without approval	☐	☑

In this case, anonymous users are not able to post or even access comments at all, but changing this is simply a case of checking the relevant boxes and clicking **Save permissions**. We won't look at this in any more detail here, but as mentioned, permissions will be dealt with in detail later on in Chapter 5.

Search

This is an interesting module to configure because there are some subtle underlying issues that require consideration when adjusting settings. For a start, the indexing process that is used to build the search in the database relies on cron (discussed in Chapter 10). Ensure this is operating correctly on a live site if you are going to implement a search feature. For more information on cron jobs and the cron.php script provided with Drupal, you can visit **System** in the **Help** section under the **Administer** menu item.

It is possible to re-index a site manually by clicking on the **Re-index site** button at the top of the search page, in **Search settings** under **Site configuration**. This will cause Drupal to go over the site's content and update its index so that any new content that you specifically wish to be included in any searches will be once the cron runs. If you wish to re-index the site immediately, run cron manually until the percentage of the site that is indexed reaches 100%.

Most of the other settings in this section relate to the performance of the system. For example, as the number of items to index per cron run will also affect the speed of the cron job, it may be prudent to make this setting a little lower if there are time-out problems. In addition, indexing shorter words adds load to the system, because it has to index that many more words in the content. It may also clutter up the search results with unwanted matches as a result of including words like *a* or *in*.

Finally, it is possible to decide on how to weigh the site search based on three criteria, namely **Keyword relevance, Recently posted,** and **Number of comments.** Work out which criterion is more important, and which one can be safely downgraded in importance. For example, the following settings:

Content ranking

The following numbers control which properties the content search should favor when ordering the results. Higher numbers mean more influence, zero means the property is ignored. Changing these numbers does not require the search index to be rebuilt. Changes take effect immediately.

Factor	Weight
Keyword relevance	5
Recently posted	4
Number of comments	2

Indicate that a higher importance is placed on the **Keyword relevance** of the content—in other words, how closely does the content match the keywords specified in the search. This importance is almost matched by how recent the content is—the most recent being the most important. Finally, the **Number of comments** is given less **Weight** and is therefore not considered quite as important as the first two criteria. Depending on your criteria, you may choose something completely different—the bottom line is to ensure that the search results are as relevant as possible to the site's users.

Dealing with modules more often than not requires us to configure their display, and for this, a working knowledge of blocks is required. Let's take a look at how to deal with them...

Working with Blocks

As we saw briefly in Chapter 2, blocks contain information or related data that is visible in various places around the site—depending on where you choose to show them. Blocks are often generated by modules, but it is also possible to create them manually. Since many modules generate blocks automatically, it is always wise to pay the **blocks** section a visit whenever a new module has been enabled, because it is likely there are some new settings to play with.

When we talk about working with blocks, what we are really saying is "*How do we want to present the functionality of the site to the user?*" Naturally, everyone should strive to make a striking and unique site, and layout configuration is a big part of that—especially since it governs how functionality is organized on the site's interface.

Keep in mind at all times that the overriding factors that govern the way to set things up when it comes to presenting the site are all about usability. Make sure that the site is intuitive, easy to follow, and never sacrifice clarity and ease of use for artistic reasons.

Luckily, Drupal is already fairly sensibly laid out by default, but that doesn't mean that there is not plenty to do. You have an exceptional amount of control over where and how everything is displayed, and correspondingly, quite a lot to work on.

One of the best ways to find out how you want things done is by looking on the Net and seeing how other people have made sites that work nicely. If there is something you like, see if it can be replicated.

Another way to learn about how you are ultimately going to set things out is to actually play around and see what works. This section will concentrate on this method and leave the first method for you to research.

Adding Blocks

Under **Site building**, click **Blocks** to bring up the list of blocks that are available for the site at present. Remember that this list will change as modules are added and removed—you will probably have to revisit it more than once. The blocks page provides a list of the available blocks and several options for each one. Drupal gives you the ability to place any of these blocks pretty much anywhere on the page, but your choices shouldn't be quite so random.

It is generally a good idea to group related information into the same places on the site, so that users can get a feel for where they might look for a specific type of content. For our current purposes, the following settings are made:

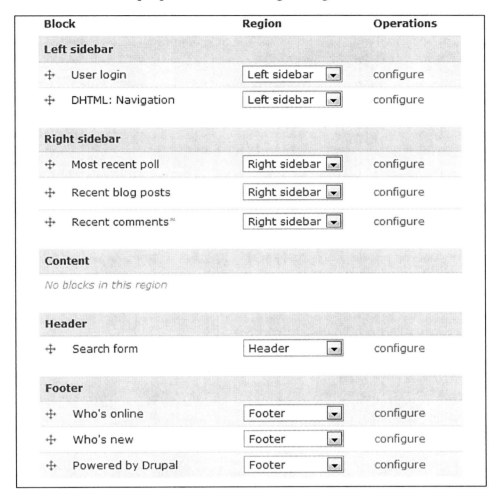

Notice that community related information, like **Who's new** and **Who's online,** is confined to the footer area of the page. While this information might be of interest, it must be relegated to the bottom of the page to avoid detracting from the main content of the site.

All content-related blocks are grouped into the right-hand sidebar. This means that if people want to quickly take a look at what new content has been added to the site, they can find it by looking here. Additionally, information is structured such that polls appear above all other information (because we generally want to encourage people to take the time to answer a poll), but we have left the **Search form** at the top of the page, because this should be one of the most useful tools once the amount of content on the site has become substantial.

Of course, some blocks remain disabled as the site does not need them for now. It is always easy to add or remove blocks at a later date. Provided you make sure there is a nice logical layout for the various blocks, you can chop and change what is and is not displayed as and when required. Try not to chop and change too often once the site is live as this impairs its usability and may lead to confusion.

Taking a look at your homepage once these changes have been saved (by clicking **Save blocks**), notice that the various blocks have now been inserted into the web pages. It's easy enough to move things around until you are totally happy with the way the page looks, but there is little point in spending hours and hours getting everything just perfect if you are going to change the theme at a later stage. Rather, make sure you understand how blocks works and come back to it after settling on a theme.

You may also have noticed that there is an **Add block** tab at the top of the **Blocks** page. Clicking this brings up a page that can be used to insert your own blocks into the site, as shown in the following screenshot:

Block description: *

> LinkDoozer - Bookmark site

A brief description of your block. Used on the block overview page.

Block title:

The title of the block as shown to the user.

Block body:

```
<a href="javascript:
void(open('http://www.linkdoozer.com/account.php?name=' +
escape(document.title) + '&close=on' + '&url=' +
escape(location.href),'LinkDoozer',' height=300, width=450, location=no,
scrollbars=yes, menubar=yes, toolbar=yes, directories=no, resizable=yes'));"
><img src="http://www.linkdoozer.com/doozer_icon.png" alt="Doozermark
Me" title="Doozermark this Page" border="0" /> Doozermark this site!</a>
```

The content of the block as shown to the user.

In this case, we have added a link provided by a free online favorites site called LinkDoozer (`http://www.linkdoozer.com`) that allows users to add sites directly to their online favorites list at the click of a button. Doing something like this is a great way to gain exposure for your site because at least in the LinkDoozer community, users can review and recommend a site to other community members.

 In general, be wary of adding 3rd party JavaScript to your pages. Make sure you trust the authors of the script before adding something like this.

Notice that the **Block title** section was left blank because this block should not take up any more valuable screen real estate than is absolutely necessary, and the link that is displayed is fairly self explanatory anyway so any name added here would simply waste space and be redundant.

It is likely that you want everyone and anyone to add your site to their favorites, so setting this block to display prominently on each page makes sense:

Clicking on the new link confirms that it is working, as evidenced by the reply from LinkDoozer:

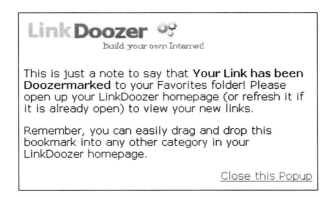

The situation becomes more complex when we start thinking about whether certain people should be allowed to access a block or not, or whether the block should be displayed on all pages or only on selected pages. In order to find out how to deal with these issues, we must look at block configuration in some detail.

Configuring Blocks

Drupal allows us to control when a block is displayed through the **configure** link at the right-hand side of each block in the list. This configuration page is split up into four main sections that deal with:

- **Block specific settings**
- **User specific visibility settings**
- **Role specific visibility settings**
- **Page specific visibility settings**

Combining these provides a sophisticated method of controlling when a block is shown, and to whom. Of course, some modules don't require any specific settings of their own; in which case you are only required to make specific decisions about users and pages.

A good example for configuring a block can be shown by the **Who's online** page. This page allows us to decide how long users can be inactive before we no longer consider them online, as well as the maximum number of people to show at any one time. That's easy enough to deal with, and really depends on the needs of the site.

The other options give us something to think about though:

```
▽  User specific visibility settings

Custom visibility settings:
  ○ Users cannot control whether or not they see this block.
  ◉ Show this block by default, but let individual users hide it.
  ○ Hide this block by default but let individual users show it.
  Allow individual users to customize the visibility of this block in their account settings.


▽  Role specific visibility settings

Show block for specific roles:
  ☑ anonymous user
  ☑ authenticated user
  Show this block only for the selected role(s). If you select no roles, the block will be visible to
  all users.


▽  Page specific visibility settings

Show block on specific pages:
  ○ Show on every page except the listed pages.
  ◉ Show on only the listed pages.
  ○ Show if the following PHP code returns TRUE (PHP-mode, experts only).

Pages:
  <front>



  Enter one page per line as Drupal paths. The '*' character is a wildcard. Example paths are
  blog for the blog page and blog/* for every personal blog. <front> is the front page. If the
  PHP-mode is chosen, enter PHP code between <?php ?>. Note that executing incorrect
  PHP-code can break your Drupal site.
```

The settings shown in the previous screenshot allow users to edit their own preference for whether they can see the **Who's online** block—leaving all roles unchecked allows the block to be displayed for all users. We will look at how to create different roles in Chapter 5 and this will require you to return to this page to re-specify the **Role specific visibility settings** if necessary.

With these settings in place, users editing their account information are presented with the following checkbox that allows them to enable the block or disable it:

Looking at the screenshot before last again, notice that the **Show on only the listed pages** option has been selected and the text **<front>** has been entered in the **Pages** text area. This means that whenever someone visits the site, they are shown who is online but as soon as they begin using the site and move away from the home page, that information is no longer visible.

People with PHP experience have the ability to add some code to determine whether or not the block is displayed. This could be in the form:

```
if (some_condition_is_true){
 return TRUE;
}else{
 return FALSE;
}
```

As always, it is recommended that you play around and attempt to show a block on a certain page but not others. For example, can you prevent a block being shown when someone is using the forums? The answer is of course to select **Show on every page except the listed pages** option, and then enter **forum*** into the text area. Make sure this is correct by trying it out on your own machine.

Completing the site's block configuration is simply a case of going through each enabled block, and making the appropriate decisions about when, where, and to whom it will be displayed. At present though, this is not quite the full picture because we have not yet discussed users, roles and permissions, so be prepared to revisit this after Chapter 5.

Menus, Primary and Secondary Links

There are three default menus that can be configured in Drupal. The navigation menu is the one we have been using up to now and is the standard menu system for traversing all the functionality the site administrator needs. At some point you might want users to have quick access to several main sections of a site, in which case the primary links may be configured to provide this feature. For less important links, generally stuff like **About us** or **Terms of use** pages, Drupal provides the secondary links menu.

Clicking on **Menus** under **Site Building** in the **Administer** section (or double-clicking for DHTML menu users) provides access to the navigation, primary and secondary link dialogs as well as the **Add menu** and menu **Settings** pages:

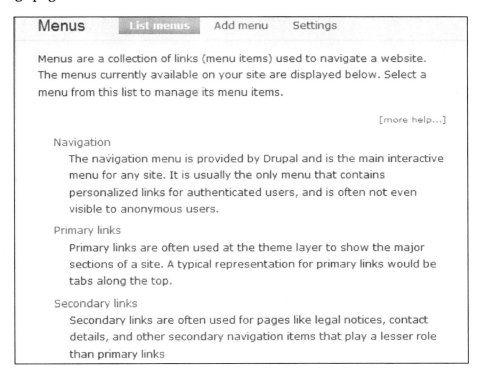

If at some point, the default menus are not sufficient for your purposes, adding a new menu is quite easy:

Any added menu will now be available to work with in the **Menu** section just like the defaults. Remember that the new menu will not show up until you tell Drupal where it should be displayed in the **Blocks** section of the **Site building** menu.

The **Settings** options, shown in the following screenshot, can be a little more difficult to fathom initially.

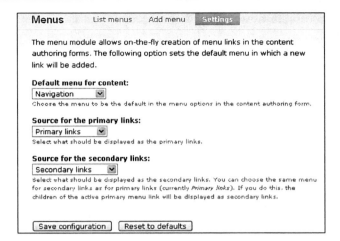

The **Default menu for content** option specifies where links that are added during content creation (for example, when creating an **About us** page) will be added. It's basically a shortcut method of adding new content to the menu because it saves you from having to post some content, find the relative path (i.e. `http://localhost/drupal/forum`), and then add that to the menu manually—although, we discuss this process in a moment.

The next few options are interesting because they control where the links displayed in a theme's primary and secondary links menus are drawn from. For each of these you can select either to show the navigation menu, primary or secondary links, or not to show the menu at all. As a quick exercise, set the **Source for the primary links** to **Navigation** and click **Save configuration**. You should find that the **Navigation** menu items are now displayed in the **Primary links** menu, like this:

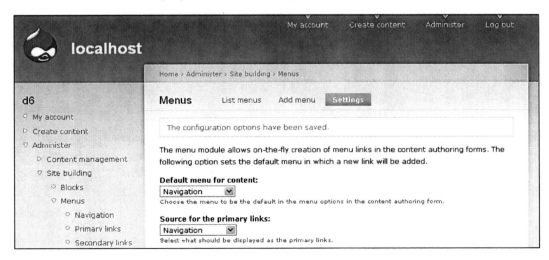

It's a bit confusing to picture what is going on before we have even looked at the primary links in any detail, so we'll clarify this in a moment. For now ensure that you reset the **Source for primary links** option to **Primary links** and click **Save configuration**.

Go back to the **List menus** option and select **Navigation** to bring up the standard menu overview dialog. From here, you can add, edit, enable, disable, or, in some cases, delete items as well as determine whether or not items should be expanded in the menu by default. In addition, items that are enabled or disabled will subsequently display a reset option that turns any configuration back to their defaults:

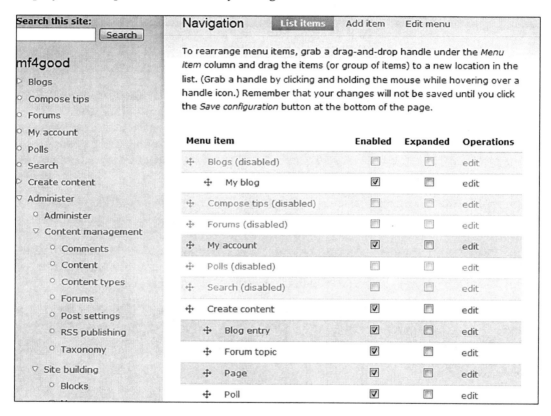

It is important to note that adding a new module does not necessarily mean that it will be added to the **Navigation** menu. Revisit this page any time you add new features and want them to show up in the menus—bear in mind that some modules will do this automatically.

For the moment, let's not mess around with the **Navigation** menu, since it is possible to make some irretrievable changes that could cause a bit of hassle later down the line. Instead, let's look at how to build up the **Primary links** menu. Click on that option under **Menus** to bring up its overview page and then select **Add item**:

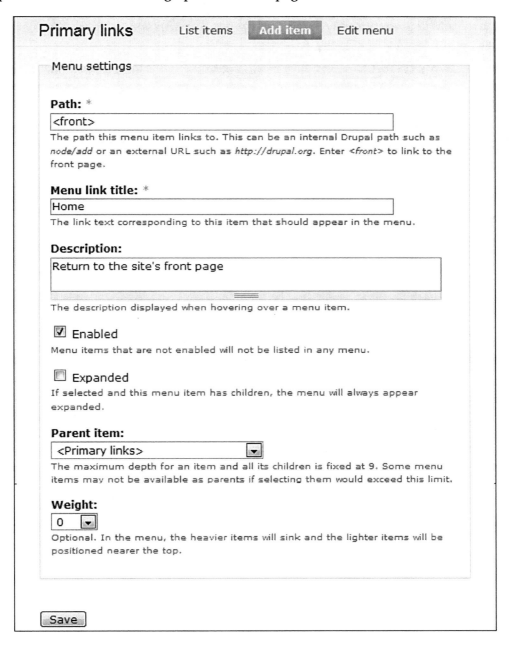

In this instance we are creating a new menu item that will take users back to the home page. The **Description** will be displayed as a tip whenever a user hovers their mouse over the link, so ensure you enter something succinct and helpful here. Since this link will not have any child links there is no point in selecting the **Expanded** option because there will be nothing to expand. The **Parent item** is of course set to **Primary links**, but modify this to the appropriate menu item depending on where in the menu you want it to appear.

Clicking **Save** adds this new link to the **Primary** links and it will be available to **edit**, **disable** or **delete** in the overview section. More importantly, looking at a page now should reveal the effect this has had:

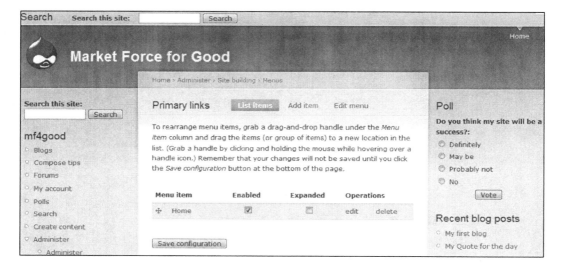

Notice there is now a **Home** link at the top right of the page. This is where the primary links are displayed in the default theme, but different themes might make any number of changes to the **Primary links** menu (including not displaying it at all). Clicking on **Home** should take you straight to the default front page, as specified when the link was added.

Try to add another menu item to the **Primary links** to make sure you can add any target page at will. Since we have created a forum, let's add the forum front page to the **Primary links** (can you guess the target **Path** we should specify?):

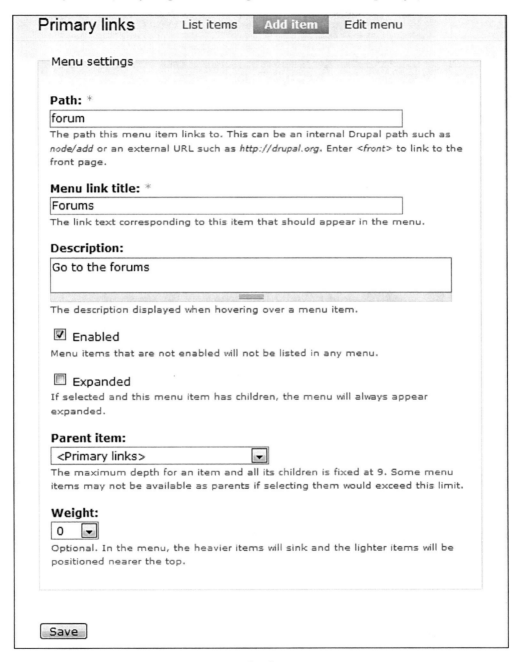

A good trick, hinted earlier, to locate the path needed for a menu item is to navigate to it directly and then cut and paste the relative path (i.e. everything in the URL after the root). For example, if we go to the forums on the site as it stands, the URL looks like this:

`http://localhost/drupal/`**`forum`**

The bold part is the relative path because `http://localhost/drupal` is the root folder (or homepage).

Now, you might decide that in addition to visiting the forum front page, you also want to add the containers to this menu so that people can go straight to their forum of choice.

After saving the forum primary link, go back to the **Add item** dialog and then add the new link as follows:

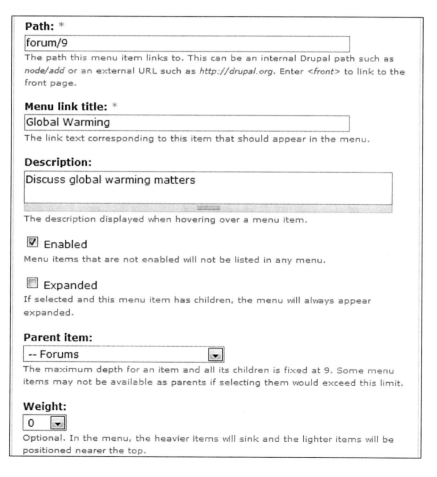

Determining that `forum/9` corresponds to the **Global Warming** container required a quick visit to the container that displayed `http://localhost/drupal/forum/9` as the URL, and from there it is a simple matter to add this to the **Path**. Remember, that we want this link to be a child item of **Forums** within the **Primary links,** so the **Parent item** needs to be changed accordingly. Be careful here because you are able to select a parent item from any of the menus, so it is possible to choose the wrong one.

With that done, click **Save** and then take a look at the **Primary links** at the top right of the page:

Of course, **Global Warming** is not immediately visible because it is a child of **Forums.** Unfortunately, clicking on **Forums** takes you to the forums and does not expose the **Global Warming** link within the Primary links as you might expect—this is because **Primary links** do not display child links.

We have a trick up our sleeves though because we can set the **Source for secondary links** to **Primary links**. This means that the **Secondary links** are sourced from the children of **Primary links**, so when we click on **Forums**, **Global Warming**, as a child element of the **Primary links**, appears in the **Secondary links**:

If things are still not clear, then perform the following exercise to highlight the other side of the coin:

1. Go back to the menu **Settings** page and select **Secondary links** as the **Source for secondary links**.

2. Go to **Secondary links** and **Add item**, ensuring it is saved with **<Secondary links>** as **Parent item**.

Take note of the changes to the **Secondary links** while performing these steps—you should find that any items added to the **Secondary links** show up as expected in the **Secondary links** area, underneath the **Primary links**. Changing the source back to **Primary links** will of course mean that **Global Warming**, or whatever other child links there are in **Primary links**, are displayed once more.

You are not constrained to stick with the conventional setup for these particular menus either. Head on over to the **Blocks** section of **Site building** and set the **Primary links** block to display in the **Left sidebar** (remember, there is also a DHTML version available if you prefer). With that saved, there is a new view of the **Primary links** menu complete with child links:

Alternatively, it is easy enough to display any of the menus you create manually in any area of the page by going to the **Blocks** page and specifying the desired region for the menu.

Having the ability to create unlimited menus and display them anywhere is a very powerful feature. There are a multitude of different combinations to try out. For example, you might wish to create a content menu that contains a listing of all the different types of content on a site—blogs, forums, stories, polls, and have this as the primary links. Alternatively, you could create an entirely new menu and add this to the **Header** region by configuring it on the **Blocks** page.

Summary

This chapter discussed the all-important topic of adding functionality and organizing it on the site. This is one of the most important tasks to undertake during development. Selecting and implementing the right functionality for the right users is a subtle art, but hopefully you found that Drupal makes it quite easy to implement.

We also got a taste of what it's like to have an entire development community to draw from, when we downloaded and installed a contributed module. Contributions are an invaluable resource for extending the functionality of a site. This facility comes with the express warning that you need to safeguard the security of your site by making backups before implementing any changes.

Drupal's power and elegance shone through when we talked about how easy it is to customize the site's menu and navigation. Having a powerful tool, combined with the flexibility of the menu system, is an extraordinary help when it comes to creating a well-designed and easy-to-use site.

One of the most important things you hopefully learned from this chapter is that, because Drupal is so flexible and customizable, there are a large number of settings that are held at different places. Keeping track of all of these might seem quite daunting at first, but will become more familiar in time.

For now though, sit back and take a quick break, happy in the knowledge of a task well done. In the following chapter we look at a fair few configuration issues—another topic crucial for your success as a Drupal website administrator.

4

Site Configuration

The most common trap people fall into when first starting out is they assume the *basics* are easy to master, and therefore don't require too much thought. Things are not quite so clean cut in reality because while your site's basic setup is, more often than not, easy to implement, the more subtle problem is knowing *what* you want to implement, and *how* you want to implement it in the first place. Discovering what you need from your site is particularly important for precisely this reason, so we cover this topic here but it is likely that you will need to revisit every now and then.

Does this mean that you should not start working directly on the site unless you know exactly what you want? Not really; like most things, it's a bit of a trade-off when it comes to starting out with the development of your Drupal website. This is because it is almost impossible to determine exactly what your site will need, and how its functionality should be provided until you have been working with it for some time. Often, you will find yourself modifying the behavior of a site based on feedback from the users.

 Have a good idea of what you're working towards, even if you're not quite sure how to get there!

At any rate, to get the ball rolling, we are going to need to talk about the following Drupal site configuration topics:

- Clean URLs
- Error reporting
- File system and file uploads
- Logging and reports
- Site information
- Site maintenance

Not everything that is available in Drupal's *Site Configuration* section is discussed in this chapter. For example, the performance settings will be discussed in more detail in their own section later on in the book, while others are very straightforward and really don't warrant our attention. However, you should look over everything in this section at least once to familiarize yourself with what is available, even if it isn't discussed here.

Assuming you have paid close attention to how you want a site to function, and how it should be used, then once the basic settings are complete the number of changes you have to make down the line are kept to a minimum.

Before We Start

It is sensible to make note of a few important things before getting our hands dirty. Make it second nature to check how the changes made to the settings in Drupal affect the site. Quite often settings you modify, or features you add, will not do precisely as expected and without ensuring that you use a prudent approach to making changes, you can sometimes end up with a bit of a mess.

Some of you might be groaning at the prospect of having to plow through setting after setting in order to get everything just right. Of course, creating a flashy new theme would probably be more exciting, but taking the time to look through and play with all the available settings is an important step towards becoming a competent Drupal administrator.

 In fact, setting up a site's configuration is akin to laying the groundwork for creating a flashy theme, because it reduces the amount of work required later down the line.

Log into your site as the administrator, and navigate to **Administer,** and then **Site configuration**. You should see something like the following page:

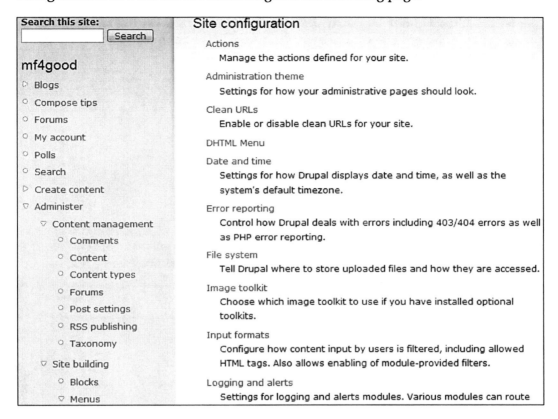

There are plenty of options to deal with (demonstrated by the sheer number of links presented on this page), and we will start, throughout this chapter, by working our way down the links provided on the right-hand side of the page—excluding any that are incorporated into later topics.

Looking at the latest screenshot actually highlights an earlier point. Notice that there is a **DHTML Menu** option now available in this section. This was only added *after* we installed the module, and is a good example of how making changes in one part of the site can lead to alterations in another. In this case, it is nothing particularly earth shattering, because clicking on the link takes us to the same configuration page that is available from the **By module** view of the **Administer** section anyway.

Clean URLs

It is important to discuss this particular topic early on because it acts as a cog in the greater machinery of not only your site, but also in how your site interacts with the rest of the Internet. The simplicity of the **Clean URLs** configuration page belies its importance:

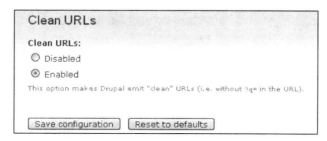

As you can see, the choice is simple — either enable or disable **Clean URLs**. Your system should also tell you whether or not it is possible to use clean URLs — if you see something like the following screenshot, then you have problems:

Your system configuration does not currently support this feature. The handbook page on Clean URLs has additional troubleshooting information.

Remember:

 It is *highly recommended* that you have **Clean URLs** enabled on your live site.

The reason for this recommendation is because you naturally want your site to be able to compete fairly with other sites when it comes time for Google and other search engines to index its web pages. Search engines use automated programs to traverse the Web (called bots) and when they come across nice, straightforward URLs like the ones displayed by Drupal when Clean URLs are enabled, http://localhost/drupal/node/2, they happily go about their business, indexing pages.

Indexing allows content to start showing up in Web searches and hence more people can find these pages and you're on your way (more or less). If however, they come across dynamic URLs (ones that contain query strings) then they often don't put the same effort into indexing that page, or worse, ignore it entirely. This can lead to a situation where you have a lot of lovely content just waiting to be read, but no one is able to find it because the search engines are ignoring all the pages of form:

http://localhost/drupal/**?q**=node/2

The highlighted part of this URL, (?q=) is what causes the problem. Drupal navigates around its own pages by a system of internal URLs that it finds using queries in the format shown in the previous URL. In other words, ?q=node/2 is asking Drupal to go and find whatever content or page is held at node/2. The problem is that the Googlebot simply sees the dynamic query and says to itself, "Hmmm, this could be a nasty trick designed to make me index the same page millions of times over so I won't pay it any mind".

> Actually, providing informative names (called aliasing) for posts is far better than relying on Drupal's default numbering system. It's worth skipping ahead and looking over the section on **Path & Pathauto** in Chapter 10 so that you get into the habit of providing user and search engine friendly aliases for all your content.

The people at Drupal realized this is the case, so if it is possible on your setup, clean URLs are enabled by default and you don't have to worry about any of this anyway. If you have installed Apache2Triad then your development machine is safe in this regard. The problem comes during deployment because it is quite possible that your Internet service provider's setup does not allow for clean URLs. Now what?

If you already know who is going to host your live site, then try test things out now by installing a copy of Drupal on the live server and ensuring it is possible to use clean URLs (see Appendix A on Deployment for more information). If you can't, consider finding another host that does. Otherwise, you will end up having to deal with their system admin guys and hang around until they can sort stuff out or eventually start ignoring you.

Whether you can or can't use clean URLs basically comes down to a configuration setting in Apache. On your development machine you have direct access to the httpd.conf file (found in the conf folder of your Apach2Triad installation) that Apache uses for its configuration—this is probably not the case on your live servers since any given host obviously doesn't want to give everyone using their servers total control to mangle everything as they see fit.

In order for Drupal to implement clean URLs, Apache needs to have mod_rewrite enabled. By way of example, open up httpd.conf and search for the line that reads:

```
LoadModule rewrite_module modules/mod_rewrite.so
```

That's the line that determines whether or not Apache can implement what Drupal requires in order to give you clean URLs. If it's commented out you will need to uncomment it and then restart Apache before any changes take effect.

If you find that at some stage you fall into the trap of having clean URLs enabled on a system that cannot implement them, causing all sorts of fun problems, then manually navigating to the following page should allow you to disable the clean URLs and use the site as normal:

`http://localhost/drupal/?q=admin/settings/clean-urls`

Remember to exchange the highlighted part for whatever is pertinent for your setup.

Error Reporting

This section allows you to broadly deal with the problem of two common site errors that may crop up during a site's normal course of operation. In particular, you may wish to create a couple of customized error pages that will be displayed to users in the event of a *page not found* or *access denied* problem.

Remember there are already pretty concise pages, which are supplied by default, but should you wish to make any changes then the process for creating an error page is exactly the same as creating any other normal page.

Let's do one very quickly. Click on **Create content** in the main menu and select **page**. Add whatever content you want for, say, the *page not found* error:

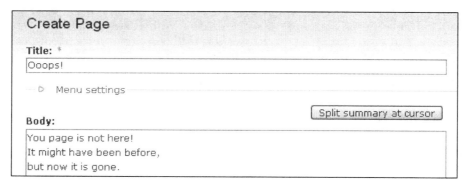

Don't worry about the host of options you have available on this page—we will talk about all of this later on. For now, simply click on **Save**, and make note of the URL of the page when it is displayed (in this instance, mine is `http://localhost/drupal/node/4`). Now, head to the **Error reporting** section of **Site Configuration** and add this URL to the **Default 404 (Not found) page** section and then click **Save configuration**:

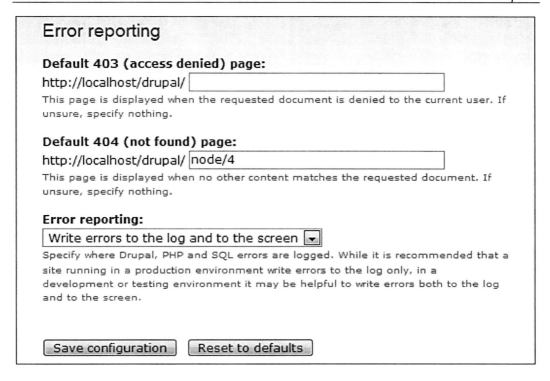

If you now navigate to a page that doesn't exist, for example, node/3333, you should receive the new error message:

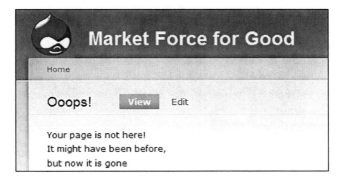

In this example we asked Drupal to find a node that does not yet exist and so it displayed the page not found error message. Since Drupal can also provide content that is private or available to only certain users, it also needs the **access denied** error to explain to would be users that they do not have sufficient permissions to view the requested page. This is not the same as not finding a page of course, but you can create your own **access denied** page in exactly the same way.

The next option, **Error reporting**, allows you to decide whether to write errors to the screen as well as to the error log or just to the log. While you are busy building the site, it useful to select **Write errors to the log and to the screen**, in order to determine what has gone wrong and when. However, once it is time to go live you should change this to **Write errors to the log** (seen in the drop-down list). This helps prevent displaying information to malicious users who might be able to use it in an attack on your site.

Check your logs on a regular basis as part of your overall strategy to ensure that the site continues to run smoothly. Error messages, warnings, and so on, are effectively a window into the operations of the site, and are an indispensable tool. We'll take a look at the *Logging and alerts* part of your site configuration as well as how to work with your logs in a moment. Before we do, let's discuss files.

File System and File Uploads

How you deal with file system settings really depends on what type of content you use to visualize your site. If you know that all files will always be available for anyone to download on your site, then leave the **Download method** under **File system** as **Public**. While it is possible to change between public and private, it is also likely that you will experience some problems due to the fact that all the file paths will change when hopping between one or other.

 Having your file access set to **Public** is probably wise, because at present, **Private** can interfere with the proper working of other parts of the site.

Public files can be accessed directly through a browser without having to go through your Drupal website. So, if someone liked a video you posted, they could reference it from their own website, causing people to visit their site to see the video but use your bandwidth to serve it—obviously, not ideal! You need to keep an eye on this and find out if your host service provides some sort of hotlinking protection to combat this, if you do notice a problem.

Assuming you *do* want to make your download method private, then you will need to move the `files` directory out of the document root so that it is not directly available over the Web. If you do this, then enter the *fully-qualified* file path to this folder instead of the *relative* path, because otherwise Drupal will try to find it in the normal place. For example, on the demo site's development machine, the following file path was entered with the **Private Download method** selected:

```
C:\apache2triad\files
```

Also ensure that the `temp` directory set is sensible, which in the case of the demo site is: `C:\apache2triad\temp`.

Before continuing, let's confirm that we can upload a file to the site without any problems. Go to the **Modules** section under **Site Building** in **Administer**, enable the **upload** module (if it's not already) and click **Save configuration**. Now when you attempt to **create content**, the following **File attachments** option is displayed:

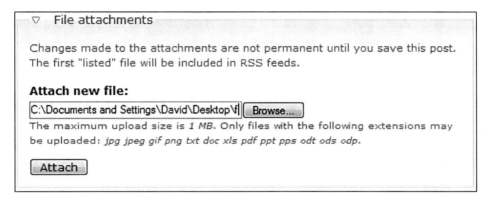

Once the file has been uploaded, you should see a confirmation message:

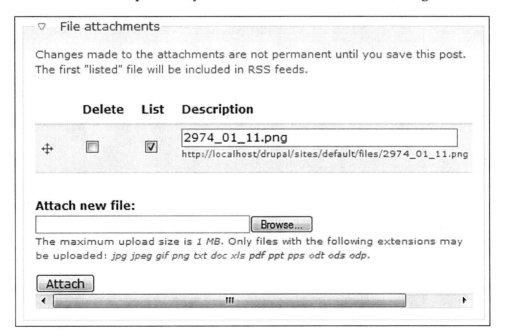

The new table shown below **File attachments** in the previous figure has
three columns:

- **Delete** gives you the option to delete the attachment from the post.
- **List** shows the uploaded file in the attachment section of the content posting.
- **Description** is the name of the file (and its location).

If you are attaching files in order to display them within a page, you will need to
ensure they are fairly small, for performance and speed. Incidentally, if you do
choose to list your attachment, by selecting the **List** option, then this is what the post
looks like:

Users can simply click the link to upload the file. If you are attaching the file to your
post so that it can be displayed from within the page, then you probably want to
disable the **List** option. For more information on file attachments, head on over to
Chapter 7, which deals with *Advanced Content*.

How Drupal controls what type of files and what size files can be uploaded is a
matter for the **File uploads** section just below **File system** in the **Site configuration**
menu. It is not really sensible to allow *any* type of file to be uploaded to the site.
The first thing that will happen if you do is that someone will upload a malicious
executable file that does something nasty when run on users' machines, causing them
in turn to say or do something nasty to you.

The page we are given:

File uploads

▽   General settings

Maximum resolution for uploaded images:

`0` `WIDTHxHEIGHT`

The maximum allowed image size (e.g. 640x480). Set to 0 for no restriction. If an image toolkit is installed, files exceeding this value will be scaled down to fit.

List files by default:

`Yes ▾`

Display attached files when viewing a post.

Default permitted file extensions:

`jpg jpeg gif png txt doc xls pdf ppt pps odt ods odp`

Default extensions that users can upload. Separate extensions with a space and do not include the leading dot.

Default maximum file size per upload:

`1` MB

The default maximum file size a user can upload. If an image is uploaded and a maximum resolution is set, the size will be checked after the file has been resized.

Default total file size per user:

`1` MB

The default maximum size of all files a user can have on the site.

Your PHP settings limit the maximum file size per upload to *16 MB*.

...provides a number of options to play with and the decisions you ultimately make should be dictated by the needs of the individual site. When in doubt, follow the tenet:

 Provide only what is absolutely necessary, and no more!

The actual settings themselves are easy enough to implement, but I suggest you remove any file extensions that you *know* the site will not need. Remember that it is possible to cloak nasty software within other file types, so the more variety you allow, the less secure things become.

PHP comes with a built-in image toolkit, GD, so you will always have the option to scale images since Drupal has native support for GD. This means you can set a maximum image width and height safe in the knowledge that anything larger than that will be nicely scaled. This can be important for maintaining a consistent layout—it is possible to end up with a very ugly mess if people can upload images wider than your page.

The default total file size per user also needs some thought because the last thing you want to do is stifle productive and active community members by disallowing more than a few uploads. Conversely, giving people complete impunity can also end up in tears.

Logging and Reports

To begin with, click on **Logging and alerts** under **Site configuration**. If there is only a blank page shown, go to the **Modules** section and enable the **Database logging** module, and then revisit it. Click on **Database logging** to see what is available for configuration:

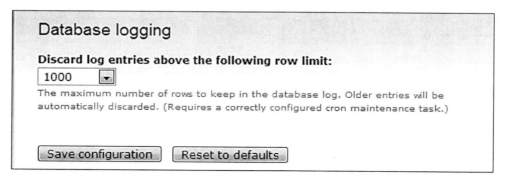

Just the one setting, which, at least to begin with, is sensible—you may wish to increase or decrease the number of records stored on the system depending on how much work you have to do in order to maintain the site properly. Remember that Drupal can properly maintain the site's event logs only if the cron jobs are being run regularly (See Chapter 10 for more on this). Having only one setting to make is not that exciting, so let's go look at the actual logs that are stored by Drupal.

In order to take a look at the logs, click **Reports** under the **Administer** menu item, and you will be presented with a list of the various types of logs and reports that are available:

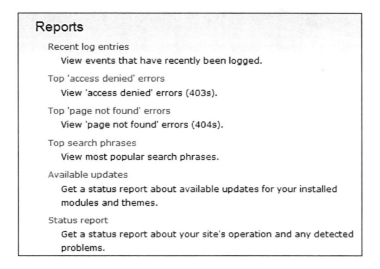

Selecting the first option, **Recent log entries**, brings up the site's log of events and you can filter these events by clicking on **Filter log messages** and then selecting any options in the boxes under the heading **Type** and then clicking **Filter**:

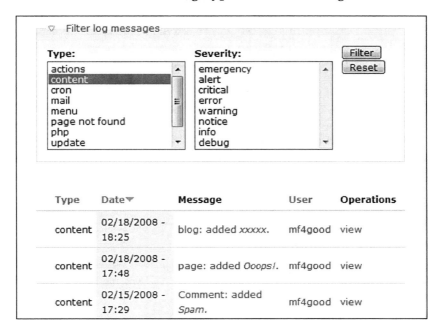

Each of the log records have several important features that help to determine their type and importance, who or what initiated them, and what the outcome of the event was. If you want to look at the details of any error report, click the link found in the **Message** column, and the details of the log report will be displayed, much like the following screenshot:

Details	
Type	update
Date	Thursday, October 25, 2007 - 12:41
User	mf4good
Location	http://localhost/drupal/admin/logs/updates
Referrer	http://localhost/drupal/admin/logs
Message	Fetched information about all available new releases and updates.
Severity	notice
Hostname	127.0.0.1
Operations	view

This logging interface gives you fairly good control over how to locate and deal with site issues. There are several other options that you should explore on your own in the **Reports** section, most notable being the **Available updates** and **Status report**—especially at the time this book gets released, because many module developers and Drupal itself will still be undergoing upgrades, and accordingly these two sections will be even more important than usual.

Frequently examining the various types of reports can help detect and isolate unusual or important happenings that can have a huge impact on your site. You might find that a certain site refers a number of people to you, and therefore may be a good candidate for pursuing a relationship with. Alternatively, hackers and spammers trying to gain access to certain pages may leave traces of their activities in these logs, giving away their IP address(es) and so on.

Site Information

This page contains a mixed bag of settings, some of which are pretty self explanatory, while others will require us to think quite carefully about what we need to do. To start with, we are presented with a few text boxes that control things like the name of the site, the mission statement, and so on.

Nothing too earth shattering, although I should point out that you might want to hold back on adding mission statements and slogans until you have at least decided on which theme you are going to implement. The reason being that different themes implement these settings differently, and some don't implement them at all:

Home › Administer › Site configuration

Site information

Name: *

Market Force for Good

The name of this website.

E-mail address: *

dave@marketforce4good.org

The *From* address in automated e-mails sent during registration and new password requests, and other notifications. (Use an address ending in your site's domain to help prevent this e-mail being flagged as spam.)

Slogan:

Your site's motto, tag line, or catchphrase (often displayed alongside the title of the site).

Mission:

Your site's mission or focus statement (often prominently displayed on the front page).

Footer message:

This text will be displayed at the bottom of each page. Useful for adding a copyright notice to your pages.

Anonymous user: *

Anonymous

The name used to indicate anonymous users.

Default front page: *

http://localhost/drupal/ node

The home page displays content from this relative URL. If unsure, specify "node".

Moving along, we see that we also have the option of defining a name for anonymous users. **Anonymous** is fairly widely used, but change it to something else if you have a compelling reason for doing so. The only thing this action will do is change the credited name of a posting from **Anonymous** to whatever you set (assuming anonymous users can post content to the site).

The final setting warrants a closer look, because many people prefer to have a defined landing page from which users can then move to their desired content — as opposed to the default behavior of adding the latest content posts to the front page.

Let's assume that there is a page of content that should be displayed as the default — before anyone views any of the other content. For example, if you wanted to display some sort of promotional information or an introduction page, you could tell Drupal to display that using this setting. Remember that you have to create the content for this post first, and then determine its path before you can tell Drupal to use it. We could, for example, specify a specific node with its identity number, but equally, a site's blogs could be displayed should you substitute node/x (in node/ID format) for blog.

A good way to determine exactly how to display the front page you want is to actually browse to the page (once it has been created). This could be a blog page, aggregated news feed (more about feeds later in the book), a forum, or anything.

Once you are looking at the content intended for the front page, take note of the **relative URL path** and simply enter that into the text box provided.

Recall that the relative URL path is that part of the page's address that comes after the standard domain, which is shared by the whole site. For example, setting node/2 works because Drupal maps this relative path to:

```
http://localhost/drupal/node/2
```

The first part of this address, `http://localhost/drupal/` is the **base URL**, and everything after that is the relative URL path.

Make sure, however, that everything works properly before moving on. Setting file paths can sometimes be a pain because it is easy to make a mistake and add an erroneous slash here and there — if you're like me, that is.

Site Maintenance

I should make the following point very clear:

 All major development or changes to a site should be performed on the development machine and thoroughly tested before being implemented or ported to the live site.

There will be times, however, when you simply have to make some changes directly to the live site—even if it is only to implement upgrades that have already been tested out on the development server. If this is the case, then rather than allow users to work on a site under maintenance, simply switch the **Site status** to **Off-line** and get on with your work.

You can add a quick message explaining why the site is currently offline so that when a user attempts to access the site they see something like the following:

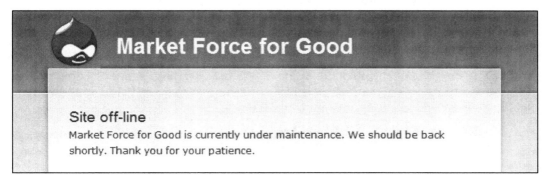

Be very careful when working on this because once you have logged out you are effectively locked out too. This is because only user 1 (that is the administrative user) can do anything on the site while it is offline. If you log off and try logging on again, you are no longer the administrative user; you are instead anonymous and are shown only this off-line message.

This is not very helpful if you do happen to be the site administrator; so Drupal allows the login page to be accessed as normal. Navigate to `http://localhost/drupal/`**user**, and you will be able to **log in** as the administrator and use the site without hindrance.

Very important:

 Make certain you know the administrator's password when setting the site's status to **Off-line**!

Everyone else is locked out until the site's status is returned to **Online**.

Summary

This chapter has covered a fair amount of ground in terms of setting up the site. We began by looking at some general configuration settings that are important in terms of getting the nuts and bolts in working order. Many of these settings will need to be revisited as the site develops, and as you become more adventurous.

Knowing that in this fiercely competitive Internet environment we need to take every SEO advantage we can find, means that enabling clean URLs is important. If worst comes to worst, it may become necessary to find a new hosting service to ensure you don't have problems with the Apache setup.

Add to this the ability to control file uploads and file handling, as well as how to deal with the multitude of events that your Drupal system can log and you should now be able to work with Drupal with some confidence.

The chapter finished with a quick look at how to provide some basic site information and switch the site into maintenance mode in the event that some behind-the-scenes work becomes necessary.

5
Access Control

It's time to look at an entirely different aspect of running a Drupal website. Up until now we have focused on adding and organizing the site's basic functionality. We have not yet given any thought to how this functionality is to be accessed, or by whom. As the site grows, you will most likely feel the need to delegate certain responsibilities to various people. Alternatively, you might organize a team of people to work on specific aspects of the site. Whatever is required, at some stage you will have to make decisions about who can do what, and Drupal makes sure that it is possible to do precisely this.

In the same vein as the previous chapter, having Drupal simplify the implementation of your access control policies does not mean that the task is a trivial one. There is still much thought that needs to go on behind the scenes in order to create a sophisticated, and above all, effective policy for controlling access to the site. Because of this, we will spend a bit of time exploring the ramifications of the various choices available, instead of simply listing them. Taking a holistic approach to implementing an access control policy will ensure you don't end up with any nasty surprises down the line.

Specifically, this chapter will look at the following topics:

- Planning an access policy
- Roles
- Users
- Access rules

Before we continue, it is worth pointing out that at the moment you are more than likely using the administrative user (user number 1) for all the site's development needs. That is absolutely fine, but once the major changes to the site are completed, you should begin using a normal administrative user that has only the permissions required to complete your day-to-day tasks. The next section will highlight the general philosophy behind user access, which should make the reason for this clear.

Planning an Access Policy

When you think about how your site should work, focus in on what will be required of yourself, other community members, or even anonymous users. For instance:

- Will there be a team of moderators working to ensure that the content of the site conforms to the dictates of good taste and avoids material that is tantamount to hate speech, and so on?

- Will there be subject experts who are allowed to create and maintain their own content?

- How much will anonymous visitors be allowed to become involved, or will they be forced to merely window shop without being able to contribute?

Some of you might feel that the site should grow organically with the community, and so you want to be extremely flexible in your approach. However, you can take it as given that Drupal's access policies are already flexible, given how easy it is to reconfigure, so it is good practice to start out with a sensible set of access rules, even if they are going to change over time. If you need to make modifications later, so be it, but at least there will be a coherent set of rules from the start.

The first and foremost rule of security that can be applied directly to our situation is (recall that we mentioned this earlier in a slightly different context):

 Grant a user permissions sufficient for completing the intended task, and no more!

Our entire approach is going to be governed by this rule. With a bit of thought you should be able to see why this is so important. The last thing anyone wants is for an anonymous user to be able to modify the personal blog of a respected industry expert. This means that each type of user should have carefully controlled permissions that effectively block their ability to act outside the scope of their remit.

One upshot of this is that it is better to create a larger number of specific roles, rather than create a generic **role** or two, and allow everyone to use those catch-all permissions.

 A role constitutes a number of permissions that define what actions any members of that role can and can't perform.

We will explore roles in detail in the next section!

Drupal gives us fine-grained control over what users can accomplish, and you should make good use of this facility. It may help to think of your access control using the following figure (this does not necessarily represent the actual roles on your site — it's just an example):

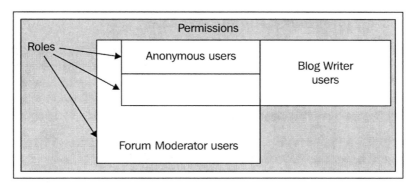

The shaded region represents the total number of permissions available for the site. Contained within this set are the various roles that exist either by default, like the **Anonymous users** role, or those you create in order to cater for the different types of users the site will require — in this case, the **Blog Writer users** and **Forum Moderator users** roles.

From the previous diagram you can see that the **Anonymous users** role has the smallest set of permissions because they have the smallest area of the total diagram. This set of permissions is totally encapsulated by the **Forum Moderator users** and **Blog Writer users** — meaning that forum moderators and blog writers can do everything an anonymous user does, and a whole lot more.

Remember, it is not compulsory that forum moderators encapsulate all the permissions of the anonymous users. You can assign any permissions to any role — it's just that in this context it makes sense that a forum moderator should be able to do everything an anonymous user can and more.

Of course, the blog writers have a slightly different remit. While they share some privileges in common with the forum administrators, they also have a few of their own. Your permissions as the primary or administrative user encompass the entire set, because there should be nothing that you cannot control.

It is up to you to decide which roles are best for the site, but before attempting this it is important to ask: *What are roles and how are they used in the first place?* To answer this question, let's take a look at the practical side of things in more detail.

Roles

It may seem a bit odd that we are not beginning a practical look at access control with a discussion on users. After all, it is all about what *users can* and *cannot* do! The problem with immediately talking about users is that the focus of a single user is too narrow, and we can learn far more about controlling access by taking a more broad view using roles. Once we have learned everything there is to know about roles, actually working with users becomes a trivial matter.

As mentioned, a user role in Drupal defines a set of rules that must be obeyed by all the users in that role. It may be helpful to think of a role as a character in a play. In a play, an actor must always be true to their character (in the same way a user must be faithful to their role in Drupal) — in other words, there is a defined way to behave and the character never deviates (no matter which actor portrays the character).

Creating a role in Drupal is very easy. Click the **User management** link under **Administer** and select the **Roles** tab to bring up the following:

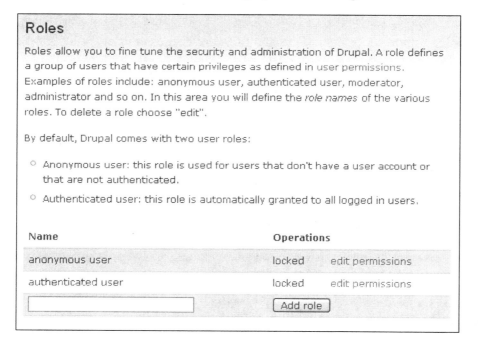

As you can see, we have two roles already defined by default—the **anonymous user** and the **authenticated user**. It is not possible to change these, and so the **Operations** column is permanently set to **locked**. To begin with, the anonymous user (this is any user who is browsing the site without logging in) has very few permissions set, and you would more than likely want to keep it this way, despite the fact it is possible to give them any and all permissions.

Similarly, the authenticated user, by default, has only a few more permissions than the anonymous user, and it is also sensible to keep these to a minimum. We will see in a little while how to go about deciding who should have which permissions.

In order to add a new role, type in a name for the role and click **Add role**, and you're done. But what name do you want to add? That's the key question! If you are unsure about what name to use, then it is most likely you haven't defined the purpose of the role properly. To see how this is done, let's assume we require a forum moderator who will be a normal user in every way, except for the ability to work directly on the forums (to take some of the burden of responsibility off the administrator's hands) to create new topics, and to edit the content if necessary.

To get the ball rolling, type in `forum moderator` and click **Add role**—actually, you might even want to be more specific and use something like **conservation forum moderator** if there will be teams of forum moderators—you get the general idea.

Now the **roles** page should display the new role with the option to edit it, shown in the **Operations** column. Click **edit role** in order to change the name of the role or delete it completely. Alternatively, click **edit permissions** to deal with the permissions for this specific role (we discuss permissions in a moment so let's leave this for now).

Our work is just beginning, because now we need to grant or deny the various permissions that the **forum moderator** role will need in order to successfully fulfill its purpose. New roles are not given any permission at all to begin with—this makes sense, because the last thing we want is to create a role only to find that it has the same permissions as the administrative user.

Chances are you will need to add several roles depending on the needs of the site, so add at least a **blogger user** that can edit their own blog—we will need a few different types to play with later on.

Let's move on and take a look at how to flesh out this new role by setting permissions.

Permissions

In order to work with permissions, click the **Permissions** link under **User management** and you should be presented with a screen much like the following (notice the new **forum moderator** role on the right-hand side of the page):

Permissions

Permissions let you control what users can do on your site. Each user role (defined on the user roles page) has its own set of permissions. For example, you could give users classified as "Administrators" permission to "administer nodes" but deny this power to ordinary, "authenticated" users. You can use permissions to reveal new features to privileged users (those with subscriptions, for example). Permissions also allow trusted users to share the administrative burden of running a busy site.

Permission	anonymous user	authenticated user	forum moderator user
block module			
administer blocks	☐	☐	☐
use PHP for block visibility	☐	☐	☐
blog module			
create blog entries	☐	☐	☐
delete any blog entry	☐	☐	☐
delete own blog entries	☐	☐	☐
edit any blog entry	☐	☐	☐
edit own blog entries	☐	☐	☐
comment module			

As you can see, this page lists all of the available permissions down the left-hand column and allows you to enable or disable that permission by checking or un-checking boxes in the relevant column. It is easy enough to see that one traverses the list, selecting those permissions required for each role. What is not so easy is actually determining what should and shouldn't be enabled in the first place.

Notice too that the permissions given in the list on the left-hand side pertain to specific modules. This means that if we change the site's setup by adding or removing modules, then we will also have to change the permissions on this page.

Most times a module is added, you will need to ensure that the permissions are set as required for that module, because by default no permissions are granted.

What else can we learn from the permissions page shown in the previous screenshot? Well, what does each permission precisely mean? There are quite a few verbs that allow for completely different actions. The following lists the more common, generic ones, although you might find one or two others crop up every now and then to cater for a specific module:

- **administer**: gives the user the ability to affect the function of a module. For example, granting administer rights to the locale module means that the user can add or remove languages, manage strings, and even export .po files. This permission should only ever be given to trusted users, and never to anonymous users.

- **access**: gives the user the ability to make use of a module without being able to affect it in any way. For example, granting access rights to the comment module allows a user to view comments without being able to delete, edit, or reply to them.

- **create**: gives the user the ability to create content of some sort. For example, granting rights to create stories allows users to do so, but does not also give them the ability to edit those stories.

- **edit any/own**: gives the user the ability to work with either anyone's content or specifically the content *they have created* — depending on whether edit any or edit own is selected. For example, granting **edit own** rights to the *blog* module means that the user can modify their own blogs at will.

- **delete any/own**: applies to content related modules such as **Node** and empowers users to remove either anyone's content or confine them to removing only content posted by themselves. For example, setting **delete own blog entry** allows users to take back any blog postings they may regret having published.

There are also other module-specific permissions available, and it is recommended that you play around and understand any new permission(s) you set.

 Previously, assigning the **edit own** permission automatically provided the **delete own** permission. For added security, **delete own** permissions for individual core content types have been removed from all roles and should be assigned separately.

How do we go about setting up the required permissions for the forum moderator user? If we look down the list of permissions shown on the **Permission** page, we see the following forum-related options (at the moment, the **forum moderator** permissions are those in the outermost column):

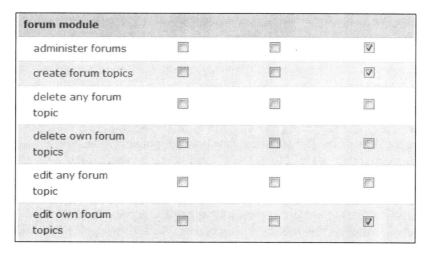

Enabling these three options, and then testing out what new powers are made available, should quickly demonstrate that this is not quite what we want.

If you are wondering how to actually test this out, you need to create a new user and then assign them to the **forum moderator** role. The following section on *Users* explains how to create new users and administer them properly. Jump ahead quickly and check that out so that you have a new user to work with if you are unsure how it is done.

The following point might make your life a bit easier:

 Use two browsers to test out your site. The demo site's development machine has IE and Firefox. Keep one browser for the administrator and the other for anonymous or other users in order to test out changes. This will save you from having to log in and log out whenever testing new permissions.

When testing out the new permissions one way or another, you will find that the forum moderator can access and work with all of the forums—assuming you have created any.

However, notice that there are **node module** permissions available, which is quite interesting because most content in Drupal is actually a node. How will this affect the forum moderator? Disable the **forum module** permissions for the **forum moderator user** and then enable all the node options for the **authenticated user** before saving and logging out.

Log back in as the **forum administrator** and it will be clear that despite having revoked the forum based options for this user, it is possible to post to or edit *anything* in the forum quite easily by selecting the **Create content** link in the main menu. Is this what you expected?

It should be precisely what you expect because the forum moderator is an **authenticated user**, so they have acquired the permissions that came from the **authenticated user**. In addition, the forum posts are all nodes, and any authenticated user can add and edit nodes, so even though the forum moderator is not explicitly allowed to work with forums, through generic node permissions we get the same result:

 Defined roles are given the **authenticated user** permissions.

Actually, the result is not entirely the same because the **forum moderator** can now also configure all the different types of content on the site, as well as edit any type of content including other people's blogs. This is most certainly undesirable, so log back in as the primary user and remove the node permissions (except the first one) from the **authenticated user** role. With that done, you can now spend some time building a fairly powerful and comprehensive role-based access control plan.

As an addendum, you might find that despite having a goodly amount of control over who does what, there are some things that are not easily done without help from elsewhere.

Users

A single user account can be given as many or as few permissions as you like via the use of roles. Drupal users are not really anything unless they already have a role that defines the manner in which they can operate within the Drupal framework. Hence, we discussed roles first.

Users can be created in two ways. The most common way is by registering on the site—if you haven't already, go ahead and register a new user on your site by clicking the **Create new account** link on the homepage just to test things out. Remember to supply a valid email address otherwise you won't be able to sign in properly. This will create an authenticated user, with any and all permissions that have been assigned to the **authenticated user** role.

The second way is to use the administrative user to create a new user. In order to do so, log on as the administrative user and click on **Users** in **User management** under **Administer**. Select the **Add user** tab and follow the instructions on that page. For example, I created a new forum moderator user by ensuring that the relevant role was checked:

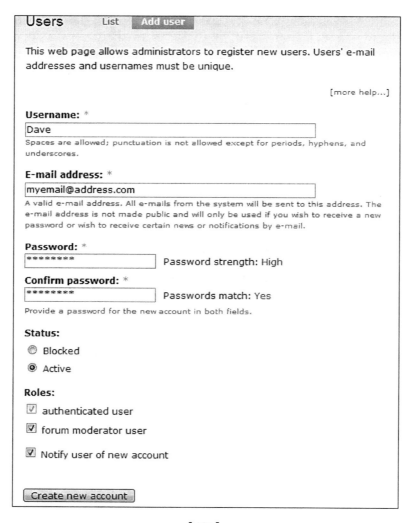

You will need to supply Drupal with usernames, email addresses, and passwords. Once there are a couple of users to play around with, it's time to begin working with them.

Administering Users

The site's administrator is given complete access to the other users' account information. By clicking on the **edit** link shown to the right of each user account (under the **Operations** column heading) in the **Users** page under **User management,** it is possible to make any changes you require to a given user.

Before we do though, it's worth noting that the administration page itself is fairly powerful in terms of being able to administer individual users or groups of users with relative ease:

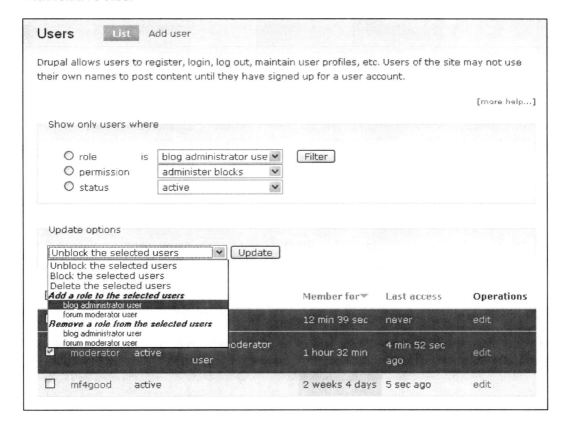

The upper box, **Show only users where**, allows you to specify several filter conditions to cut down the result set and make it more manageable. This will become more and more important as the site accumulates more and more users. Once the various filter options have been implemented, the **Update options** allow you to apply whatever changes are needed to the list of users selected (by checking the relevant checkbox next to their name).

Having both broad, sweeping powers as well as fine-grained control over users is one of the most valuable facilities provided by Drupal, and you will no doubt become very familiar with this page in due course.

Click on the **edit** link next to the **forum moderator user** and take a look at the **Roles** section. Notice that it is now possible to stipulate which roles this user belongs to. At present there are only two new roles to be assigned (yours might vary depending on which roles have been created on your setup):

```
Roles:
  ☑ authenticated user
  ☑ forum moderator user
```

Whenever a user is added to another role, they obtain the **combined permissions** of these roles. With this in mind, you should go about delegating roles in the following fashion:

1. Define the most basic user of the site by setting the **anonymous user** permissions.

2. Set permissions for a basic **authenticated user** (i.e. any Tom, Dick or Harry that registers on your site).

3. Create special roles by only adding the *specific additional permissions* that are required by that role, and no more. Don't re-assign permissions that the authenticated user already has.

4. Create new users by combining whatever roles are required for their duties or needs.

If you follow the steps above, you will be sure to always give the correct permissions to each role by avoiding redundancy and only applying permissions incrementally by role. Basically, you are building up a user's permissions from the most basic to the most complex without having to assign every single permission each time. It should be commonsense (although not a technical obligation) that a forum moderator would have all the permissions of an anonymous and authenticated user, plus a few more. Looking back to the first diagram in the section *Planning an Access Policy* you can see that, in this case, we would:

1. Define the **anonymous user** and **authenticated user** role permissions—an authenticated user should have all the permissions of an anonymous user, plus whatever else is needed by a basic site user.

2. Create new roles with only the additional permissions needed for both the **forum moderator** and **blog user** respectively—other than those given to the authenticated user.

3. Assign blog writers to the **blog user** role (they are automatically given the permissions granted to an authenticated user), and do the same for forum moderators and their role.

Other than using that strategy for assigning roles to users, the rest, as they say, is history. Play around with any new roles you create to ensure they behave as you expect and then move on.

User Settings

This section looks at how the site treats users, rather than discussing what users can and cannot do. However, you will find that some of the information in this section is important for the look and feel of the site.

Click on **User settings** under the **User management**. The following set of options is provided, beginning with **user registration settings**, as follows:

User settings

User registration settings

Public registrations:

○ Only site administrators can create new user accounts.

○ Visitors can create accounts and no administrator approval is required.

◉ Visitors can create accounts but administrator approval is required.

☑ Require e-mail verification when a visitor creates an account

If this box is checked, new users will be required to validate their e-mail address prior to logging into to the site, and will be assigned a system-generated password. With it unchecked, users will be logged in immediately upon registering, and may select their own passwords during registration.

User registration guidelines:

Thanks for taking a moment to register with us. We look forward to having you join our community...

REMEMBER - once you have verified your email address by clicking on the link provided, YOU MUST SET YOUR OWN PASSWORD!

This text is displayed at the top of the user registration form. It's useful for helping or instructing your users.

You might want to consider which of the first three options to select quite carefully, depending on how you envisage the site functioning. For example, allowing everyone to read and post comments to the forums, or do whatever, without needing to register first may be ideal. If this is the case, then it is likely that the only people who would need to register are going to be performing some sort of administrative duties, in which case you would probably want to select the first option, or at least the third option.

If you do go for the third option, then check the user list regularly in order to unblock new users as soon as possible. Note that Drupal can be configured to email the site administrator automatically whenever there is a new user registration application—see the section entitled *Actions & Triggers* in Chapter 9 for more information:

Additionally, if you enter a message into the **User registration guidelines** text area then this will appear during the registration process, as shown in the following screenshot:

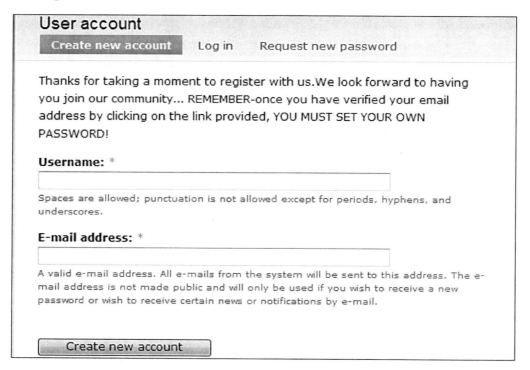

I specifically added this note in here because it is fairly well known that new users often log in with the one-time password generated by Drupal, but then fail to add their own password before logging off. When they return, they are then locked out because the one-time password has expired and there is no new one set.

The next section on this page deals with the process of user email customization for the various different type of emails that Drupal sends out. There is an interesting facet to this in that Drupal makes certain variables available for use within the static text that is entered. Let's take a look at how to modify a line or so in order to get the feel for how it works.

By way of example, we will change the **Welcome, no approval** text from:

Account details for !username at !site

to a slightly sprightlier:

Congratulations !username, you have registered with the !site on !date!

Nothing too complicated here! The keywords preceded by the ! sign are simply placeholders for other values that are inserted into the email, according to how they are set at that particular time. This gives you the ability to personalize correspondence. In this case, the subject of the welcome email for a user registered as **David M** is now displayed as follows:

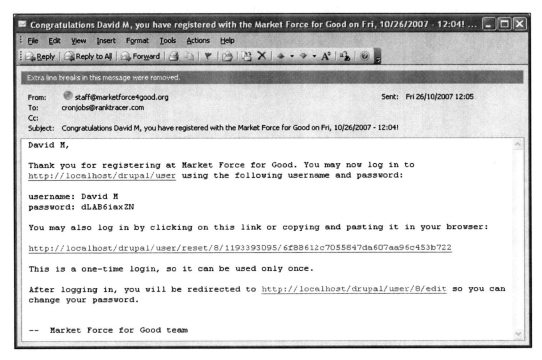

The **!username**, **!site**, and **!date** placeholders have been correctly changed to reflect the contents of the variables for that particular setup. There are settings available for several standard emails such as **password recovery** and **welcome (awaiting admin approval)**. The defaults are fairly sensible and easy to change should you need to. Remember the placeholders that are available for each piece of text are mentioned below the section heading, so play around with them until you are comfortable with their usage:

> ▽ Welcome, no approval required
>
> Customize the welcome e-mail message that is sent to new members upon registering when no administrator approval is required. Available variables are: !username, !site, !password, !uri, !uri_brief, !mailto, !date, !login_uri, !edit_uri, !login_url.

The final two sections deal with **Signatures** and **Pictures**. If you wish to enable **Picture support** for users, then select **Enabled** from the list, provide a default picture (if you want one), and click **Save configuration** (the other settings are fairly self explanatory and sensible, and you can come back at any stage to change them if they are not suitable).

Drupal will set up a `pictures` folder to hold all of the pictures within the `files` folder in your Drupal installation. Once everything is done, users will have a new section added to the **edit** tab of their **my account** page, like the following figure:

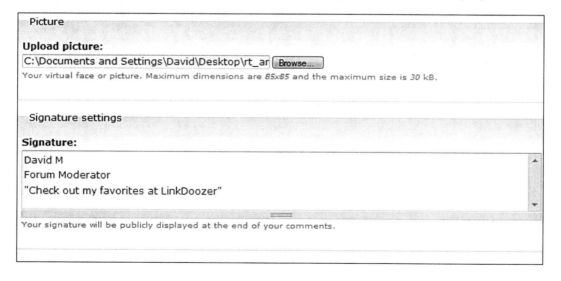

When the picture has been successfully uploaded, it will appear on the **my account** page, and with the user's blog and forum posts on the site. If the image does not appear and you end up seeing a link, something like the following:

...then you will need to ensure that you set the correct **upload module** permissions on the **Permissions** page, as follows:

Remember that since the **forum administrator** user automatically receives all the permissions of the **authenticated** user, it is not necessary to enable the **view uploaded files** permission for the **forum administrator** as this would be redundant and would make the purpose of your user less clear.

It is possible to control where the user pictures are displayed by selecting the **Configure** tab of the **Themes** page under **Site building** and checking the relevant picture related checkboxes, as shown in the following figure:

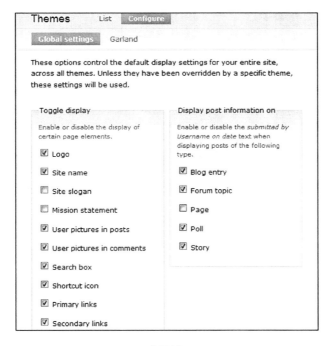

Allowing users to incorporate pictures into a site is a good way for people to be able to personalize their contributions, and also gives everyone something visual to associate posts with. This is a great way to foster a community, as it helps give different users an identity of sorts.

Changing the picture is easy! Simply modify it in the **Picture** section of the user's edit page, as shown in the following screenshot:

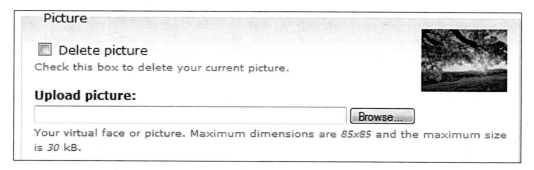

That is pretty much the end of the line for configuring users. There are still a few more things we need to discuss with regards to security before we can move on though.

Access Rules

So far it should seem like Drupal has things more or less covered when it comes to ensuring that it is possible to control who does what on the site. This is certainly the case, but there are a few more situations that we have not yet discussed, and may well end up affecting the site at some stage. For example, what happens if there is a company that repeatedly spams your forums with advertisements and marketing information? Or, what happens if only people from a certain company should have access to your site?

Problems of this nature can really be a thorn in the side. Access problems can even end up driving community members away—unless you have the ability to set access rules.

There are some techniques that can be used to set access rules via the **Access rules** link under **User management**. To implement any access rules you will need to select the **Add rule** option, which brings up the following page:

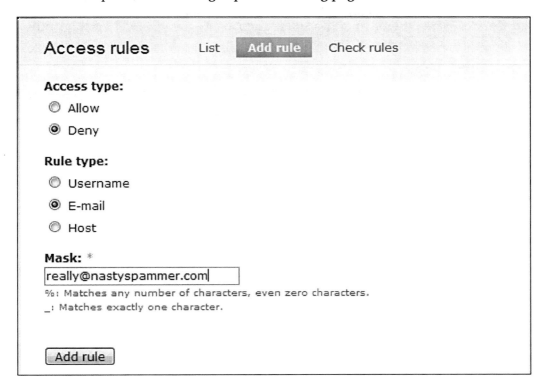

From this you can see that I am in the process of making a rule that denies access based on an email address—more specifically, really@nastyspammer.com. Before we continue on this line, it is important to note that there are both **Allow** and **Deny** options available, and these will act based on a supplied **Username, E-mail,** or **Host** address given in the **Rule type** section. The final option, **Mask**, allows you to specify the actual name of the user or host to which the rule will apply.

In the above case, the email address really@nastyspammer.com will have a **deny** rule created after **Add rule** has been clicked.

Go ahead and create a rule like this one, and notice that the rule now appears under the **list** tab. Now that there is a **deny** rule in place, how do we go about using it? The answer is that it is already being used. If someone tries to register with the email address supplied in the rule, they will be denied access. As it stands, this is probably not very helpful, because it is unlikely you will know ahead of time what specific email addresses to block.

In order to cater for the times when you aren't entirely sure of the specific address, there are two wildcard characters provided that can serve as generic strings or characters. Imagine you wanted to ban someone who runs a small spamming business. Simply blocking their current email address is not really sufficient, because they can easily create another address and use that one to register. If you know that the addresses come from one location, such as:

```
<some characters>@irritating_spammer.com
```

...you could use the % character to match whatever characters are present before the @ sign, effectively stopping anyone from that email server from registering, like so:

```
%@irritating_spammer.com
```

If you have a Hotmail account, or something similar, try blocking any address that ends with @hotmail.com and then attempt to register an account on the site. Drupal will dutifully display the following message:

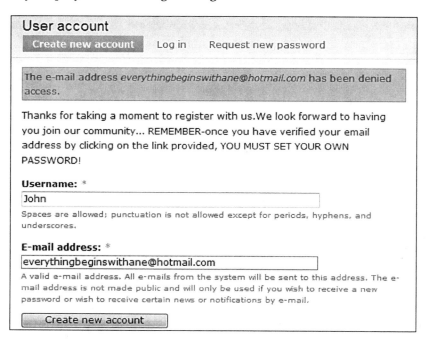

A new problem rears its ugly head when it so happens that you don't want to allow Hotmail addresses on the site, with the exception of a close personal friend who is traveling around the world and can only access Hotmail addresses. In this case, you need to set an **Allow** rule as well. If, for example, the email address of the person is good_friend@hotmail.com, then you could set the **Allow** rule by selecting the appropriate options to cater for this on the **add rule** page.

The rules would then look something like the following:

Access type ▲	Rule type	Mask	Operations	
deny	e-mail	%hotmail.com	edit	delete
allow	e-mail	good_friend@hotmail.com	edit	delete

What this does is ban all Hotmail addresses from the site. However, because *an* **allow** *rule takes precedence over a* **deny** *rule*, the one and only Hotmail address specified in the single **allow** rule shown in the screenshot will work fine. Now when your good friend attempts to register, everything will go swimmingly well.

After adding plenty of rules, things can sometimes become slightly confusing and it is simply not feasible to continue attempting to register new names all the time, to ensure that they work according to plan. In this case, use the **Check rules** tab on the right-hand side of the **Access rules** page. This allows names of users, email addresses, and hosts to be entered in order to check whether they have access or not. Simply compare these results with your expectations to determine if everything is working as planned.

One final thing to bear in mind is that if you deny access using the host criteria, then this will be enforced throughout the site and not just on the registration pages. For the case of the spammer, you would probably want to deny access to the site in general; so you would select the **host** option with something like this for the **Mask**:

```
%irritating_spammer%
```

This would then match to any host with `irritating_spammer` in it. For example:

```
www.really_irritating_spammer.com
www.mildly_irritating_spammer.com
www.extremelyirritating_spammer.org
www.unbelievably_irritating_spammer.comms.org.co.sz
```

...and so on.

It is important to realize that this only applies to the host criteria:

 If an undesirable user has already registered with an **email address** that is *subsequently* blocked, then no action will be taken against them.

Remember to check that all the added rules have the desired effect on the site's access policy. It would be a shame to make a rule that prevented potentially valuable community members from accessing content, causing them to go elsewhere.

I would be remiss if I didn't mention, before finishing off, that there are a number of other **user access/authentication**-related modules available on the Drupal website. It is probably worthwhile to check these out at `http://drupal.org/project/ Modules/category/74` in case there is something that is particularly suited to your needs.

Summary

This chapter provided a good grounding in the basics of controlling access to your site's content. Drupal comes with a large number of facilities and options to ensure proper maintenance of the site by retaining overall control with the administrative user, as well as delegating important jobs to trusted users via the use of roles.

We looked at how to go about planning an access policy. This is not only an important requirement, in terms of making sure the site runs smoothly, but also helps to solidify how the site will eventually work by forcing you to consider many eventualities. A tour of the fundamental aspects of access control in Drupal saw us discussing roles, permissions, and users, and learning how to plan and implement an access policy based on the requirements of the site.

Access rules were then introduced as a further way of controlling who gets into the site, with a discussion on how to use the wildcard characters effectively. Planning, and above all, testing, will help ensure that everything works as intended.

With that, we are done with access control, although you are strongly urged to spend some time playing around with the various options until you are comfortable with being able to make changes and understanding their effects.

The next two chapters take an in-depth look at content—the beating heart of Drupal!

6
Basic Content

Everything we have dealt with so far, as important as it may be in terms of creating a unique site, must take a back seat when it comes to the topic of content and content management in Drupal. After all, content *is* what this is all about! With the explosion in the number of sites offering dynamic content, it is now an absolute necessity to provide meaningful, dynamic, and relevant information on your site in order to prosper. How this is done behind the scenes is really of no concern to a site's users, but if you can make their browsing experience hassle free and relevant to them, they will stick with you.

Content needs to be easy to find, which in turn means it needs to be well organized. It should be well presented and easy to interact with—in other words, simple to use. Most of this is taken care of already by Drupal, and for very little additional effort, we can provide some very powerful functionality. However, before we look at adding more functionality, we must have a good grasp of how to use what is already in place.

To this end, this chapter will provide a good grounding in the basics of content management before it moves on to look at a few interesting and powerful features of Drupal. Specifically, we will look at the following:

- Content overview
- Content types
- Working with content
- Content-related modules

Once we are done here, it will be time to look at how to put together some neat new content types using CCK, how to use HTML and PHP to create content, as well as the all important task of working out how to classify and categorize content to provide a sophisticated and intuitive content management system. All this is to come in the following chapter. For now, let's get on with familiarizing ourselves with Drupal from the content management perspective.

Content Overview

It's worth looking at how Drupal organizes itself in terms of presenting you, the site administrator, with a powerful content management environment. The menu system itself is dynamic in that it automatically adds and removes features and menu options that are available depending on what functionality you add, enable or remove. While this sounds intuitive, it can make life tricky if you don't get into the habit of doing a comprehensive check whenever important changes are made (such as adding a new content type).

In fact, there are three separate areas related to content within the main menu:

1. Modules—from here you can add or remove the functionality that implements the various content types.

2. Content management—perform a variety of content related administrative tasks.

3. Create content—add any content that has been enabled and/or configured in the first two sections.

By way of demonstration, take a look at the **Content management** section under **Administer**:

Content management

Comments
   List and edit site comments and the comment moderation queue.

Content
   View, edit, and delete your site's content.

Content types
   Manage posts by content type, including default status, front page promotion, etc.

Forums
   Control forums and their hierarchy and change forum settings.

Post settings
   Control posting behavior, such as teaser length, requiring previews before posting, and the number of posts on the front page.

RSS publishing
   Configure the number of items per feed and whether feeds should be titles/teasers/full-text.

Taxonomy
   Manage tagging, categorization, and classification of your content.

There are quite a few options that deal with a wide variety of topics here, which we will discuss in due course in this chapter and the next. Now, go back to **Modules** and enable the **Book** module. Then look at your **Content management** page once more. You should find that it now has an additional option:

Content management

Books
  Manage your site's book outlines.

Comments
  List and edit site comments and the comment moderation queue.

Content
  View, edit, and delete your site's content.

Naturally, the **Create content** page also responds to whatever modules you have enabled or disabled. Looking at the **Create content** page of the main menu, brings up the list of content types that you may work with:

Create content

Blog entry
  A *blog entry* is a single post to an online journal, or *blog*.

Book page
  A *book page* is a page of content, organized into a collection of related entries collectively known as a *book*. A *book page* automatically displays links to adjacent pages, providing a simple navigation system for organizing and reviewing structured content.

Forum topic
  A *forum topic* is the initial post to a new discussion thread within a forum.

Page
  A *page*, similar in form to a *story*, is a simple method for creating and displaying information that rarely changes, such as an "About us" section of a website. By default, a *page* entry does not allow visitor comments and is not featured on the site's initial home page.

Poll
  A *poll* is a question with a set of possible responses. A *poll*, once created, automatically provides a simple running count of the number of votes received for each response.

Story
  A *story*, similar in form to a *page*, is ideal for creating and displaying content that informs or engages website visitors. Press releases, site announcements, and informal blog-like entries may all be created with a *story* entry. By default, a *story* entry is automatically featured on the

---

As expected, the **Book page** content type is available to work with because we have just enabled it. It's important to remember that that is how things work for you as the site administrator, and for the standard content types that are part of the core Drupal distribution. However, contributed content modules might have slightly different implementations and you should always go over the README file carefully before installing and using these.

Furthermore, the situation gets a little more complicated when you consider different types of users, and the access privileges that have been granted to them. When adding a new content type, you need to ensure that not only is it configured correctly, but that you provide roles with the necessary permissions required to utilize it. We have already covered roles and access permissions, but for completeness sake, head on over to the **Permissions** page under **User management** and look for the new **Book** related permissions:

book module				
access printer-friendly version	☐	☐	☐	☐
add content to books	☐	☐	☐	☐
administer book outlines	☐	☐	☐	☐
create new books	☐	☐	☐	☐

You can determine precisely who can do what here depending on the needs of the site, and how you want the content to be created and maintained. Remember it is better to create a new role with its own role specific permissions than to hand out new permissions to all and sundry.

Understanding that content management in Drupal is a multi-faceted discipline is the key factor here. Try to get into the habit of checking all the distinct aspects of any content type, including user permissions, whenever you deal with content as a whole.

Talking of content, let's take a look at what's available...

Content Types

We need to have a good idea of the types of content that can be created in Drupal, and then look at the various ways these content types can be put to use. Knowing this will help determine the best way to go about implementing whatever functionality you have in mind.

The following table lists the content types that ship with Drupal by default:

Content Type	Description
Blog entry	A blog, or weblog, is an author-specific content type that is used as a journal or diary, among other things, by individuals. In Drupal, each blog writer can, depending on the site's settings and their permissions, add attachments, HTML, or PHP code to their blog.
	A good example of a blog can be found at: `http://googleblog.blogspot.com/`, which demonstrates an interesting use of the blog content format.
Book page	A book is an organized set of book page types (actually any type can be used nowadays), which are intended to be used for collaborative authoring. Book pages may be added by different people in order to make up one single book that can then be structured into chapters and pages, or in whatever structure is most appropriate, provided it is in a hierarchical structure.
	Because pretty much any data type can be added to a book, there is plenty of scope for exciting content (think of narrated or visual content complementing dynamic book pages, created with PHP and Flash animations, to create a truly unique Internet-based book—the possibilities are endless!).
	A good example of a book is the documentation provided for developers on the Drupal site, found at: `http://drupal.org/node/316`. This has been built up over time by a number of different authors.
	You will notice that if you have the **Book** module enabled, an additional **outline** tag is presented above all/most of the site's posts. Clicking on this tab allows you to add that post to a book—in this way, books can be built up from content posted to the site.
Forum topic	Forum topics are the building blocks of forums. Forums can only consist of forum topics and their comments, unlike books, which can consist of pretty much any content type. Information in forums is categorized in a hierarchical structure, and they are extremely useful for hosting discussions as well as community-based support and learning.
	Forums are abundant on the Internet and you can also visit the Drupal forums to get a feel for how they operate.
Page	The page type is meant to allow you to add basic, run-of-the-mill web pages that can be found on any site. **About us** or **Terms of use** pages are good candidates for the page type, although you can spruce these up with a bit of dynamic content and HTML.
	Just look on any website to see examples of such pages.

Content Type	Description
Poll	The poll type provides the facility to ask questions, and supply a set of answers that are then presented in graph format. Many different enterprises make use of polls in order to collect political or marketing information, or to conduct research, among other things.
	Polls by nature generally have a limited life span; so you will have to search for your own examples. Many news sites such as Time magazine conduct polls to determine public opinion; so these may be your best bet for seeing how polls can be put to good use.
Story	A story page is more or less the same thing as a standard page type. However, you might want to distinguish the two by using story types for short-lived pages, such as news or notices.

Comments are not the same as the other node types discussed in the previous table.

 While there may be exceptions, the terms 'node' and 'content' are synonymous with respect to Drupal.

While, technically, they are content, consider the fact that one cannot create a comment without first having another node to add the comment to. Instead, you can tack comments onto other content types, and these are very popular as a means to stimulate discussion among users.

 You can see comments in action by logging into the Drupal forums, `http://drupal.org/forum`, and posting or viewing comments on the various topics there.

It's important to check out what contribs are available to provide new content types, because as Drupal 6 matures, you can be sure that there will be some pretty neat multimedia types amongst many, many others. At the time of writing, lamentably, there are few to mention, so we will move directly along.

Every time new content is created, using the appropriate content type in the **Create content** page, there are several options available for you that control how that content post is managed. These options are displayed in the list that appears below the body of the post. Depending on the permissions of a given user, certain options are available and others are not. For example, if upload permissions are enabled for authenticated users, then they will be able to decide whether to attach a file to any content they create.

As the administrator, your powers are substantial; so let's go through the default options available when creating a standard page content type. Be aware that different types of content may also have additional options available for them. For example, if you create a new poll, you will have to decide how long the poll is to run for by setting the **Poll duration** in the poll type's unique **Settings** section.

To make things ever so slightly interesting, the choices that are made available on a content posting page not only rely on the situation as discussed, but also change depending on which modules are enabled. This is because there are several value-add modules here and there that can modify how, when, and where content is displayed.

The content options discussed in the following section are representative of most types.

Working with Content

This section takes a slightly more in-depth look at how to both edit and configure content to reflect the needs of the site. We have already worked with content in previous chapters, and so, are familiar with bits and pieces of this already. However, the intention here is to provide a single, cohesive point of reference from which to learn.

There are a few different aspects to working with content, and we will begin by looking at how to set up the correct default options whenever you create something new. Following this, it is important to look at the **Content** facility under **Content Management**, and to round everything off, we will have a brief look at issues to look out for in general.

Working with Content Types

It is possible to specify some default behavior for each of the content types. To do this, go to **Content types** under **Content management** to bring up the following page:

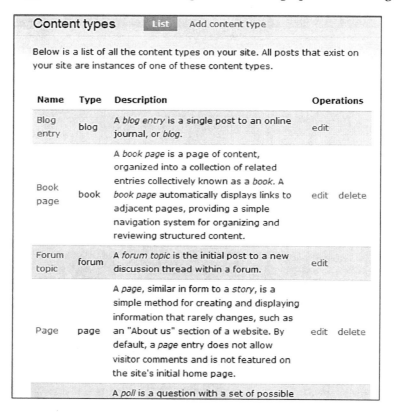

Each content type has a set of editable configuration parameters, so to get a good idea of how they work, click on the **edit** in the **Book page** row. The edit page is broken up into four sections dealing with the following:

- **Identification** – Allows you to specify the human readable name and the name used internally by Drupal for the associated content type, as well as add a description to be displayed on the content creation page.

- **Submission form settings** – Allows you to set the field names for the title and body (leaving the body blank removes the field entirely) as well as specify the minimum number of words required to make the posting valid. Again, it is possible to add in submission guidelines or notes to aid those users posting this content type.

- **Workflow settings** – Allows you to set default publishing options, multilingual support, and specify whether or not to allow file attachments.

- **Comment settings** – Allows you to specify default comment settings such as **read** or **read/write**, whether or not comments are allowed, whether they are to appear expanded or collapsed, in which order and how many, amongst other things.

By way of demonstration, the following **Workflow settings** were used for the **Book page** content type:

Obviously, your settings may well differ depending on how you want to use book pages (if at all), but, for example, opting to enable revisions helps ensure that all changes are recorded automatically to prevent the risk of losing data or corrupt content being published.

Changes made here will be visible whenever a user attempts to post content—see the next section on *Creating Content* for more information. In this example, the default posting page now has the **Create new revision** checkbox automatically checked.

 Users with permission to administer a given content type can override these default settings at will.

It is also possible to add your own completely new content type by selecting the **Add content type** tab on the **Content types** page. Looking over the new page should be quite familiar to you as it is exactly the same configuration page that is presented for any other *content type*, so we won't talk about this in much depth for the moment. However, we will come back to this when we look at how to create more advanced and complex content types.

Creating Content

Drupal makes it very easy to post new stuff:

- Click on **Create content**
- Select the type of content you need
- Enter the content into the fields provided and set the desired properties and options.

The first screenshot in the **Content Types** section highlights the generic list of options available to you, as someone who has all the requisite permissions together with an enabled **Book** module—if the **Book** module is disabled, the **Book outline** content option will disappear from this list.

There is one additional option that is presented above the main body of the content, namely **Menu settings**:

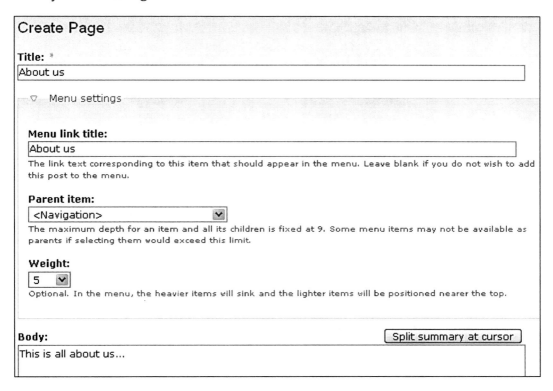

Adding a **Menu link title** tells Drupal that this content is to be added to one of the site's menus. In this instance, the page is an **About us** page that we would like to add to the bottom of the main navigation panel. Equally, we could have added it to the **Primary** or **Secondary links**. Clicking on **Save** now adds this page to the menu as one would expect:

Most often, content posted to the site will not form part of the menu so you can safely ignore this option. However, if you ever wish to remove or edit this menu item again, look at the same **Menu settings** section, and there will be a new checkbox, automatically available, to delete it:

One of the nice usability features of Drupal 6 allows for easy specification of the summary content. Leave the cursor sitting after whatever content is to appear as the summary, and click the **Split summary at cursor** button. This will split the page into a summary and content:

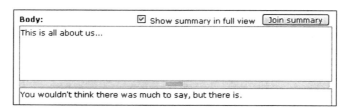

Now, the **Input format** section is presented as follows (if the **Input format** link is minimized, click on it to bring up the full version):

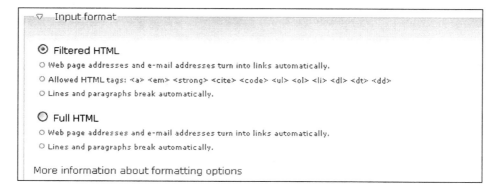

By default, the **Filtered HTML** option is selected. Unless you have a good reason to use the other available option, stick with the default. Especially be wary of allowing any user to add PHP to their content (although, this now has to be done by enabling the **PHP Filter** module first), as this could put your site at serious risk. Remember that even **Filtered HTML** is not entirely safe, as users could still add links to malicious web addresses within their posts, which amounts to the same thing as having it on your site.

Before continuing, I should mention that in the following chapter we will discuss how to create custom input formats, because the default options might not always be suitable for the site's requirements. It's also worth noting that not all users will be granted access to all the different input formats available, depending on the access policy and roles in place.

The **Book outline** section really forms part of a discussion on working with the **Book** module, so we will leave this for the section entitled *Book* later on in this chapter.

The next option, **Revision information**, allows you to specify whether Drupal should create a new version of the content if it is being updated or revised:

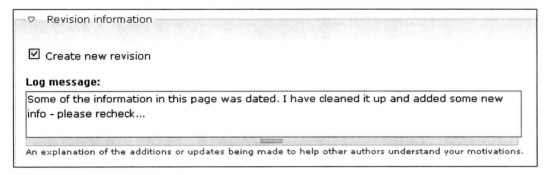

This means that the old version of the content is retained as well as making a new version. This is useful if you want to keep track of what changes are being made to documents. If a new revision has been created and tracked then, assuming you have sufficient permissions, you will notice a new **revisions** tab on the page as follows:

Using this **Revisions** page, it is now possible to review content's history quite easily. For example, you can decide which revision should be the active one (displayed to the public) by clicking on **revert**, or you can **delete** revisions altogether. Notice that the log message that was added to the content type is also displayed at the bottom of each revision. This is a very powerful feature that is quite important for maintaining good version control in content that is often modified.

Next, **Comment settings**, allows you to determine whether other users will be able to add comments to the content or not, as shown here:

The first option, **Disabled**, is useful if you are posting content for which comments are not appropriate — perhaps, like me, you are averse to criticism about your poetry, or something similar. The second allows only those with administration rights to post comments to this content, although other users can view the comments. The final option allows all users with sufficient permissions to pass comment on your wonderful poetry (or whatever).

File attachments are by now easy to work with and we have already seen them in action, so we'll discuss this option no further.

Authoring information has only two options. The first names the author of the content and the second gives the date on which the content was first created — these are automatically given the correct options but there are times when it is necessary to change them. Naturally, modifying the content will not change the **Authored on** date.

The **Publishing options** can be tricky to get right, depending on how things are set up. This is what they look like at the moment:

In the following section on *Administering Content,* it is possible to decide whether content of certain types coming from certain users needs to be moderated before it can be allowed onto the site for general consumption. If this is the case, you or a designated user will have the ability to go through a moderation queue in order to confirm that any and all the content meets the site's requirements.

In the previous screenshot, the content being added is being published directly without the need for moderation, although you could uncheck this if, for example, you wanted to leave it on the site without it being available to the general public.

Enabling the second option, **Promoted to front page**, will cause the content being created to appear on the front page of the website when it is first published (unless you have set a specific node to be displayed here already).

It is unlikely that by default you would want, for example, new book pages to appear on the front page ahead of say blogs from industry experts; so enable this option only for the content types that should capture some of the limelight.

The final option, **Sticky at top of lists**, causes the node to remain at the top of its list regardless of how many other postings there are. This is extremely useful for posting important messages to forums. For example, if there is some confusion about how to do something on a given forum, write a note explaining the procedure, and select this option to pin it to the top of that forum. In this way, you ensure that it is the first thing everyone sees whenever they visit.

 Not every content type honors the **Promoted to front page** request — page, forum and taxonomy lists will however.

That about wraps it up for default content options — there's plenty more to learn, so keep your thinking cap on as we venture into the world of content administration.

Administering Content

Assuming a user does not have **administer** permissions enabled on nodes, he or she will not have the power to modify the publishing options, and will simply have to click **Submit** in order to send their page for moderation or publication.

To see this in action, do the following:

- Give anonymous users the ability to post pages to the site by checking the **Create page content** option under the **node module** in **Permissions**, then click **Save permissions**.

- Edit the **Page** content types by unchecking the **Published** option and click **Save content type**.

Now, log out and post a page as an anonymous user. You should find that the page just submitted will not appear anywhere because it has not been published. In order to see what's going on, we need to log back in and visit the **Content** page under **Content management**, that shows a list of all the content on the site along with a variety of options in order to work with it, like so:

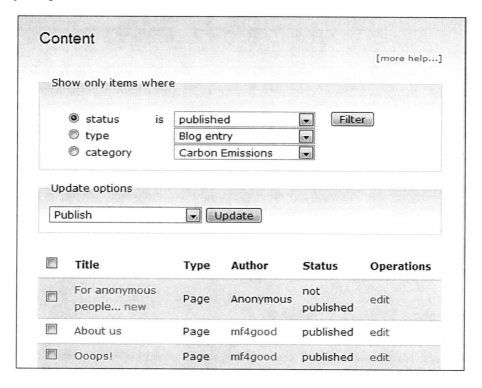

Notice that in this screenshot, the first submission was posted by an anonymous user (the rest being published by the site administrator for the demo site, **mf4good**). This page has not yet been published because the default settings require it to first be moderated. Before we do get a round to publishing this particular post, let's explore the anatomy of this page more closely.

The content filter shown towards the top of the page, above **Update options**, is a very important tool in your administrative workshop. It allows you to display only those nodes that satisfy certain requirements. There are four filter criteria provided: **status, type, category**, and **language**. These filter all the content on the site, presenting only those items that meet the specific requirement set in the drop-down list to the right of the selected method.

To locate a node that has already been published, check the **status** criterion, and then select the **published** option from the drop-down list (as shown in the previous screenshot) before clicking **Filter**. The displayed list would then be filtered and only published content would be displayed. Easy enough to do!

What if we want to show only those published posts that are of the **Blog entry** type? The way to do this is perform a nested, or refined, search. This involves searching for one criteria and then refining those results using another criteria. In this case, we would:

- Select the **published status** and click **Filter**
- Select the **Blog entry type** and click **Refine**

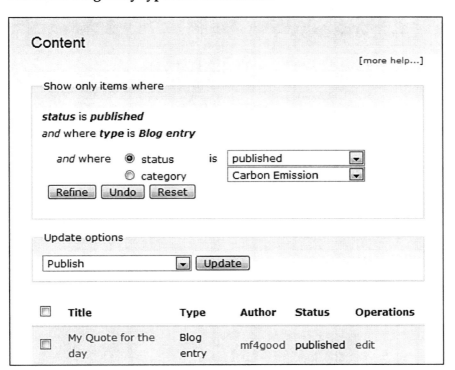

Notice that Drupal provides a readable version of the filter criteria that have been applied in order to display the current content results. In this instance, there is only one content posting that has **status published** and **Blog entry** type. It is possible to further refine the filter by selecting other filter types or even loosen it by one notch by clicking **Undo**.

 Remember to click **Reset** before embarking on a brand new search.

That's all good and well, but where is the moderation queue? If you look at the drop-down list provided with the **status** criterion, you will notice that there is a **not published** option. Selecting this and clicking **Filter** will present the following results:

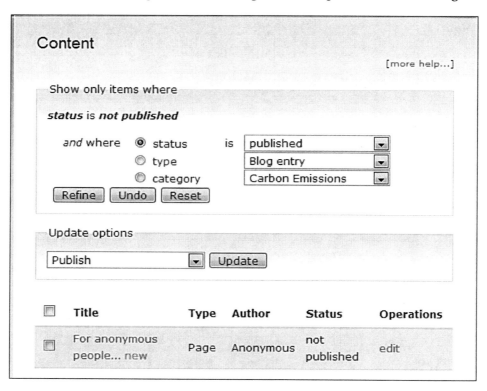

As expected, there is only one posting in this category at the moment because we have only posted a single page using the anonymous user, with the default published option unselected for this content type. This is precisely what this page is telling us, and you can now either view the content by clicking on the title or edit it by clicking on **edit**.

Once you are happy, or even unhappy, with the posting you can perform a number of update options by checking one from the **Update options** dropdown list and clicking **Update**. The options presented in this list are fairly self-explanatory and you can do everything from add or remove stickiness, force the content to be displayed or remove from your site's front page or even delete the content entirely.

It's worth remembering that selecting unpublish and delete will have the same effect in terms of effectively removing content from the site. The difference, however, is that deleting the content is irreversible, completely gone, while unpublishing is reversible and can be published again at a later stage.

For example, let's say we now wanted to allow the anonymous page to be published and displayed on the front page because after a bit of editing, we are happy with it. Check the box to the left of the **Title**, and then, in the **Update options** section directly above the list, select the relevant option, as shown here:

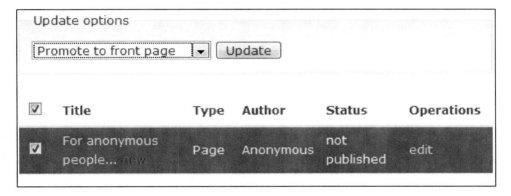

Clicking on **Update** will ensure that the page is now published as intended. You can confirm this by viewing the page on the site as per normal—simply navigate to the homepage to see it.

Finally, in the event that it is not possible to easily locate content, use the search tool provided by the **Search** module. Bear in mind that you can make use of the * wildcard character to match any characters in order to broaden your search.

The **Advanced search** link on this page also provides you with several other options to specify conditions for your search:

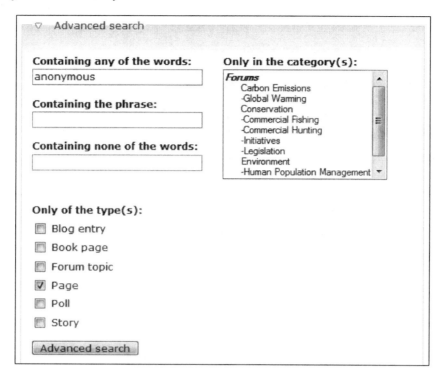

New content will not be searchable until your cron run has been completed Cron and scheduled tasks are discussed in detail in Chapter 10.

Play around with the search options in order to become familiar with how each one functions.

Content-Related Modules

It's a safe bet that there are far more content-related modules available than we can safely discuss in this chapter. However, if there is something specific you need to do, it is always worth checking out what modules are available in Drupal before building anything yourself. There are hundreds and hundreds of modules to choose from and even if there isn't one that does exactly what you need, you can often get fairly close with the available modules and then work from there.

This section will look over a couple of content modules that you will likely need at some stage…

Aggregator

One of the greatest opportunities available to web-based communities is the ability to share information. All that is required is a set of guidelines for how that information is to be presented, and once you have that, the rest is easy. So easy, in fact, that it is now possible to include news and articles of interest on your site from many well known sources with just a few clicks.

What makes it so easy to include other people's news, documents, articles, or any other content is a standard called **Rich Site Summary (RSS)**. This allows aggregators (programs that consume RSS feeds) to understand how to present content on web pages due to the way in which the RSS feed is structured. Drupal comes with one of these aggregators built in—simply enable it in the **Modules** section under **Administer**, and you will find that a few extra menu items pop up, allowing you to administer and view the content once it has been added.

Let's assume that the demo site would like to provide some news relating to wildlife from the *National Geographic* website. We pop along to the news site at `http://news.nationalgeographic.com/` and look for where the RSS feed icons are presented on the site. In this case, they look like the following:

Clicking on the **RSS** link here will bring up the following page (it may appear in a number of formats depending on your browser)—luckily Drupal takes care of all the dirty work for us, and we don't even need to understand the XML in order to consume this feed:

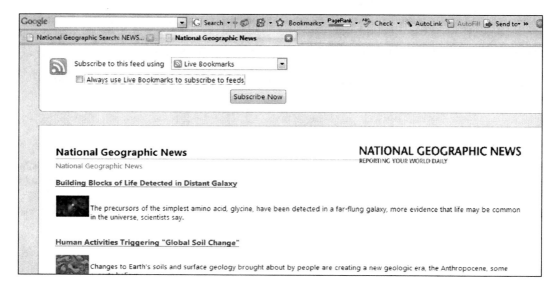

This may not seem to interesting at the moment, but it serves to confirm that there is at least a feed available for use at this URL.

We can now head back to our site and look for the **Feed aggregator** link under **Content management** in order to begin adding this feed to the site. This will bring up the as yet blank list of feeds along with everything else we need. On this page, clicking on the **Add category** tab brings up the following form:

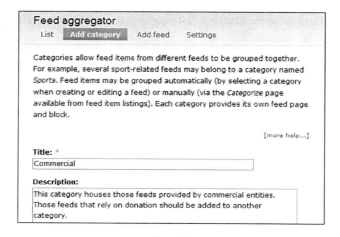

Assuming you intend to make use of a variety of feeds, it is probably prudent to categorize your content right from the start. Remember, providing access to timely and interesting news is a value-added service for your site and encourages users to return time and again.

Once finished, click **Save**, and then click on the **Add feed** tab to bring up the following:

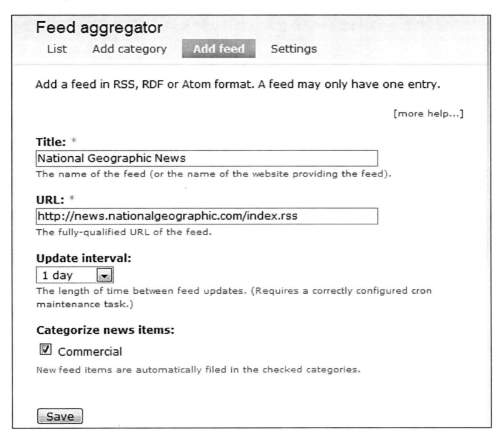

As you can see, we have:

1. Specified a title for the new feed.
2. Supplied Drupal with the location of the RSS feed (check this against the URL of the RSS feed page we visited on the actual *National Geographic* site a bit earlier).
3. Given an **Update interval** of one day, making this a daily news feed.
4. Associated this feed with the newly created **Commercial** category.

There are a number of things to consider when filling out this form. First, ensure that you are not infringing any licensing issues that will be supplied by the creator of the source feed. If there are restrictions as to what can and cannot be done with the feed, please ensure you abide by those restrictions.

Next, there is no point in setting an update interval of one hour if you are only running the cron script once a day—cron can at most only update the script once a day in this case. By the same token, there is no point in using cron to update a feed every ten minutes if the feed itself is only updated on a weekly basis—check how often the feed providers recommend it is updated.

[Some feed providers will ban you from their service if you persist in querying their feeds too regularly—it is your responsibility to honor their stipulations.]

Having taken these factors into account you can now click on **Submit** to add the feed. Now the aggregator homepage has something to tell us, and should look like this:

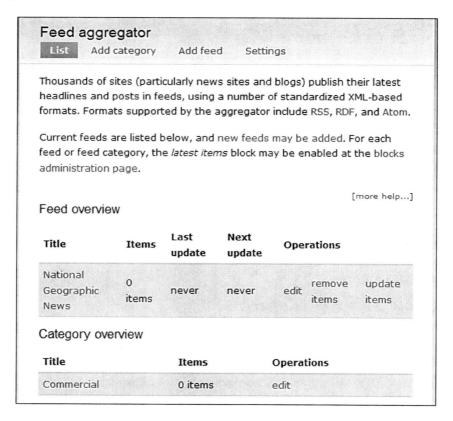

As yet, there are no items in the feed because the `cron.php` script hasn't been run. You can either wait for it to be accessed by your scheduled task or crontab, or if you are not keen to hang around, click the **update items** link to the right of the feed listing, or alternatively, navigate to the **Status report** page under **Reports** and click the **Run cron manually** link.

Once that is done, you should get something like this:

| Feed aggregator | List | Add category | Add feed | Settings |

Thousands of sites (particularly news sites and blogs) publish their latest headlines and posts in feeds, using a number of standardized XML-based formats. Formats supported by the aggregator include RSS, RDF, and Atom.

Current feeds are listed below, and new feeds may be added. For each feed or feed category, the *latest items* block may be enabled at the blocks administration page.

[more help...]

Feed overview

Title	Items	Last update	Next update	Operations		
National Geographic News	11 items	7 sec ago	*23 hours 59 min left*	edit	remove items	update items

Category overview

Title	Items	Operations
Commercial	11 items	edit

Success! The feed now contains **11 items** as of the last update, which occurred **7 sec ago**. As well as this, you can also **edit** the feed, **remove items** from the feed, or manually update the feed by clicking **update items** — this will update the feed to reflect any recent changes on the source site. That's all there is to it!

You can, of course, now view the content of the feed on the site. As an exercise, grant permission to access the feeds to anonymous and authenticated users alike. Now when someone visits and clicks on the **feed aggregator** link in the main menu, they are presented with something like the following:

Feed aggregator

Building Blocks of Life Detected in Distant Galaxy
National Geographic News - Tue, 02/05/2008 - 05:30

The precursors of the simplest amino acid, glycine, have been detected in a far-flung galaxy, more evidence that life may be common in the universe, scientists say.

Categories: Commercial

Human Activities Triggering "Global Soil Change"
National Geographic News - Tue, 02/05/2008 - 05:30

Changes to Earth's soils and surface geology brought about by people are creating a new geologic era, the Anthropocene, some experts believe.

Categories: Commercial

"Stay at Home" Baboon Dads Raise Healthier Kids
National Geographic News - Tue, 02/05/2008 - 05:30

Young yellow baboons that spend time with their dads early in life may experience less stress and mature more quickly—a distinct survival advantage.

All users have instant access to all the content provided by National Geographic. Nothing stops you from gathering information from any number of other feeds, and what is interesting is that provided you are not infringing any licenses, your feeds can be made available to other sites. Doing this is easy—enable the **Syndicate** block in **Blocks** under **Site Building** before trying it out.

Scroll down to the bottom of the feed page until you see a small icon that looks like this:

Click it in order to display your own feed page that is provided at the following URL (in the case of the demo site): `http://localhost/drupal/aggregator/rss`. This is how Drupal content can be syndicated (shared with others). You aren't limited to syndicating online feeds you have obtained—any content can be syndicated.

It's worth noting that feed sources can be revealed in the navigation column by clicking on the **Sources** link under **Feed aggregator**. In this case, we are presented with the following:

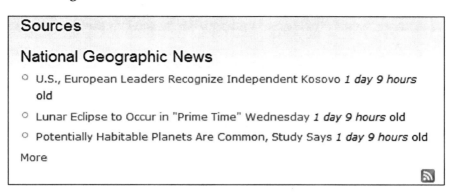

This presents us with a nice summary of feeds from each source. So far so good, but what does the **More** link do? Clicking on the **More** link for the National Geographic News source brings up the following page:

The feeds associated with this source are listed on the page below the title box for easy access. Following which, all the feeds from this source are listed in a slightly more comprehensive form. There are also two tabs at the top of this page. The **Categorize** tab opens a new page that allows us to put individual feed items into a variety of different categories (assuming you have created a variety of categories, in the same way we created **Commercial**).

This following screenshot shows a feed item being assigned two categories, namely **Commercial** and **Special**:

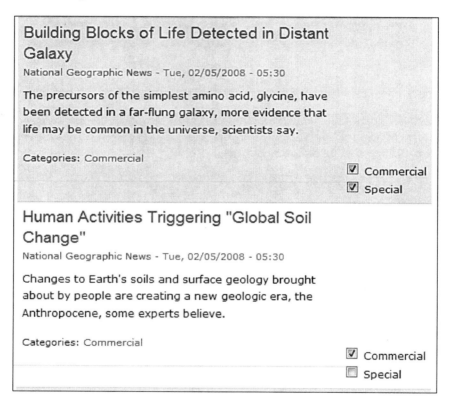

In this case, the **Special** category was created with a specific purpose in mind. Because there is news every now and then that will hold special interest for the site's readers, all items that are tagged in the **Special** category should be displayed in a special block on the website (we'll see how this is done in a moment) so that every user can see the special news when viewing any page on the site.

The final tab on the **Sources** page, entitled **Configure**, brings up the same page that was used in order to create the feed. From here, you can make any changes you require to the feed with ease.

It is entirely possible you would like to display some of the latest feeds in a block somewhere on the site, so **Aggregator** provides this functionality, automatically. Head on over to **Blocks** under **Site building** and enable one of the new blocks so that it displays its latest items:

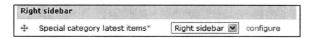

Once this is done, you will see the new feed, along with a selection of its items on Drupal's web pages. You can configure the number of news items displayed in the **Block specific settings** on its configuration page (click on **configure** to open this up)—for our purposes, the default option of five feeds is just fine.

Assuming that a user has blogging permissions and the feed license allows for it, you can add feed items to blogs, by clicking on the little **b** icon that appears next to each item, as shown here (the **Blog** module must first be enabled):

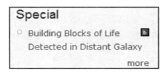

Adding a news item to your blogs gives the article more permanency as it will not be lost when, or if, the list of items in the feed is cleared. The aggregator has one more important section to look at—configuration! If you click on the **Settings** tab of the **Feed aggregator** page under **Content management**, the following is displayed:

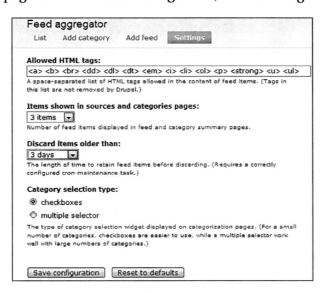

This interface provides control over the type of HTML that is allowed within the feeds that are to be consumed. This should be sufficient for most, if not all, the feeds you want to aggregate, but on the off chance that there are problems with some feeds, it is likely that they are using tags that are not specified in this section.

For example, you may wish to have images shown through your feeds. As it stands, this is not possible because the aggregator is not set to allow the **<img>** tag. Adding this tab to the list, and clicking **Save configuration** means that users can now see any images that are presented along with the feeds:

Feed aggregator

Building Blocks of Life Detected in Distant Galaxy

National Geographic News - Tue, 02/05/2008 - 05:30

The precursors of the simplest amino acid, glycine, have been detected in a far-flung galaxy, more evidence that life may be common in the universe, scientists say.

Categories: Commercial, Special

Human Activities Triggering "Global Soil Change"

National Geographic News - Tue, 02/05/2008 - 05:30

Changes to Earth's soils and surface geology brought about by people are creating a new geologic era, the Anthropocene, some experts believe.

Categories: Commercial

Next, the number of items to be shown with each feed in general as well as how long to hold onto old feed items can be specified. It is easy enough to make sensible selections here. The final section stipulates whether the category selection interface (on the **Categorize** tab of the **Sources** page) should use checkboxes or the multiple selector. We have already seen checkboxes in use but if **multiple selector** was enabled, the category selections would look like this:

Before we move on, it is worth mentioning again that having interesting and informative news on your site makes it a more attractive destination for users. Further, providing your own content that others can utilize through RSS feeds builds popularity as people follow RSS feed summaries back to your site to read the full article—it's a good way of immersing your site into the Internet community as a whole.

Book

Earlier in this chapter we used the **Book** module to demonstrate how enabling a module can lead to changes in a variety of areas of the site administration. However, we neglected to give complete coverage of this useful module so let's elaborate on this here quickly.

A book, in the Drupal context, is a navigable structured document that can be authored collaboratively – provided that more than one person has permission to create book pages. It can consist of pretty much any type of content, including the default **Book page** and imbues its content with a number of features that make them part of the book. For example, navigation links are added to each book page allowing readers to traverse the book structure with ease.

Creating a book is fairly easy. After ensuring that the **Book** module is enabled, click on **Create content** and select **Book page**:

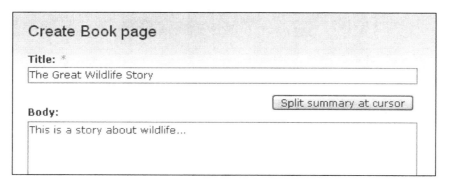

Adding a title for the book and a brief summary of what it is about is really no different from creating any other type of content. The difference comes in setting up where in the book's structure this page is going to be placed. Scroll down the page and open up the section entitled **Book outline**:

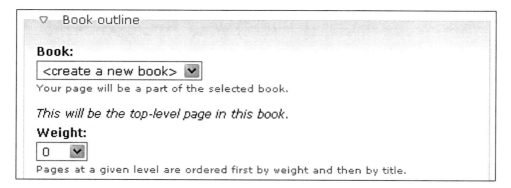

Selecting **<create a new book>** from the drop-down list indicates that we wish this page to be the start of a new book—Drupal dutifully informs us that this will therefore be the top level page in the book. With that done, go ahead and save the changes—if you intend on working on the book regularly, perhaps consider adding it to the navigation menu for easy access in the **Menu settings** section first.

When viewing this page it now becomes clear how the rest of the book can be built by adding pages:

Click on **Add child page** and call the new page **Chapter 1**. The important part of adding any content to a book comes in the **Book outline** section where we can specify where in the book this page must be added:

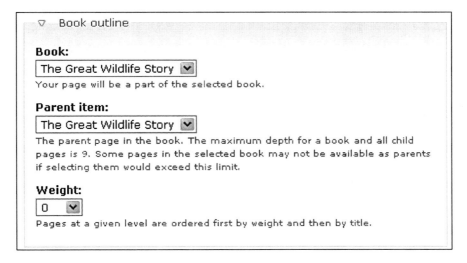

In this instance, we want this page to be part of the new book, and more importantly, its parent item must be the original book page. Click on **Save** and then create a few more chapter pages so that you end up with something like this when viewing the book:

It is easy enough to then begin adding content to each chapter by adding sections or articles, and Drupal actually mentions on the content creation page that it will accept up to 9 levels of depth in the content. Of course, adding content to each chapter requires us to specify the chapter in the **Book outline** section:

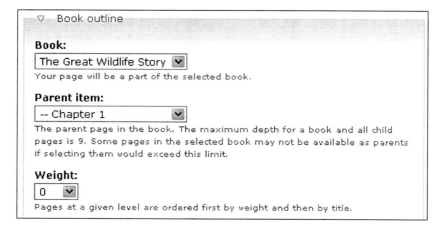

With this new child page added to Chapter 1, the book outline now tells us that there is something contained within the chapter by modifying the bullet:

Clicking this link now brings up the child page(s) along with the book's associated navigation:

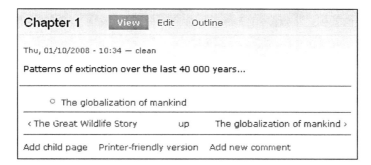

That's all there is to it!

Remember that any content you like can be added to a book, so you are not limited to having to build each piece of content up in the way we have done here. Take a look at any piece of content that has been created on the site—it can be a blog post, a poll, whatever—it will have an **Outline** tab, which when clicked brings up a dialog that can be used to add the content to any book on the site:

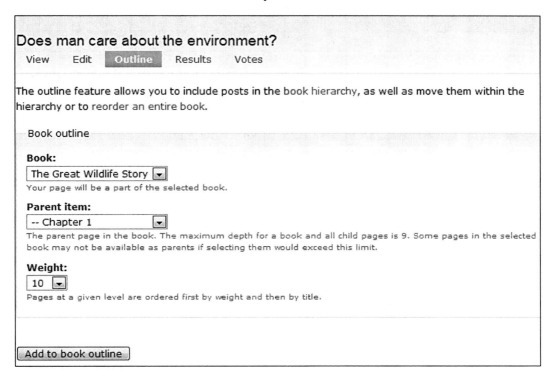

Note that this poll has been added to **Chapter 1** of **The Great Wildlife Story** book. It has also been assigned a large weight to push it to the back of the chapter—just as one would expect in, say, an instructional document that provides thought-provoking questionnaires at the end of each important section for students.

Now Chapter 1 has the following structure:

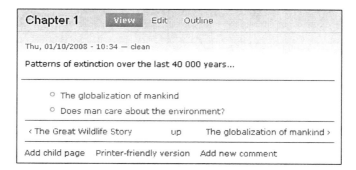

What if, realizing that we need to add a whole bunch of questions to the end of each chapter, we now want to have a questionnaire section that contains all the polls? The answer is to add a weighted page to the chapter entitled **Questionnaires** and then edit each of the polls' **Book outline** options to insert them into their correct parent item.

Before we round off this section, it is important to note that the behavior of each book can be controlled by visiting the **Books** section under **Content Management**. This page presents a list of all the books on the site and provides a graphical interface utilizing drag-and-drop features for editing a book.

For example, the one we created has the following edit page:

The Great Wildlife Story			
Title		**Operations**	
⊕ Chapter 1	view	edit	delete
⊕ The globalization of mankind	view	edit	delete
⊕ Questionnaire	view	edit	delete
⊕ Does man care about the environment?	view	edit	delete
⊕ Chapter 2	view	edit	delete
⊕ Chapter 3	view	edit	delete

Save book pages

Finally, the **Books** page also has a **Settings** tab that can be used to specify the default page type for books, as well as which content types are to be allowed and disallowed. As the administrator, it is possible to add any content type to a book by default, but you may wish to consider disallowing some types if the book is to be created collaboratively.

Summary

Knowing how to deal with content efficiently and quickly is a highly desirable trait when it comes to working with CMS systems such as Drupal. To this end, this chapter set the foundation for you to work from by giving an overview of the fundamentals. To start with, we took a brief look at the various types of content that can be implemented using Drupal and then discussed how to work with that content using the administration tool.

At the moment, content management might seem fairly straightforward, but as the site grows larger, the job becomes slightly harder. Ensuring that you spend time learning about the content-related administrative areas of the **Administer** menu will ensure that you stay on top of things as you begin attempting more complex content-oriented tasks.

The second half of this chapter demonstrated some of the powerful functionality that ships with Drupal or is provided by contributions. We saw that it is possible to create books and aggregate RSS feeds with relative ease, and in turn syndicate content so that it is made available to other sites to consume. Having the ability to do this with only the minimum of fuss is a quantum leap for the Internet as a whole, and Drupal makes it a breeze.

Armed with a solid understanding of how to work with content, as well as the type of things available to use, we are now ready to look at some slightly more advanced content issues. The next chapter will talk about how to create your own dynamic and attractive content, as well as talk about how to categorize content.

7
Advanced Content

Most of our dealings with content up till now have been fairly basic—they require us only to learn which settings to enable and what text to enter. There is a fundamental difference between that and what is coming in this chapter, mainly because the content in this chapter requires us to think ahead, and plan what we want ahead of time, in order to prevent things going awry at a later date.

One of the most important aspects to managing content is the manner in which it is best organized for expedient retrieval—and for this, we need to to discuss taxonomy. Taxonomy is what makes Drupal's classification system so powerful, and it is left for us to decide how best to implement. It might sound a little strange at first, but we will see later on in the chapter why this faculty of Drupal is one of the features that distinguishes it from everything else out there—it's really a good thing!

Being able to categorize information is one thing, but the ability to create entirely new content types and post complex pages will also come in handy at some stage. Accordingly, this chapter discusses the following subjects:

- Taxonomy
- Content Construction Kit (CCK)
- HTML, PHP, and Content Posting

The skills learned during the process of content classification, creation, and management will prove useful not only for this website but also in other aspects of life—whether it is creating and managing office reports for your boss, building a new website, or even writing a book. That is because, by and large, we are now going to learn *how content should be managed and created* rather than how to enable or disable settings.

Taxonomy

At first glance, it might seem that taxonomy is yet another term indicating that your job is going to be more complex for some reason or other. After all, it's perfectly reasonable to set up a website to allow blog writers to blog, forum posters to post, administrators to administer, or any other type of content producer to produce content and leave it at that. With what we have covered so far, this is all quite possible, so why does Drupal insist on adding the burden of learning about new concepts and terms?

If your site is never going to gather a substantial amount of content (perhaps it is only meant as a more static, placeholder type of site), then spending time working with taxonomies and so on is probably not going to bring much advantage—go ahead and enable whatever content types you require and let users add whatever they want.

However, the aim is not generally to remain in obscurity when creating a website, so assuming that you do want to attract a community of users, then the method of categorizing content in Drupal makes it one of the most sophisticated content management systems around.

Take the time to master working with taxonomy in Drupal, because not only will this help you to work out how to manage content better, but it will also really set your site apart from others because of the flexible and intuitive manner in which the content is organized. These attributes allow you to manage a site of pretty much any size imaginable (just in case what you are working on is *"the next big thing"*).

What and Why?

Taxonomy is described as the science of classification. In terms of how it applies to Drupal, it is the *method by which content is organized* using several distinct types of relationship between terms. Simple as that! This doesn't really encompass how useful it is, though, but before we move on to that, there is a bit of terminology to pick up first:

- **Term**: A term used to describe content (also known as a *descriptor*)
- **Vocabulary**: A grouping of related terms
- **Thesaurus**: A categorization of content that describes *is similar to* relationships
- **Taxonomy**: A categorization of content into a hierarchical structure
- **Tagging**: The process of associating a term (descriptor) with content
- **Synonym**: Can be thought of as *another word for* the current term.

It may help to view the following diagram in order to properly grasp how these terms inter-relate.

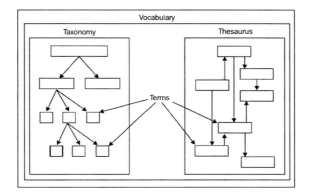

This serves to illustrate the fact that there are two main types of vocabulary. Each type consists of a set of terms, but the relationships between them are different in that a *taxonomy* deals with a hierarchy of information, and a *thesaurus* deals with relationships between terms. The terms (shown as small boxes) and their relationships (shown as arrows) play a critical role in how content is ogranized.

We have already seen an example of a taxonomy when the **Forum** module was discussed. In this case, there was a hierarchical relationship between forum containers and the forum topics they contained. But what would we need thesauri for? For one thing, if you were working on creating a scientific document and wanted to allow plenty of references between terms, so that users could browse related pages (which didn't necessarily have child-parent relationships), then you would go for this type of structure.

What we have discussed so far is how to *control a taxonomy* from the administrator's point of view. It is also possible to pass that control onto everyone who uses the site by creating a *free taxonomy*. One of the things that makes the Drupal taxonomy system so powerful, is that it allows content to be categorized on the fly (as and when it is created). This unburdens administrators because it is no longer necessary to moderate every bit of content coming into the site in order to put it into pre-determined categories.

We'll discuss these methods in some detail in the coming sections, but it's also worth noting quickly that it is possible to tag a given node more than once. This means that content can belong to several vocabularies, at once. This is very useful for cross-referencing purposes because it highlights relationships between terms or vocabularies through the actual nodes.

Let's begin…

Implementing Controlled Taxonomies in Drupal

The best way to talk about how to implement some form of categorization is to see it in action. There are quite a few settings to work with and consider in order to get things up and running. Let's assume that the demo site has enlisted a large number of specialists who will maintain their own blogs on the website so that interested parties can keep tabs on what's news according to the people in the know.

Now, some people will be happy with visiting their blog of choice and reading over any new postings there. Some people, however, might want to be able to search for specific topics in order to see if there are correlations or disagreements between bloggers on certain subjects. As there is going to be a lot of content posted once the site has been up and running for a few months, we need some way to ensure that specific topics are easy to find, regardless of who has been discussing them on their blogs.

Introduction to Vocabularies

Let's quickly discuss how vocabularies are dealt with in the administration tool in order to work out how to go about making sure this requirement is satisfied. If you click on the **Taxonomy** link under **Content management,** you will be presented with a page listing the current vocabularies. Assuming you have created a forum during the last few chapters, you should have something like this:

Taxonomy   List   Add vocabulary

The taxonomy module allows you to categorize your content using both tags and administrator defined terms. It is a flexible tool for classifying content with many advanced features. To begin, create a 'Vocabulary' to hold one set of terms or tags. You can create one free-tagging vocabulary for everything, or separate controlled vocabularies to define the various properties of your content, for example 'Countries' or 'Colors'.

Use the list below to configure and review the vocabularies defined on your site, or to list and manage the terms (tags) they contain. A vocabulary may (optionally) be tied to specific content types as shown in the *Type* column and, if so, will be displayed when creating or editing posts of that type. Multiple vocabularies tied to the same content type will be displayed in the order shown below. To change the order of a vocabulary, grab a drag-and-drop handle under the *Name* column and drag it to a new location in the list. (Grab a handle by clicking and holding the mouse while hovering over a handle icon.) Remember that your changes will not be saved until you click the *Save* button at the bottom of the page.

[more help...]

Name	Type	Operations		
Forums	Forum topic	edit vocabulary	list terms	add terms

Before we look at editing terms and vocabularies, let's take a look at how to create a vocabulary for ourselves. Click on the **add vocabulary** tab to bring up the following page that we can use to create a vocabulary, manually:

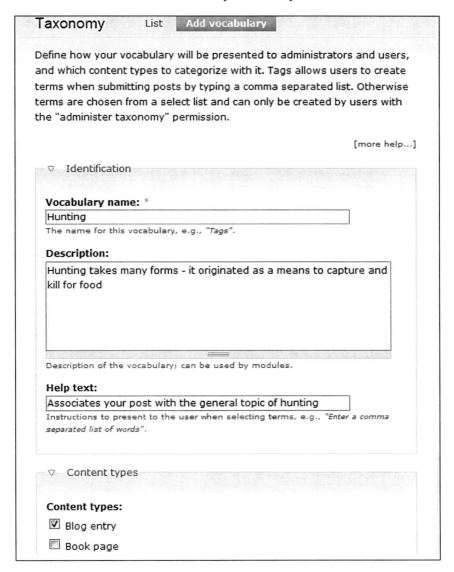

By way of example, this vocabulary will deal with the topic of hunting. This vocabulary only applies to blog entries because that is the only content (or node) type for which it is enabled—you can select as many or as few as you like, depending on how many content types it should apply to.

Looking further down the page, there are several other options that we will discuss in more detail, shortly. Clicking on **Submit** adds this vocabulary to the list, so that the main page now looks like this:

Created new vocabulary *Hunting*.

The taxonomy module allows you to categorize your content using both tags and administrator defined terms. It is a flexible tool for classifying content with many advanced features. To begin, create a 'Vocabulary' to hold one set of terms or tags. You can create one free-tagging vocabulary for everything, or separate controlled vocabularies to define the various properties of your content, for example 'Countries' or 'Colors'.

Use the list below to configure and review the vocabularies defined on your site, or to list and manage the terms (tags) they contain. A vocabulary may (optionally) be tied to specific content types as shown in the *Type* column and, if so, will be displayed when creating or editing posts of that type. Multiple vocabularies tied to the same content type will be displayed in the order shown below. To change the order of a vocabulary, grab a drag-and-drop handle under the *Name* column and drag it to a new location in the list. (Grab a handle by clicking and holding the mouse while hovering over a handle icon.) Remember that your changes will not be saved until you click the *Save* button at the bottom of the page.

[more help...]

Name	Type	Operations		
✛ Forums	Forum topic	edit vocabulary	list terms	add terms
✛ Hunting	Blog entry	edit vocabulary	list terms	add terms

Save

So far so good, but this will not be of much use to us as it stands! We need to add some terms (descriptors) in order to allow tagging to commence.

Dealing with Terms

Click on **add terms** link for the **Hunting** vocabulary to bring up the following page:

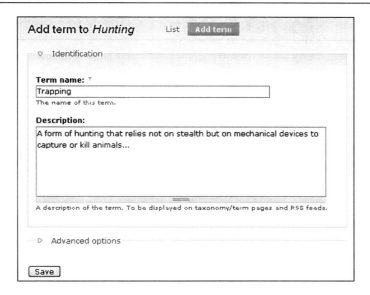

The term **Trapping** has been added here, with a brief description of the term itself. We could, if we choose, associate the term **Poaching** with **Trapping** by making it a related term or synonym (of course, you would need to create this term first in order to make it a related term). Click on the **Advanced options** link to expose the additional features, as shown here:

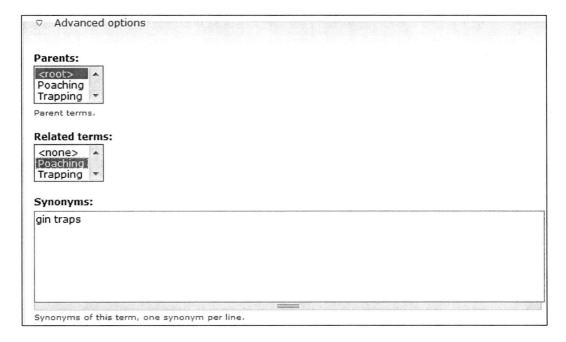

In this case, the term **Trapping** is specified as being related to **Poaching** and by way of example, **gin traps** is a synonym. Synonyms don't actually do anything useful at the moment, so don't pay too much mind to them yet, but there are modules that expose additional functionality based on related terms and synonyms, such as the **Similar by Terms** module.

The **Parents** option at the start of the **Advanced options** warrants a closer inspection, but as it relates more closely to the structure of hierarchies, we'll look at it in the section on *Hierarchies* that's coming up.

For now, add a few more terms to this vocabulary so that the list looks something like this:

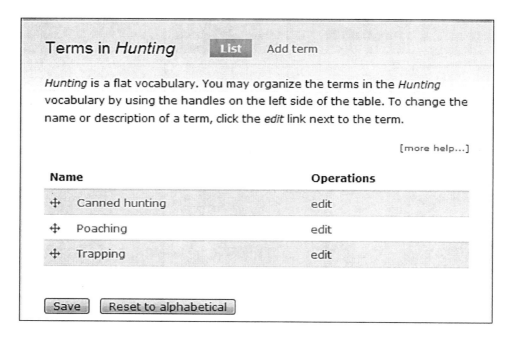

It's now time to make use of these terms by posting some blog content.

Posting Content with Categories Enabled

Using any account with the requisite permissions to add blog content, attempt to post to the site. You should now be able to view the newly inserted **Hunting** category, as shown here:

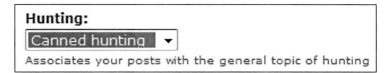

Now comes the clever bit! Once this blog node has been posted, users can view the blog as normal, except that it now has its term displayed along with the post (bottom right):

Campaign against Canned Hunting wins prestigious award

Wed, 02/27/2008 - 14:20 — mf4good

Recently, Adv Mercer and his non-profit campaign against canned hunting in South Africa was given a shot in the arm when it was awarded the Marchig foundation's annual award for outstanding service in the field of conservation.

Add new comment   Canned hunting

Where does the descriptor link take us? Click on the term, in this case **Canned hunting**, and you will be taken to a page listing all of the content that has been tagged with this term. This should really have you quite excited, because with very little work, users can now find focused content without having to look that hard — this is what content management is all about!

Hierarchies

What we have seen so far is really only the tip of the iceberg. You can build an entire hierarchy of terms in a vocabulary to give you a fairly complex taxonomy. Remember that if it is a hierarchy you are building, then the broadest terms should be towards the top of the pile, with the more focused terms near the bottom. At the moment, though, we don't really have a *hierarchy*, but rather, more of a *flat* structure.

What if we wanted a set of more specific terms that would allow bloggers to tag their content (which focuses on specific types of *Trapping*, for example)? The answer lies in restructuring the vocabulary by dragging and dropping its terms not only up and down the list, but right to left — this is done when viewing the **list terms** page of the vocabulary.

For this example, I added a term entitled **Snaring** to the vocabulary, and then dragged it under and to the right of the term **Trapping** to indicate that it is lower in the hierarchy:

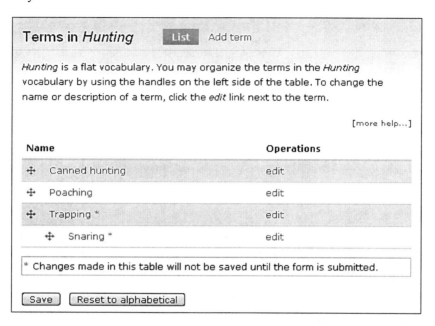

Saving this change leaves us with the same page, only the description of the hierarchy has moved from flat to single:

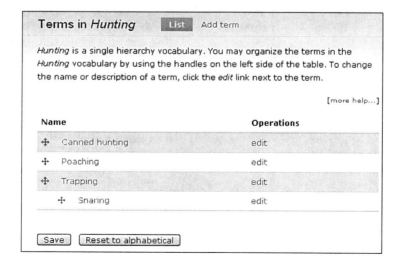

That was fairly easy to do, and now we are free to create either flat hierarchies or single depth ones (i.e. one parent term with one child term—no grandchildren). If you wanted to create a deep hierarchy structure, then this is easily achieved by dragging either additional terms under **Snaring**, or moving **Trapping** under something else, like this:

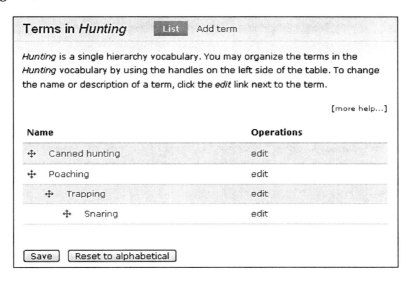

This should not be confused with creating multiple hierarchies—notice that the hierarchy description in this screenshot still describes **Hunting** as a single hierarchy vocabulary.

But what happens if your topic is slightly more complex than a straightforward hierarchy? For example, it's quite possible that the terms **Pits** (referring to hunting pits) could be equally at home under both **Trapping** and **Poaching** (which in turn may also have multiple parents). In the event that one term has several parent terms, the phrase used to describe this structure is *multiple hierarchy*.

Recall that when dealing with terms previously, there was an **Advanced option** in the term edit page that allowed us to specify one or more parent terms. Selecting more than one parent, like so:

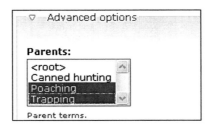

...leads Drupal to warn us with the following page:

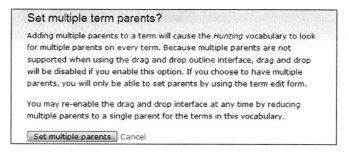

Basically, it is necessary to warn users that the normal drag and drop facility for vocabularies are not implementable when terms have a complex hierarchy involving several parents—that said, drag and drop will still be enabled if it is at all possible, and the structure will still be shown on the **List** page. If you want a multiple hierarchy, then the structural editing of the hierarchy must be done by hand in each term's **edit** form.

Go ahead and click **Set multiple parents**—you might want to add a few terms and set each of these to have multiple parents, to make the structure a little more complex. With that done, note that the drag-and-drop features of the list page are disabled:

Name	Operations
Canned hunting	edit
Pits	edit
Poaching	edit
gin traps	edit
Pits	edit
Pits	edit
Trapping	edit
gin traps	edit
Pits	edit

The hierarchy structure is useful when the topics of discussion fall fairly neatly into some sort of natural hierarchy—forums are the best example of this. However, it may well be that a given piece of content overlaps several terms and should really be tagged with more than one term. To achieve this, head back to the vocabulary editing page and select the **Multiple select** option in the **Settings** section:

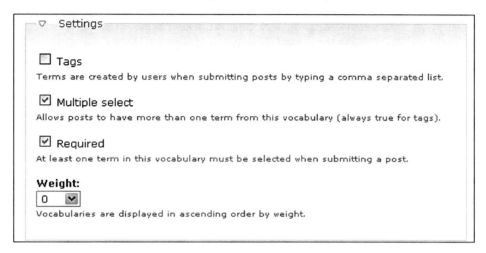

Save this and then post some new content. Now, instead of being presented with a single term to associate with the post, it is possible to select as many as are relevant:

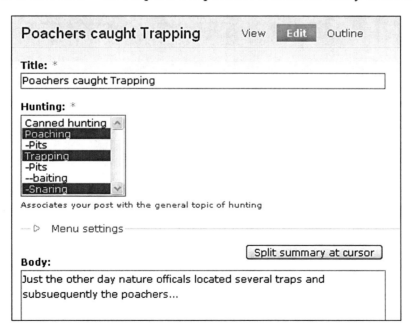

When this post is viewed on the site, it has several tags associated with it, and users can click on any of these tags to immediately locate more content that is of specific interest to them:

Notice that the terms presented do not, in any way, indicate their underlying structure to the reader—it simply tells them that these are all terms of this bit of content.

Content Structure

What if, in the demo site's case, we have the term **Trapping** available to tag content with (blog posts in this case), but someone is really talking about something other than hunting entirely, and there happens to be some sort of content overlap? An example scenario might be as follows:

- Several specialists are contracted to maintain blogs about the African continent.
- They tag their content using a new **Africa** vocabulary that contains terms like **nature, gazelle, predators, lakes, rivers, mountains, hunting, weather,** and **tourism.**
- You wish to be able to allow material that is created from the Africa blogs to be cross-referenced by hunting-related topics in the **Hunting** specialists' blogs.

In order to achieve this, it is necessary to create a new vocabulary called **Africa**. Attach this vocabulary to the blog content type, and then create several terms, ensuring that one of them is entitled **Hunting**, as follows:

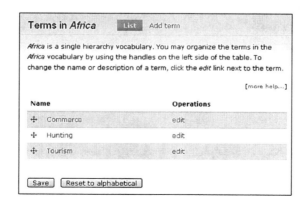

Now, when users attempt to post content, they are presented with not one but two options to classify their content, and assuming you have correctly ordered the vocabularies on the **Taxonomy** page, you can apply a kind of hierarchy to the tags. For example, a blog post on poaching by one of the **Africa** bloggers might look like this:

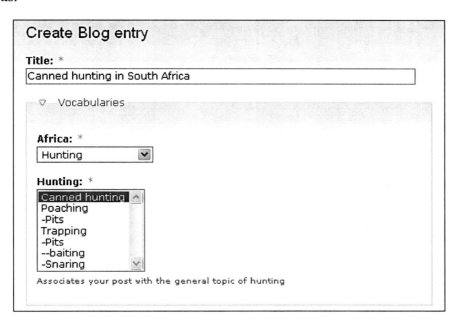

Once this is posted to the site, it is then possible to view both categories on the content page, instead of just one. In other words, the node has been tagged with several terms in what is known as **faceted tagging**.

Faceted tagging uses a *bottom up* system of classification, where facets or properties of the content are described by the terms. In this way, a very intuitive method of classifying content can be created without users needing to understand the top-down path of a content hierarchy in order to find the content they are after. In this case, the specific method of tagging used here helps to elucidate the hierarchy of terms too (i.e. **Canned hunting** is a child of **Hunting**):

Taking a look at this posting on the site confirms that users can now go directly to both the **Hunting** and **Canned hunting** category pages by clicking on the links provided in the posting.

What happens if one of the **Hunting** bloggers simply wants to make an entry and tag it with the **Canned hunting** term from the **Hunting** vocabulary, without having to first specify that this content also belongs to the **Africa** vocabulary? The answer lies once again in editing the vocabulary page, which contains a **Required** checkbox right at the bottom. If this option is enabled, then posters must select at least one tag from the vocabulary, but if we leave it unselected, then posters can choose whether to include a term from that vocabulary or not.

Talking of new options, there is one more that we should take a look at quickly—tagging. Since tagging has a number of considerations to consider before implementation, we treat it in its own section.

Implementing Thesuari in Drupal (Tags)

Tagging is an interesting option because it allows posters to choose their own terms for their content. While posters effectively have free reign when it comes to tagging their posts, Drupal understands that a hundred different people might come up with a hundred different terms to describe the same post, and this can be very detrimental to the usability of the site.

In order to combat this effect, Drupal provides helpful clues to keep the tagging of posts as uniform as possible, without placing restrictions on what can and is used for tagging. Enabling **Tags** for the **Hunting** vocabulary, for example, means posters are given the following category options when creating a blog entry:

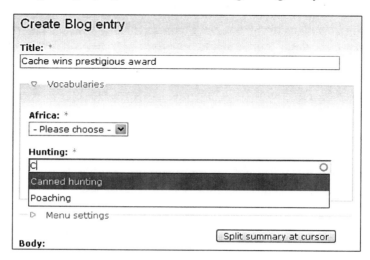

Notice that there is a red asterisk superscript above the **Hunting** category. This is because, despite the fact that we are using free tagging, the **Required** option on the **edit vocabulary** page is still enabled—so something *has* to be entered here. Secondly, there is a drop-down list of all the tags available (containing with whatever letter(s) you type). This means that giving people free reign to type in their own tags is not as random as it may at first seem, because they can still be guided as to what terms are already available using this drop-down list. In this way, Drupal can encourage a more coherent body of terms.

"But **Poaching** doesn't being with a C", some of you may be remarking. That is quite correct, but **Poaching** contains a **c** so it is displayed here nevertheless—it's a good way to provide a range of available tags that narrows down quickly as the user types.

Tagging has some pros in that it is far more flexible. People can tag their content exactly as they please—making the tagging system fit the content far more snugly. The problem is, however, that the vocabulary may well become unwieldy, because similar content could be tagged with entirely different terms, making it hard for users to find what they are looking for.

 Allowing free tagging is a very powerful method for categorizing content. Be wary though, it can lead to a lot of redundant tags that in turn lead to content that is hard to find.

You should make note of the fact that it is not possible to create a hierarchy of terms using the free tagging system, because every new tag is on the same level as all the other tags. So what you end up with is really a *thesaurus*, instead of a taxonomy (hence this section's heading).

Remember that it is still possible to moderate a thesaurus because any and all terms that posters create will still be added to the list of terms in the vocabulary, and they can be viewed, edited or deleted as you like.

It is interesting to note that a middle ground between controlled taxonomies and free tagging is achievable using the already mentioned **Multiple select** option and disabling **Free tagging**. This allows users to tag their posts with as many terms as are made available by the creator of the vocabulary—giving you control over the terms used, and posters the freedom to choose which ones they make use of.

With that we come to the end of the discussion on taxonomy. As mentioned when we first began working on this section, it may take a little while to get the hang of things, because the way in which the categorization works in Drupal is not always immediately intuitive. However, once you have mastered it, you will find that your content is readily accessible and well organized with very little effort.

Content Construction Kit (CCK)

It is likely that at some stage, you will want to upgrade at least some content from plain text to something that looks a little *out of the ordinary*. Drupal provides the CCK module as a way to build custom content types that can be tailored to suit your needs. In effect, it gives you control over which *fields* are presented to a user whenever they post content using custom content types.

[The term *field* refers to a given piece of content within a node. Conversely, a node is a collection of fields.]

In addition to the basic field types provided by the CCK module, you should also keep an eye out for contribs that extend CCK functionality to provide a huge range of useful field enhancements. Everything from Brazilian ID numbers to validated email fields, voting widgets and Amazon ASINS have been made available in the past.

There are also a number of other modules that make use of CCK in a variety of ways. Most important among these is *Views*. Views provide administrators with the means to modify how Drupal displays lists of content, and CCK exposes its fields to the **Views** module, making them perfect partners when it comes to creating custom content and then displaying that content in a highly configurable manner.

At the time of writing, *Views* is not available for Drupal 6 (although the module is being actively developed and should hopefully be ready by the time you read this) so it is left as an exercise to download and install it, and create at least one new *View*, utilizing fields created in the following sections.

Installing CCK

CCK is available, so go ahead and download the latest version and extract the file to your **modules** folder. CCK adds its own section to the **Modules** page under **Site building**:

There are a number of interdependent sections for this module, but all of them rely on the first option, **Content**, so go ahead and enable this first. We are going to look over all the features provided by CCK, by default, in this section. So go ahead and enable those modules that rely only on **Content**. With that done, enable the remaining options so that you end up with everything working, like this:

Notice that some of the options are disabled to prevent us from inadvertently disabling an option that is required by something else. If, for example, you wish to disable **Text**, then disable **Node Reference** and **User Reference** first.

Working with CCK

With all the options enabled, we can now go ahead and create a new content type. Actually, it is possible to create new content types without the use of CCK, it's just that the new content types will look pretty much like the standard content types already available, because there are no really interesting fields to add.

Head over to **Content types** under **Content management** and select the **Add content type** field to bring up the following page:

Content types   List   **Add content type**   Fields   Export   Import

To create a new content type, enter the human-readable name, the machine-readable name, and all other relevant fields that are on this page. Once created, users of your site will be able to create posts that are instances of this content type.

Identification

Name: *

Endangered Species

The human-readable name of this content type. This text will be displayed as part of the list on the *create content* page. This name must begin with a capital letter and contain only letters, numbers, and **spaces**. This name must be unique.

Type: *

species

The machine-readable name of this content type. This text will be used for constructing the URL of the *create content* page for this content type. This name must contain only lowercase letters, numbers, and underscores. Underscores will be converted into hyphens when constructing the URL of the *create content* page. This name must be unique.

Description:

Provides the vital statistics of species found on the endangered list...

A brief description of this content type. This text will be displayed as part of the list on the *create content* page.

The identification section is pretty straightforward. You can go ahead and fill in whatever new content settings are appropriate. Of special interest is the **Submission form settings** below this that allows you to decide whether the default **Title** and **Body** fields should be changed or even retained (in the case of the **Body** field):

In the case of the **Endangered Species** content type, it doesn't really make sense to have a species **Title**, rather a **Common name** makes more sense. Leaving the **Body field label** blank will cause this field to be omitted completely in the event that it is not suitable for the type of content you have in mind.

You may have noticed that there are several additional tabs to the right of **Add content type** tab that provide additional functionality. These options are discussed a little later on in this section. So for now, go ahead and fill out the **Name**, **Type**, and **Description** fields and click **Save content type** to add this to the default list:

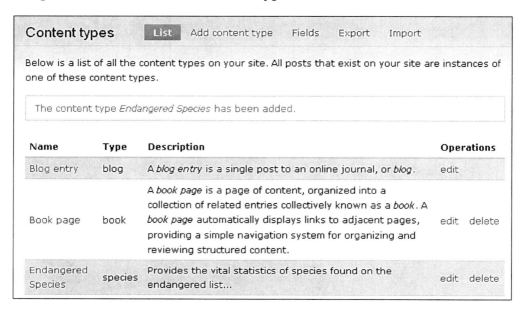

We are now ready to begin customizing this new type utilizing whatever options are available—depending on what is or is not enabled. It is possible to customize *any type* that is available on Drupal, including the default ones like **Blog entry** or **Poll**, but to begin with it is best to leave these alone.

To begin working on the new content type, click on **edit** in the **Endangered Species** row. We can now look at the various aspects of working with content types, beginning with…

Adding Fields

Select the **Add field** tab to bring up the following page:

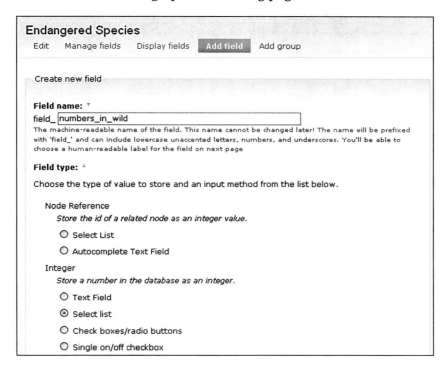

This dialog allows you to specify the new field's machine readable name and then select what type of input it is going to be.

Presently, only the **Create new field** section is displayed on this page, because we have yet to add new fields. Once there is at least one custom field available, this page will have an additional section allowing existing fields to be added directly from any content type (you can come back here once there are a few saved fields):

Regardless, the **Create new field** list presently comprises of the following options:

- **Node Reference** – Allows the poster to reference another node using its ID value
- **Integer, Decimal, Float** – Allows posters to store numbers in various formats
- **Text** – Allows posters to enter content
- **User Reference** – Allows posters to reference other users

Remember that this list is subject to change, depending on whether you disable various components of the default package, for example, **Node Reference** or **User Reference**, or include additional modules that add field types such as **Date** or **Fivestar**.

Each value type comes with a set of options for how that data should be entered. Looking at the **Integer** type, we can see that users can be prompted for an integer with a **Text Field, Select list, Check boxes**, and **radio buttons** – in this case, the **Select list** is going to be used.

Be careful about how information is stored – it is important to be efficient. For example, don't store information as text when there is only a certain number of options available, instead, store them as a number and provide the right input type to display the various options appropriately.

To demonstrate this point, consider that at the moment, the **numbers_in_wild** field is set as an integer with the **Select list** input type. We are not going to provide a select list of every possible integer, but we are going to represent a range of numbers with an integer. For example, the value 1 will correspond to the range 1-10, 2 will correspond to 11-100, and so on.

With the new field created, the configuration page for this field (Click on **configure** in the **Operations** column of the **Manage fields** page) now displays the current settings available. To begin with, the options in the **Endangered Species settings** are not of much interest as we have not specified what data this field will hold. To do this, scroll down the page to the **Global settings** section. From here, you can decide on how the data will be presented to the user and whether or not the field itself will be compulsory or not:

Global settings

These settings apply to the *field_numbers_in_wild* field in every content type in which it appears.

☑ Required

Number of values:

[8 ▾]

Select a specific number of values for this field, or 'Unlimited' to provide an 'Add more' button so the users can add as many values as they like.

Warning! Changing this setting after data has been created could result in the loss of data!

Minimum:

[   ]

Maximum:

[   ]

Prefix:

[   ]

Define a string that should be prefixed to the value, like $ or €. Leave blank for none. Separate singular and plural values with a pipe (pound|pounds).

Suffix:

[   ]

Define a string that should suffixed to the value, like m², m/s², kb/s. Leave blank for none. Separate singular and plural values with a pipe (pound|pounds).

▽   Allowed values

Allowed values list:

```
1|1-10
2|11-100
3|101-500
4|501-1000
5|1001-5000
6|5001-10000
7|100001-50000
8|50000+
```

Along with the **Allowed values list** used to input key-value pairs, there are a few other settings that may be of use, depending on what data the field should capture. **Minimum** and **Maximum** values along with **Suffix** and **Prefix** values allow for some minor input validation, as well as some useful display properties like currency denominations or physical units of measurement.

The **Global settings** section is type-specific. If, for example, you wanted to save a field in text format, you will find that the following options are presented instead of the **Prefix** and **Suffix** options:

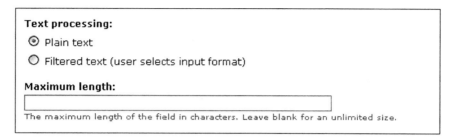

In our case, there is a specified list of eight values that denote the range of animal numbers in the wild. Clicking on **Save field settings** should now display the field type in a drag-and-drop representation of the content type, as it will appear when users attempt to use it:

It's easy enough to move things around to place them exactly as required on the page—although you must remember to click **Save** to implement the changes.

To get back to the field's configuration page, click on **configure**. Now we can implement some of the **Endangered Species settings** that were skipped the first time round.

Endangered Species settings

These settings apply only to the *field_numbers_in_wild* field as it appears in the *Endangered Species* content type.

Widget: *

○ Text Field

◉ Select list

○ Check boxes/radio buttons

○ Single on/off checkbox

Label: *

Estimated Numbers in the Wild

▽ Default value

field_numbers_in_wild: *

```
1-10
11-100
101-500
501-1000
1001-5000
5001-10000
100001-50000
50000+
```

▷ Php code

Display in group:

<none> ▾

Select a group, in which the field will be displayed on the editing form.

Help text:

Please provide the best estimates for the numbers(not including those in captivity or breeding programs)of this species...

In this case, an informative, human readable name has been provided along with a default value for the select list. Initially, no default value options could be presented because there were none specified in the **Global settings** section. At present, we have no groups so the **Display in group** option is left as is. It is possible to use PHP to determine what the default value should be, by clicking on the **Php code** link and entering it into the space provided—unless you have an exceedingly pressing reason to use this, stay clear.

Go ahead and save the changes by clicking on **Save field settings**, and head on over to the **Create content** section and create a new **Endangered Species** post:

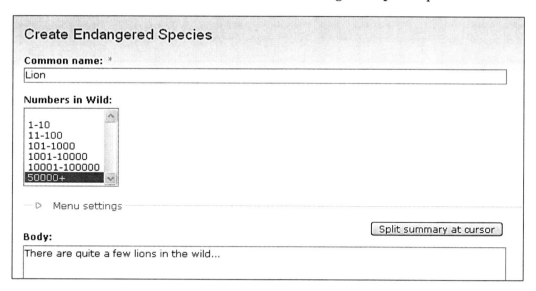

We now have, in addition to the default fields provided, a perfectly good method of specifying the number of animals in the wild by selecting the appropriate values from the select list. Furthermore, the data stored in the database is only an integer and not the entire range; so, this is a pretty efficient way of doing things.

Be aware that representing information with an integer, while efficient, means that if you do decide to change your data, then all legacy content will reflect these changes (because the data stored is only a representation and not the actual text information being displayed).

What if, in addition to the estimated numbers of the species, a field for entering the scientific name for the animal in genus species format is required. It may also be nice to have the number of breeding pairs in captivity, the total number of captive animals, the number of wild breeding pairs, and any other statistical information people might want about the species.

The species name is not really a statistic, so ideally, it would be presented separately from the stats about the animal. CCK provides a way on intuitively grouping information like this through the use of groups...

Adding Groups

To create a group, click on the **Add Group** tab and fill out the form according to how it should be presented—options that are required should always be open, but it may be better to present less important options in collapsed form, so that users can quickly scroll over them if they are not going to fill them out:

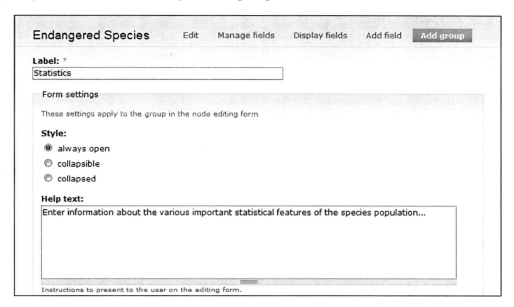

This screenshot shows the **Statistics** group that will hold the vital statistics of a given endangered species. Once you have filled out the form, click **Add** to include it in the content type. The group will now be present on the drag-and-drop list of the **Manage fields** tab, and is presented with **configure** and **remove** options, as shown here:

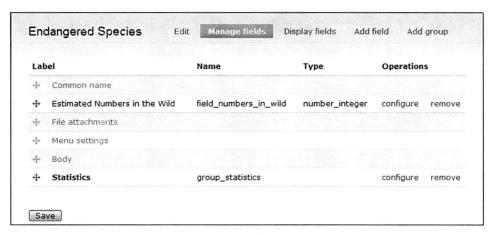

With the group added to the content type, we can now go ahead and create the other fields that will constitute the input data for this group. This includes **Estimated Numbers in the Wild,** so click on its **configure** link and modify the **Display in group** section of the **Endangered Species settings** like so:

Click **Save field settings**, and the field is now contained within the **Statistics** group:

Label	Name	Type	Operations	
⊹ Common name				
⊹ File attachments				
⊹ Menu settings				
⊹ Body				
⊹ **Statistics**	group_statistics		configure	remove
⊹ Estimated Numbers in the Wild	field_numbers_in_wild	number_integer	configure	remove

After creating a few more fields, including the **Species name**, and adding them to the **Statistics** group, we now have something like this:

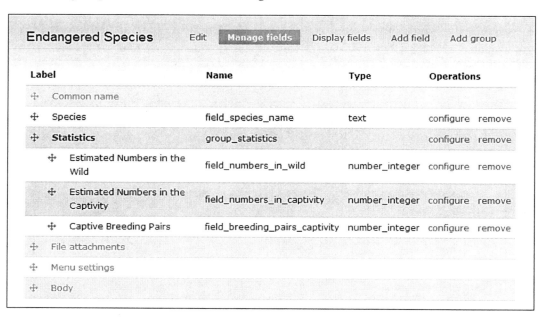

You can re-order fields within a group, in the same way fields and groups are re-ordered within the content type. Once everything is in the right place, go back to the **Create content** and look at the new post page:

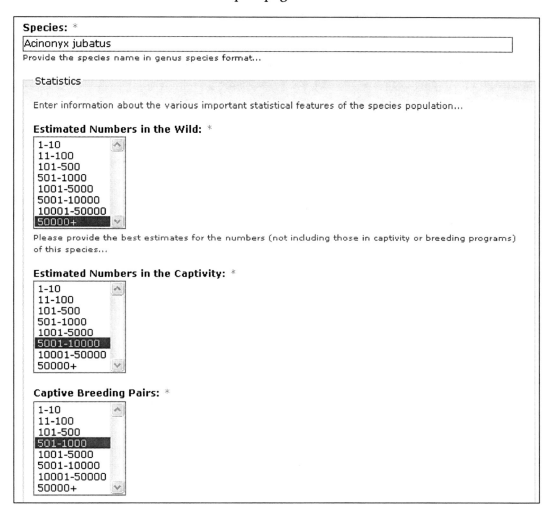

The **Species** (anyone know what **Acinonyx** means?) field is presented above the **Statistics** group with each field in the correct order, as specified in the **Manage fields** page. So the **Manage fields** page allows us to control how the fields are presented on the content creation page, but this still leaves us with the task of presenting the captured data correctly in its various forms—be it in search results, teasers or full pages.

Displaying Fields

In order to determine how input data should be displayed on screen, click on the **Display fields** tab next to **Manage fields**, when editing a content type. This brings up two tabs that cater for **General** and **Advanced** settings, respectively:

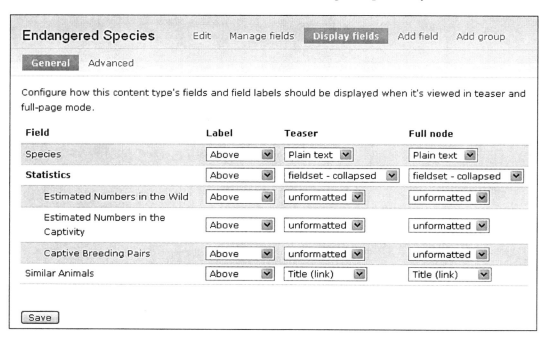

The **General** tab allows the **Teaser** and **Full node** fields and their labels to be displayed according to the settings made here. In the same way, the **Advanced** tab deals with the display of this content type in RSS items, the search index, and search results. Each field and group has a **Label** option to determine where the label is displayed, relative to the data it contains. For fields, the three options are **Above**, **Inline** or **Hidden**. Groups only have two options, **Above** and **Hidden**—Inline would not make much sense for a group.

Setting the **Species Label** to **Above**, as shown in the previous screenshot, displays its field content like this:

Setting it to **Inline** gives:

> **Cheetah**
> Wed, 01/23/2008 - 15:49 — clean
>
> **Species:** Acinonyx jubatus

And finally, setting it to **Hidden** gives:

> **Cheetah**
> Wed, 01/23/2008 - 15:49 — clean
>
> Acinonyx jubatus

As an exercise, try out the different options available for each of the fields (and group) in the **Full node** section. For example, changing the option to **Hidden** here, produces this result:

> **Cheetah**
> Wed, 01/23/2008 - 15:49 — clean

It's important to realize that different fields have different options, depending on what underlying type they are. An example of this is the **Node reference** type that can display the **Title(Link), Title(no link), Full node, Teaser,** and **Hidden.** As mentioned earlier, the **Node reference** type allows posters to reference another node, and in this case, I added a **Similar Animals** field to the **Endangered Species** content type.

Selecting the **Title(Link)** option in the **Full node** column for this type and ensuring that a few nodes have been referenced in a new post, like so (incidentally, this **Node reference** field was created with the **Autocomplete** option that allows posters to begin typing in the name of a post and select which of the available options are presented in the drop-down list—the actual node number is automatically added when a choice is made):

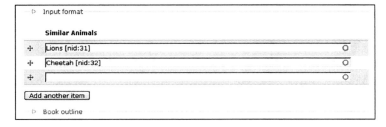

...displays the following when the content is viewed:

As requested, the user is presented with the titles of two other **Endangered Species** posts in the form of links that will take the user to their content. This is a really nice feature for providing connected and relevant content. Just as easily, we could have specified **Full node** for the **Similar Animals Node reference** field in the **Full node** column:

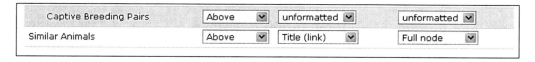

...in which case, the entire nodes would be displayed instead of the title links in any content that referenced them:

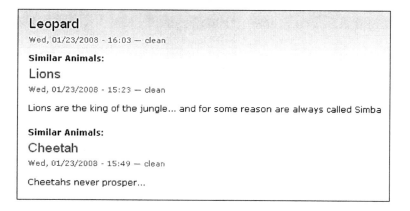

How you choose to present content is really up to your own preferences and what is most expedient and useful for users in the context of how they utilize your site. It is left as an exercise to go through the settings available under the **Advanced** tab and to make use of all the default field types in the process. Remember that you need to run the cron script before any new content will show up in search results (just in case you want to play around with the **Search Result** column and view the results).

Export & Import

Earlier in this section, we saw that there were additional tabs added to the **Content type** page under **Content management**. The first one, **Fields**, provides a list of all the fields added to the various content types and doesn't warrant much explanation here. The other two, **Export** and **Import** provide a powerful facility to effectively *copy and paste* content types, whole, or piece by piece.

For argument's sake, let's assume that the **Endangered Species** content type is close but not quite the same as an **Extinct Species** content type that is going to be added. Instead of recreating the new content type from scratch, we can duplicate the **Endangered Species** type and modify it during the **Export** process, before importing it as the new type.

Click on the **Export** tab and select the **Endangered Species** content type, and click **Submit**. This brings up a list of field and group definitions that should be included in the export:

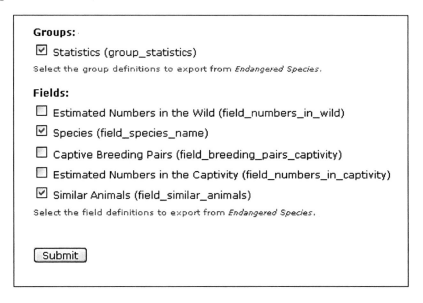

For somewhat macabre reasons, we no longer need to include any of the fields previously held in the **Statistics** group. Although, the **Statistics** group itself can be used to house other stats about the extinct species. Accordingly, only the **Species** and **Similar Animals** fields need to be exported to the new content type.

Clicking on **Submit**, brings up the **Export data** text area, containing the information that will be used by the **Import** feature to build the new content type. Copy this code and then click on the **Import** tab and paste it into the space provided:

```
Content type:
<Create>                 [v]
Select the content type to import these fields into.
Select <Create> to create a new content type to contain the fields.

Import data: *
    'nid' => '',
   ),
  ),
 ),
 'default_value_php' => '',
 'group' => false,
 'required' => '0',
 'multiple' => '1',
 'previous_field' =>
'a:13:{s:10:"field_name";s:21:"field_similar_animals";s:9:"type_name";s:7:"species";s:16:"
null";b:0;}}s:6:"active";s:1:"1";s:19:"referenceable_types";a:9:{i:1;i:1;i:0;i:1;s:4:"blog";b:
Animals";s:6:"weight";i:0;s:11:"description";N;s:6:"module";s:13:"nodereference";s:4:"type
    'referenceable types' =>
```

In this instance, the **Content type** is left as the default option, **<Create>**, because we do not want to import these group and field definitions into any of the current content types. If you did want to add a field or two into one of the existing content types, you would select that **Content type** from the drop-down list and add the new field definition (obtained from your own site or someone else's site — wherever) into the **Import data** section.

The export definition contains the content type value. In this case, we can't directly import the new definition because the **species** content type already exists, so Drupal would report a failure to import the type because is already there. To get around this, edit the first few values of the **Import data** as follows:

```
$content[type]   = array (
  'name' => 'Extinct Species',
  'type' => 'extinct',
  'description' => '',
  'title_label' => 'Common name',
  'body_label' => '',
```

Now we are effectively importing a completely new type of content (called **extinct**) that happens to be based on the existing **species** content type. Clicking **Submit** will add the new type to your list and you can now view it as expected.

Content types	List	Add content type	Fields	Export	Import

Below is a list of all the content types on your site. All posts that exist on your site are instances of one of these content types.

Name	Type	Description	Operations
Blog entry	blog	A *blog entry* is a single post to an online journal, or *blog*.	edit
Endangered Species	species	Description of currently endangered species...	edit delete
Extinct Species	extinct	Description of recently extinct species...	edit delete

You might find that there are field definitions in other content types (yours or someone else's) that could be imported instead of being recreated when modifying content types. In this case, go through the process again, selecting the relevant content type to export from, and then, choose the field to export, copy the export code across to the **Import** section, and add the field to the relevant content type.

Adding Contributed Fields

One of the great things about CCK is that anyone can build and add custom field types that can be incorporated into your own content types. Let's take a quick look at an example of this. Head on over to the Drupal site and download both the **Voting API** and **Fivestar** modules—the **Fivestar** module provides a custom field type that we can use to add rating facilities to content, but it requires the **Voting API** module to be enabled first.

Go ahead and extract both modules ensuring to first enable **Voting API** and then **Fivestar**. With that done, head on over to the **Content types** page under **Content management** and click **edit** for the content type that you would like users to be able to rate—for argument's sake, I will go with **Endangered species**. Click on the **Add field** tab, enter a field name (something like **field_rating**), and scroll down the page till you get to the **Fivestar Rating** option:

Choose an option and click **Create field** to add it to the content type, and then, ensure that you set the configuration options to something appropriate for you—each option is fairly well explained. Bear in mind that the **Node ID** field is the most important because it determines exactly, the node that receives the value of the rating. In this case, it's time to dust off your PHP skills and use it to dynamically select the appropriate node ID—admittedly, this isn't ideal but it does serve to illustrate the process for adding a contributed field, regardless of what it is.

As an addendum, **Fivestar** actually provides a nice rating widget that can be enabled for a content type—on it's **Edit** page, in the list of settings categories, towards the bottom of the page:

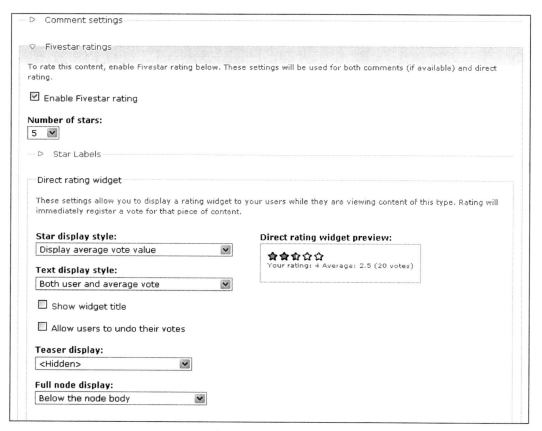

While not shown in the previous screenshot, there is also a Fivestar comment rating widget that can disabled, optional or required. Like the **Direct rating widget**, there is a preview available on the right-hand side of the page. With your choices made, click **Save** settings and then go post a piece of content for the type that now has the Fivestar rating enabled.

For example, a post of the **Endangered species** type, with **Fivestar** enabled, looks like this:

Whenever a user makes a vote, the widget registers it for that specific node. How these votes are tallied, displayed, and so on, can all be configured from the **Fivestar** and **Voting API** pages under **Site configuration**.

Don't be surprised if you click the widget only to find the vote is not registered immediately. It is possible to set the widget to update straight away, but more than likely you can leave this to update with the cron run using the **Voting API** section in **Site configuration**. By playing around with **Fivestar** settings, the rating widget can end up looking like this:

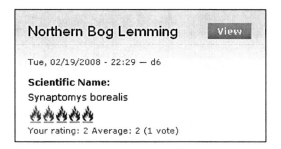

In this case, **Fivestar** actually provides dual functionality, in that it is possible to provide a voting widget for users to rate a given piece of content, as well as a contributed field type that is utilized by posters of content—this could be useful if, for example, a danger level rating should be supplied with each **Endangered species** post.

Of course, each contributed field will come with its own entourage of settings and configuration parameters, so be careful to ensure that you are entirely clear on how the contrib functions work before making it available to the site's content posters.

HTML, PHP, and Content Posting

In the event that you can't find a suitable module to do a task for you, or simply want to create something yourself quickly, it's important to look at how to harness the power of HTML and PHP to get the job done.

If it's layout you are talking about, then HTML is the order of the day. Alternatively, if you want to create some dynamic content that can change depending on the state of your site, or respond to user interaction, then PHP is the way forward. More than likely, you will end up using a combination of both.

Unfortunately, we can't possibly hope to give you a comprehensive introduction into either technology in the space we have here (although we will look over HTML quickly in a moment). However, there are many online resources available to learn about HTML and PHP for free, and we will list a bunch of them throughout this section.

For now, we will look at how to achieve some fairly useful tasks by way of demonstrating how to create an *About us* page that will contain links to other useful sites, pictures of the imaginary site team, as well as some dynamic content.

Input Formats and Filters

It is necessary to stipulate the type of content we will be posting, in any given post. This is done through the use of the **Input format** setting that is displayed when posting content to the site—assuming the user in question has sufficient permissions to post different types of content.

In order to control what is and is not allowed, head on over to the **Input formats** link under **Site configuration**. This will bring up a list of the currently defined input formats, like this:

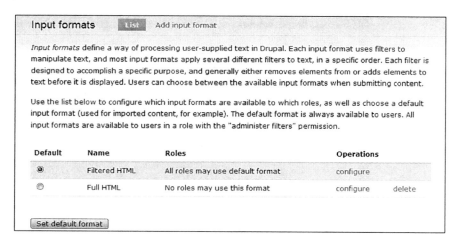

At the moment, you might be wondering why we need to go to all this trouble to decide whether people can add certain HTML tags to their content. The answer to this is that because both HTML and PHP are so powerful, it is not hard to subvert even fairly simple abilities for malicious purposes.

For example, you might decide to allow users the ability to link to their homepages from their blogs. Using the ability to add a hyperlink to their postings, a malicious user could create a Trojan, virus or some other harmful content, and link to it from an innocuous and friendly looking piece of HTML like this:

```
<p>Hi Friends! My <a href="link_to_trojan.exe">homepage</a> is a great
place to meet and learn about my interests and hobbies. </p>
```

This snippet writes out a short paragraph with a link, supposedly to the author's homepage. In reality, the hyperlink reference attribute points to a trojan, `link_to_trojan.exe`. That's just HTML! PHP can do a lot more damage—to the extent that if you don't have proper security or disaster-recovery policies in place, then it is possible that your site can be rendered useless or destroyed entirely.

Security is the main reason why, as you may have noticed from the previous screenshot, anything other than **Filtered HTML** is unavailable for use by anyone except the administrator. By default, PHP is not even present, let alone disabled.

When thinking about what permissions to allow, it is important to re-iterate the tenet:

Never allow users more permissions than they require to complete their intended tasks!

As they stand, you might not find the input formats to your liking, and so Drupal provides some functionality to modify them. Click on the **configure** link adjacent to the **Filtered HTML** option, and this will bring up the following page:

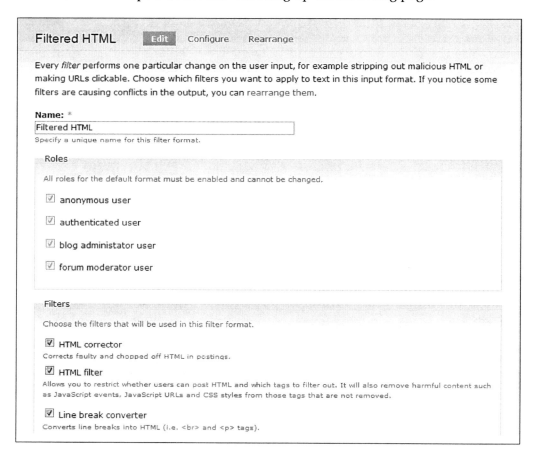

The **Edit** tab provides the option to alter the **Name** property of the input format; the **Roles** section in this case cannot be changed, but as you will see when we come around to creating our own input format, roles can be assigned however you wish to allow certain users to make use of an input format, or not.

The final section provides a checklist of the types of **Filters** to apply when using this input format. In this previous screenshot, all have been selected, and this causes the input format to apply the:

- **HTML corrector** – corrects any broken HTML within postings to prevent undesirable results in the rest of your page.
- **HTML filter** – determines whether or not to strip or remove unwanted HTML.

- **Line break converter** – Turns standard typed line breaks (i.e. whenever a poster clicks **Enter**) into standard HTML.

- **URL filter** – allows recognized links and email addresses to be clickable without having to write the HTML tags, manually.

The line break converter is particularly useful for users because it means that they do not have to explicitly enter `<br>` or `<p>` HTML tags in order to display new lines or paragraph breaks—this can get tedious by the time you are writing your 400th blog entry. If this is disabled, unless the user has the ability to add the relevant HTML tags, the content may end up looking like this:

> ### Give me a break...
> Wed, 02/27/2008 - 11:36 — mf4good
>
> Hi, there! This text should be broken up nicely. For example: This was written on a new line! So was this! But everything got bunched up...

Click on the **Configure** tab, at the top of the page, in order to begin working with the **HTML filter**. You should be presented with something like this:

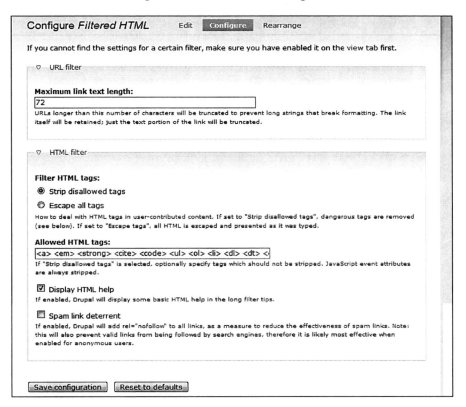

The **URL filter** option is really there to help protect the formatting and layout of your site. It is possible to have quite long URLs these days, and because URLs do not contain spaces, there is nowhere to naturally split them up. As a result, a browser might do some strange things to cater for the long string and whatever it is; this will make your site look odd.

Decide how many characters the longest string should be and enter that number in the space provided. Remember that some content may appear in the sidebars, so you can't let it get too long if they is supposed to be a fixed width.

The **HTML filter** section lets you specify whether to **Strip disallowed tags,** or escape them (**Escape all tags** causes any tags that are present in the post to be displayed *as written*). Remember that if all the tags are stripped from the content, you should enable the **Line break converter** so that users can at least paragraph their content properly. Which tags are to be stripped is decided in the **Allowed HTML tags** section, where a list of all the tags that *are* to be allowed can be entered — anything else gets handled appropriately.

Selecting **Display HTML help** forces Drupal to provide HTML help for users posting content — try enabling and disabling this option and browsing to this relative URL in each case to see the difference: filter/tips. There is quite a bit of helpful information on HTML in the long filter tips; so take a moment to read over those.

 The filter tips can be reached whenever a user expands the **Input format** section of the content post and clicks on **More information about formatting** options at the bottom of that section.

Finally, the **Spam link deterrent** is a useful tool if the site is being used to bombard members with links to unsanctioned (and often unsavory) products. Spammers will use anonymous accounts to post junk (assuming anonymous users are allowed to post content) and enabling this for anonymous posts is an effective way of breaking them.

This is not the end of the story, because we also need to be able to create input formats in the event we require something that the default options can't cater for. For our example, there are several ways in which this can be done, but there are three main criteria that need to be satisfied before we can consider creating the page. We need to be able to:

1. Upload image files and attach them to the post.
2. Insert and display the image files within the body of the post.
3. Use PHP in order to dynamically generate some of the content (this option is really only necessary to demonstrate how to embed PHP in a posting for future reference).

We have already seen how to perform task one when we discussed *Upload* in Chapter 3 on *Adding Functionality*. So assuming that you are able to attach files to posts, this leaves us to deal with the second and third criterion. There are several methods for displaying image files within posts. The one we will discuss here, does not require us to download and install any contribution modules, such as **Img_assist**. Instead, we will use HTML directly to achieve this, specifically, we use the <img> tag.

Take a look at the previous screenshot that shows the **configure** page of the **Filtered HTML** input format. Notice that the <img> tag is not available for use. Let's create our own input format to cater for this, instead of modifying this default format.

Before we do, first enable the **PHP Filter** module under **Modules** in **Site building** so that it can easily be used when the time comes. With that change saved, you will find that there is now an extra option to the **Filters** section of each input format configuration page:

It's not a good idea to enable the **PHP evaluator** for either of the default options, but adding it to one of our own input formats will be ok to play with. Head on back to the main **input formats** page under **Site configuration** (notice that there is an additional input format available, called **PHP code**) and click on **Add input format**. This will bring up the same configuration type page we looked at earlier. It is easy to implement whatever new settings you want, based on how the input format is to be used.

For our example, we need the ability to post images and make use of PHP scripts, so make the new input format as follows:

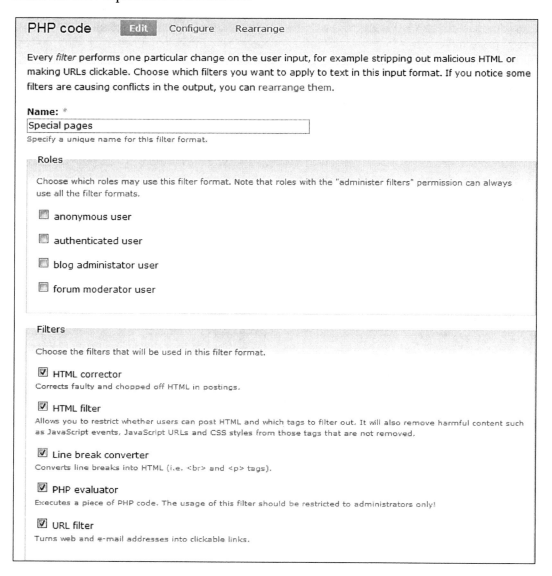

As we will need to make use of some PHP code a bit later on, we have enabled the **PHP evaluator** option, as well as prevented the use of this format for anyone but ourselves—normally, you would create a format for a group of users who require the modified posting abilities, but in this case, we are simply demonstrating how to create a new input format; so this is fine for now.

PHP should not be enabled for anyone other than yourself, or a highly trusted administrator who needs it to complete his or her work.

Click **Save configuration** to add this new format to the list, and then click on the **Configure** tab to work on the **HTML filter**. The only change required between this input format and the default **Filtered HTML**, in terms of HTML, is the addition of the `<img>` and `<div>` tags, separated by a space in the **Allowed HTML tags** list, as follows:

Allowed HTML tags:
`<img> <div> <a> <em> <strong> <cite> <code> <ul> <ol> <li:`

As things stand at the moment, you may run into problems with adding PHP code to any content postings. This is because some filters affect the function of others, and to be on the safe side, click on the **Rearrange** tab and set the **PHP evaluator** to execute first:

Name	Weight
✛ PHP evaluator	-10 ▼
✛ HTML filter	-9 ▼
✛ Line break converter	-8 ▼
✛ URL filter	-7 ▼
✛ HTML corrector	-6 ▼

Since the **PHP evaluator**'s weight is the lowest, it is treated first, with all the others following suit. It's a safe bet that if you are getting unexpected results when using a certain type of filter, you need to come to this page and change the settings. We'll see a bit more about this, in a moment.

Now, the PHP evaluator gets *dibs* on the content and can properly process any PHP. For the purposes of adding images and PHP to posts (as the primary user), this is all that is needed for now. Once satisfied with the settings save the changes.

Before building the new page, it is probably most useful to have a short discourse on HTML, because it is a requirement if you are to attempt more complex postings.

HTML

For a browser to render the neatly laid out and colorful pages it needs instructions on what goes where and what color to give everything. This is the domain of **HyperText Markup Language (HTML)**, and Drupal is no exception in its use of HTML here.

Let's have a quick crash course on the various aspects of HTML before we go any further:

- **Simplicity**: From tables and frames to lists and images, as well as specifying fonts and styles, HTML is a convenient and readily understandable convention for web-page creation and layout.

- **Platform independence**: HTML is platform independent (although not all browsers are exactly the same), which makes sense if you think about it; the last thing you would want, as the builder of a website, is to have to cater for every different type of machine that could make use of HTML.

- **Tags**: HTML comes in the form of opening and closing tags that tell your browser how to display the information enclosed within them. For example, the title of a page would be enclosed within the title tags like this: `<title>My Title Page</title>`. Notice that a forward slash is used to distinguish a closing tag from an opening tag.

- **Attributes**: Tags can have attributes that modify, identify or define certain aspects of a tag's behavior. For example, the `style` attribute in the following HTML snippet defines the color of the paragraph, `<p style="color: blue;">I have a blue font</p>`, when it is rendered in a browser.

- **Sections**: An HTML page is enclosed within `<html></html>` tags and is divided into `<head></head>` and `<body></body>` sections. The body tags enclose the bulk of the page and contain the information seen on the actual web page. In our case, we need not worry about this because all content is automatically posted between the `<body>` tags.

This gives us a fair overview of what HTML is and does, but for practical purposes, it is important to see what can be achieved right here and now, using the HTML that is available to us. Actually, all HTML tags are available for you as the administrator to use, but recall that you should only use this account during development; once the site has gone live, you should post content using an input format that is designed for the task.

The following table discusses each of the default allowed tags, along with the `<img>` and `<div>` tags that have just been added. Bear in mind that it is not really practical to show each and every attribute for each tag here, so if you would like to learn more about each tag individually, then please take a look at `http://www.htmlhelp.com`, which is an excellent resource for all things HTML and more.

Tag	Description	Important Attributes
`<img>`	The `<img>` tag, unlike other tags, does not require a closing `</img>` tag. It is used to display images within HTML pages, and through the use of optional attributes can accurately control the appearance and layout of images.	`src`: gives the path to the image file. `alt`: holds a description of the image.
`<div>`	The `<div>` tag is the basic building block of a page's layout. It is used to define divisions or section within a page and can be controlled through the use of attributes.	`style`: used to specify a number of stylistic issues such as background. Remember to make use of CSS and class and id attributes for anything but simple or once off style issues.
`<a>`	The anchor element facilitates the creation of hyperlinks or bookmarks, which can be navigated by users.	`href`: specifies the destination URL of the link. `name`: allows bookmarks to be created within web pages. `target`: defines where to open the link—most often this is a new page, `_blank`, or the same page, `_self`.
`<em>`	The emphasis tag converts standard text to italics.	
`<strong>`	The strong tag renders text in bold.	
`<cite>`	The citation tag allows text to be referenced as coming from another source or author. It is often rendered in italics.	`title`: can be used to specify the source or author of the citation in question.
`<code>`	The code tag changes the style of the enclosed text to mimic computer code's style.	
`<ul>`	The unordered list creates a list of bullet points—it requires the use of the `<li>` tag to stipulate items in the list.	`type`: defines the type of bullet point to be used: `disc`, `square`, or `circle`.

Tag	Description	Important Attributes
`<ol>`	The order list creates a numbered list of bullets — it requires the use of the `<li>` tag to stipulate items in the list.	
`<li>`	The list item tag creates a new item within either an ordered or unordered list; because of this it is contained within `<ul></ul>` or `<ol></ol>` tags.	
`<dl>`	The definition list tag creates a structured list of items that are defined by the `<dt>` and `<dd>` tags.	
`<dt>`	The definition term tag creates a term within a definition list. It is contained within `<dl></dl>` tags.	
`<dd>`	The definition description tag creates a description of its parent term — it is contained within `<dl></dl>` tags.	

This table really only lists a fraction of all the tags that are available to you to use. Most tags also have a wide variety of required or optional attributes that you can play around with in order to achieve the desired effect.

With that out of the way, we are ready to begin creating a slightly more advanced posting than all the previous ones.

Creating a Feature-Rich Page

One of the cool things about creating a new page like this is that once it is done, it can be reused pretty much anywhere else, substituting in only those values or content that need to change. Obviously, you want the site to look fairly uniform, and this supports the principle of code reuse — at least in terms of HTML.

It is quite likely that at some stage, you will want to create more than just one standalone page. If this is the case, simply cut and paste whatever page is created here and make whatever modification you need, before posting. Doing things in this way will lend all your pages a similar look-and-feel above and beyond the attributes already given to them by the current theme. The *About us* page is going to have the following features:

- Well-structured content
- List of objectives
- Inline pictures of the team
- Information about the project
- List of important links
- Some dynamic, PHP-based content
- Advertising

In order to meet the requirements stated, we are going to need to make use of the following tags:

- `<div>`
- `<ol>`
- `<ul>`
- `<img>`
- `<a>`

...along with a few others that we will use to demonstrate the various types of available font styles. In order to create a slightly more complex page like this, consider working with a proper code/HTML editor (a search on Google will turn up many results) that can indent code automatically as well as color-code the various tags and content, to make life easier.

Before we begin let's look at the resulting page to get a good idea of what we are working towards. The following screenshot shows the bulk of the page:

1. To provide an online meeting place for like-minded people

2. To discuss and monitor global conservation and wildlife activities

3. To influence policy and effect change in hard-hit areas

4. To support front-line activists like SeaShepherd

5. To raise funds for animal relief efforts and care

Meet the Team

In no specific order, the following people constitute the bulk of the full-time staff here at MF4Good (You can email them by clicking on the names shown below):

- Tolis Welch
- David Mercer
- Bronagh Casey
- Nic Malan
- Brian Reid
- Rochelle Reid

At MF4Good we strive to do the *right thing*! Please take the time to look over the site and register in order to start interacting with the community - our natural world needs all the help it can get.

If you are interested in getting involved in any one of the number of critically important organizations around the world, then please feel free to browse any of the links given below.

Our Friends

- Sea Shepherd
- World Wildlife Fund
- The Royal SPCA

Our Sponsors

I hope you'll agree that this page is fairly pleasing to the eye—no comments on the photo please! For very little work, it is quite easy to achieve a look and layout such as this. What isn't apparent from this page, is that the list of names given here, along with their email links, was provided by a short PHP script that was embedded into the HTML page.

Let's get on with the code—to start with, we have the following:

```
<div style="text-align: center;">
    <strong>The MF4Good</strong>
</div>
<div>
The <em>Market Force 4 Good</em> was started by a group of individuals
in <cite title="South Africa">Cape Town</cite>. Through hard
work, dedication and plenty of play time, they have built a truly
international community that strives to effect change with regards to
all things related to our biosphere.
</div>
<div>
    <p>
      We have the following goals:
    </p>
</div>
```

This first section is used to declare div regions that are ultimately responsible for laying out all the content. Notice that I have used the **text-align** attribute to make the heading move to the center of the page.

If you look past this snippet of code in the previous listing, you will notice the use of the `<cite>` tag, with a `title` attribute defined. This is here to show you a novel use for providing references. If a user hovers their cursor over the text contained within the `<cite>` tag (in this instance, `Cape Town`), the text defined in the `title` attribute (in this case, `South Africa`) will be displayed on screen. In this way, you can clarify or explain important terms without cluttering up your pages.

Continuing along, we get the following ordered list of goals:

```
<ol>
    <li>To provide an online meeting place for like-minded
    people</li>
    <li>To discuss and monitor global conservation and
    wildlife activities</li>
    <li>To influence policy and effect change in hard-hit areas</li>
    <li>To support front-line activists like SeaShepherd</li>
    <li>To raise funds for animal relief efforts and care</li>
</ol>
```

As you can see, each list item contains exactly one line of content (or one goal, in this case), and all are contained within the `<ol>` and `</ol>` tags. The next section is where we meet some PHP code, as well as insert our image of the team:

```
<div style="text-align: center;">
    <strong>Meet the Team</strong>
```

```
</div>
<div>
        In no specific order, the following people constitute the bulk
of the full-time staff here at MF4Good (You can email them by clicking
on the names shown below):
</div>
<div style="float: right;">
    <img src="http://localhost/mf4good/sites/default/files/
    team.jpg" alt="The Team" width="250" />
</div>
<div>
    <ul>
<?php
    $team = array('Tolis Welch', 'David Mercer', 'Bronagh Casey',
    'Nic Malan', 'Brian Reid', 'Rochelle Reid');
    foreach($team as $item){
    $name = explode(" ", $item);
    echo '<li><a href="mailto:' . $name[0] . '@mf4good.org">'
    . $item . '</a></li>';
    }
?>
    </ul>
</div>
```

To summarize, in this section we:

1. Added an inline image with `<img>` and aligned it to the right of the page.
2. Created an unordered list with the `<ul>` tag.
3. Opened up a PHP script by using the `<?php` tag.
4. Created an array of team member names.
5. Used a PHP `foreach` loop, to iterate through each name in the array.
6. Obtained the first name of each member by using the built-in PHP `explode` function.
7. Echoed the results, replete with HTML tags to the screen.

The actual email links were created using the `<a>` tag and the special `mailto` option within the `href` attribute.

 If you have the **URL filter** enabled, then Drupal would automatically make any email addresses clickable without the need for the **<a>** tag.

As you can see, there are three attributes used here to get the image properly displayed. The first, src, gives the path to the image file to be displayed; the second gives a description of the photo so that if, for some reason, the picture is not displayed, then the text **The Team** will be shown instead. Finally, we picked a size for the width of the photo in order to fit it to the page properly. Take note:

 Keep image files small! You can reduce their quality and size using image editing software—large images slow down your site.

The email addresses were built from the first name of the team member so the first two addresses are Tolis@mf4good.org and David@mf4good.org. This is slightly contrived as you might not have such an ordered system to your email addresses, but it serves to demonstrate how PHP can be embedded into pages quite easily.

The following section of HTML prints out a list of links to a few other organizations that may be of interest to users:

```
<div>
<p>At MF4Good we strive to do the <em>right thing</em>! Please
take the time to look over the site and register in order to start
interacting with the community - our natural world needs all the help
it can get.</p>
<p>If you are interested in getting involved in any one of the number
of critically important organizations around the world, then please
feel free to browse any of the links given below.</p>
</div>
<div align="center">
    <strong>Our Friends</strong>
</div>
<div>
    <ul>
      <li>
        <a href="http://www.seashepherd.org">Sea Shepherd</a>
      </li>
      <li>
        <a href="http://www.worldwildlife.org">World Wildlife Fund</a>
      </li>
      <li>
        <a href="http://www.rspca.org.uk">The Royal SPCA</a>
      </li>
    </ul>
</div>
```

This part is fairly straightforward, so we move onto the last item on the page—the advertisement:

```
<div  style="text-align: center;">
    <strong>Our Sponsors!</strong>
</div>
<div  style="text-align: center;">
    <a href="http://www.packtpub.com">
        <img src="http://localhost/mf4good/sites/default/files/
        PacktLogoSmall.png" alt="Packt Publishers" />
    </a>
</div>
</table>
```

This makes use of both a hyperlink and an image file. In effect, we have turned the image, the *Packt* logo, into a hyperlink by enclosing it within <a> and </a> tags. This means that people can not only view the sponsor's logo, but if they wish, they can also visit the sponsor's site directly by clicking on the image.

With that done, you not only have a nice, shiny new *About us* page, but also a rough template from which to make other pages with a similar look and feel. There is a lot more that goes into giving pages their look and feel, but this involves the use of themes, which we have not yet discussed.

 It is generally a bad idea to include absolute file paths in content because if you move your site to another host, or deploy it after development, these links can break. Consider using the **Inline** module or something similar to prevent this.

With the page completed, we are not quite finished yet, because it still needs to be added to the site. In order to do this, we need to look at how to actually work with the content we are adding.

Posting a Feature-Rich Page

This brief section will outline the process for getting pages up and on the site. The following list shows the steps required:

1. Create a new post, or edit one that is to be modified. In our case, we have an *About us* page already, so as the administrator, we can simply click on the **edit** tab when viewing the *About us* page.

2. Enter or modify the title of the page accordingly.

3. Select the correct input format. In this case, we have a specially created a format called **Special pages**.

4. Copy and paste the HTML into the **Body** text area.

5. Ensure the **Authoring information** and **Publishing options** are all correct.

6. For something like the *About us* page, it is probably best to disable comments, as you really want this to be a standalone page and not subject to any debate from the rest of the community.

7. Next, ensure that the **Menu settings** are appropriate for the page being added. In this case, we have the following settings in place:

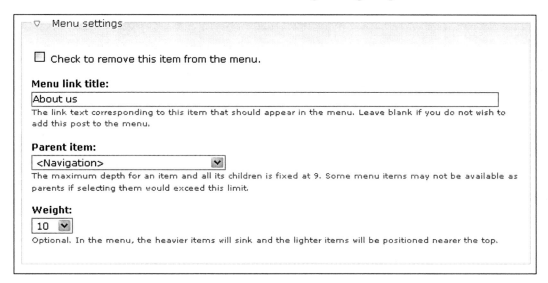

That's it! Once you are ready to view the page, click on **Preview**, and if everything looks in order, submit it. Remember that it can easily be edited again if anything is wrong.

Obviously, if you are not familiar with either HTML or PHP, you will need to practice a bit with these, but the following links should provide a start:

- http://www.php.net
- http://www.phpbuilder.com
- http://www.htmlgoodies.com
- http://www.w3schools.com

Hopefully, you now feel quite confident about incorporating more complex pages into your site.

Summary

With this chapter out of the way, you should have a good understanding of the tasks that lie ahead in creating a fully functional, content-focused website. If you are not already familiar with HTML and PHP, then I recommend you spend some time learning a bit about HTML before continuing on with the next chapter. That said, you have seen how to create input formats to allow different types of HTML or PHP content into posts, as well as looking at how to create a fairly nice HTML-based dynamic web page.

While this is certainly important in terms of creating an aesthetically pleasing site, the real nuts and bolts of your content management lesson came with the discussion on taxonomy. Drupal's taxonomy system sets it apart from other CMS technologies and provides the flexibility and power to implement pretty much any type of structure that we can imagine for our content. With powerful features like tagging available at the click of a button, you are sitting at the controls of one of the best systems around.

CCK is another powerful feature of Drupal that can provide a vast array of new and interesting content types to cater for virtually any type of content. As time goes by, more and more CCK related contributions will become available, and you are urged to keep checking the available modules. Unfortunately, at the time of writing, the **Views** contrib was not available to work in conjunction with CCK but please take the time to check it out when it does arrive.

With much of the hard work out of the way, we can turn our attention to the most creative and, in my opinion, fun part of creating a Drupal site. The following chapter will discuss themes and how to create a unique and appealing look for the new site.

8
Drupal's Interface

Working on a site's interface to make it distinctive and attractive not only requires some technical know-how when it comes to Drupal, but as with any design-like task, it also needs some creativity. Your site, at the moment, is fully functional and doesn't look awful—it's a bit plain, but it will get the job done. With a bit of effort, creating something entirely new is not out of the question, and Drupal comes with a host of features to make our lives easier.

If, like me, you enjoy working on the more creative aspects of a website, then this is really the chapter you have been waiting for. It's time to design, plan, and implement the visual environment in which users will be immersed. Creating a pleasing atmosphere in which to interact will certainly do a lot in terms of ensuring users are happy.

This chapter will discuss the following:

- Planning a web-based interface
- CSS
- Themes

There is quite a lot involved in coming up with an entirely fresh, pleasing, and distinct look for a site. There are lots of fiddly little bits to play around with, so you should be prepared to spend some time on this section—after all, a site's look and feel is really the face you present to the community, and in turn, the face of the community presents to the outside world.

Take some time to look at what is already out there. Many issues that you will encounter while designing a site have already been successfully dealt with by others, and not only by Drupal users of course. Also, don't be scared to treat your design as an ongoing process—while it is never good to drastically change sites on a weekly basis, regular tweaking or upgrading of the interface can keep it modern and looking shiny new.

Planning a Web-Based Interface

The tenet *form follows function* is widely applied in many spheres of human knowledge. It is a well understood concept that states the way something is built or made must reflect the purpose it was made for. This is an exceptionally sensible thought, and applying it to the design of your site will provide a yardstick to measure how well you have designed it.

That's not to say one site should look like every other site that performs the same function. In fact, if anything, you want to make it as distinctive as possible, without stepping over the bounds of what the target user will consider *good taste* or *common sense*.

How do you do that? The trick is to relate what you have or do as a website with a specific target audience. Providing content that has appeal to both sexes of all ages across all nationalities, races, or religions implies that you should go with something that everyone can use. If anything, this might be a slightly flavorless site because you wouldn't want to marginalize any group of users by explicitly making the site bias towards another group. Luckily though, to some extent your target audience will be slightly easier to define than this, so you can generally make some concessions for a particular type of user.

Visual Design

There's no beating about the bush on this issue. Make the site appear as visually simple as possible without hiding any critical or useful information. By this, I mean don't be afraid to leave a fairly large list of items on a page— if all the items on that list are useful, and will be (or are) used frequently. Hiding an important thing from users—no matter how easy it appears to be to find it on other pages—will frustrate them, and your popularity might suffer.

How a site looks can also have a big impact on how users understand it to work. For example, if several different fonts apply to different links, then it is entirely likely that users will not think of clicking on one type of link or another because of the different font styles. Think about this yourself for a moment, and visualize whether or not you would spend time hovering the pointer over each and every type of different content in the hope that it was a link.

This can be summed up as:

[Make sure your site is visually consistent, and that there are no style discrepancies from one page to the next.]

By the same token, reading a page of text where the links are given in the same font and style as the writing would effectively hide that functionality.

There are quite a few so-called rules of visual design, which can be applied to your site. Some that might apply to you are: the rule of thirds, which states that things divided up into thirds—either vertically or horizontally—are more visually appealing than other designs; or the visual center rule, which states that the visual center of the page (where the eye is most attracted to) is just above and to the right of the actual center of the page.

You may wish to visit the website *A List Apart* at http://www.alistapart.com/ that has plenty of useful articles on design for the Web, or try searching on Google for more information.

Language

Now this is a truly interesting part of a site's design, and the art of writing for the Web is a lot more subtle than just saying what you mean. The reason for this is that you are no longer writing simply for human consumption, but also for consumption by machines. Because machines can only follow a certain number of rules when interpreting a page, the concessions on the language used must be made by the writers (if they want their sites to feature highly on search engines).

Before making your site's text highly optimized for searching, there are a few more fundamental things that are important to consider. First off, make sure your language is clear and concise. This is the most important; rather sacrifice racy, stylized copy for more mundane text if the mundane text is going to elucidate important points better. People have very short attention spans when it comes to reading Web copy so keep things to the point.

Apart from the actual content of your language, the visual and structural appearance of the copy is also important. Use bold or larger fonts to emphasize headings or important points, and ensure that text is spaced out nicely to make the page easier on the eye, and therefore easier to read and understand—we saw an example of this in the previous chapter when we posted a well formatted and laid out *About us* page.

Images

Working with images for the Web is very much an art. I don't mean this in the sense that generally one should be quite artistic in order to make nice pictures. I mean that actually managing and dealing with image files is itself an art. There is a lot of work to be done for the aspiring website owner with respect to attaining a pleasing and meaningful visual environment. This is because the Web is an environment that is most reliant on visual images to have an effect on users—because sight and sound are the only two senses that are targeted by the Internet (for now).

In order to have the freedom to manipulate images, you really need to use a reasonably powerful image editor. Gimp, `http://www.gimp.org/`, is an example of a good image-editing environment, but anything that allows you to save files in a variety of different formats and provides resizing capabilities should be sufficient.

If you have to take digital photographs yourself, then ensure you make the photos as uniform as possible, with a background that doesn't distract from the object in question—editing the images to remove the background altogether is probably best. There are several areas of concern when working with images, all of which need to be closely scrutinized in order to produce an integrated and pleasing visual environment:

- One of the biggest problems with images is that they take up a lot more space and bandwidth than text or code. For this reason, having an effective method for dealing with large images is required—simply squashing large images into thumbnails will slow everything down because the server still has to download the entire large file to the user's machine.

- One common mistake people make when dealing with images is not working on them early on in the process to make them as uniform in size and type as possible. If all the images are of one size and of the same dimension, then you are going to have things a lot easier than most. In fact, this should really be your aim before doing anything involving the site—*make sure your images are all as uniform as a given situation allows.*

- Deciding what type of image you actually want to use from the variety available can also be a bit of an issue because some image types take up more space than others, and some may not even be rendered properly in a browser. By and large, there are really only three image types that are most commonly used—GIF, PNG, and JPG.

- The intended use of an image can also be a big factor when deciding how to create, size, and format the file. For example, icons and logos should really be saved as PNG or GIF files, whereas photos and large or complex images should be saved in the JPG format due to how efficiently JPG handles complex images.

Let's take a quick look at those here.

GIF, or Graphics Interchange Format, is known for its compression and the fact that it can store and display multiple images. The major drawback to GIF is that images can only display up to 256 distinct colors. For photographic-quality images, this is a significant obstacle. However, you should use GIFs for:

- Images with a transparent background
- Animated graphics
- Smaller, less complex images requiring no more than 256 colors

PNG, or Portable Network Graphics, is actually designed as a replacement for GIF files. In general, it can achieve greater file compression, give a wider range of color depth, and quite a bit more. PNG, unlike GIF files, does not support animations. You can use PNG files for anything that you would otherwise use GIFs for, with the exception of animations.

 IE6 will not render transparency in PNG images correctly, so be aware that this may affect what people think about your site—having ugly shaded regions around images can make your site appear to be of poor quality when in fact it is an aspect of their dated browser that causes the problem.

Incidentally, there is also an MNG format that allows for animations—you might want to check that out as an alternative to animated GIFs.

JPG, or JPEG (Joint Photographic Experts Group), should be used when presenting photo-realistic images. JPG can compress large images while retaining the overall photographic quality. JPG files can use any number of colors, and so it's a very convenient format for images that require a lot of color. JPG should be used for:

- Photographs
- Larger, complex images requiring more than 256 to display properly

Be aware that JPG uses lossy compression, which means that in order to handle images efficiently, the compression process loses quality.

Before we begin an in-depth look at themes that are responsible for just about everything when it comes to your site's look-and-feel, we still need to cover one last vital component technology. Having already discussed both PHP and HTML, we are left with CSS, so let's look at that now.

CSS

The pages in a Drupal site obtain their style-related information from associated stylesheets that are held in their respective theme folders. Using stylesheets gives designers excellent, fine-grained control over the appearance of web pages, and can produce some great effects. The appearance of pretty much every aspect of the site can be controlled from CSS within a theme, and all that is needed is a little knowledge of fonts, colors, and stylesheet syntax.

It will make life easier if you have a ready-made list of the type of things you should look at setting using the stylesheet. Here are the most common areas (defined by HTML elements) where stylesheets can be used to determine the look-and-feel of a site's:

- Background
- Text
- Font
- Color
- Images
- Border
- Margin
- Padding
- Lists

Besides being able to change all these aspects of HTML, different effects can be applied depending on *whether* certain conditions, like a mouse hovering over the specified area, are met—this will be demonstrated a little later on. You can also specify attributes for certain HTML tags that can then be used to apply styles to those specific tags instead of creating application-wide changes. For example, imagine one paragraph style with a `class` attribute set, like this:

```
<p class="signature"></p>
```

You could reference this type of paragraph in a stylesheet explicitly by saying something like:

```
p.signature {
   color: green;
}
```

Analyzing this line highlights the structure of the standard style-sheet code block in the form of a:

- **Selector**: in this case `p.signature`
- **Property**: in this case `color`
- **Delimiter**: always `:`
- **Value**: in this case `green`

Note that all the property/value pairs are contained within curly braces, and each is ended with a semi-colon. It is possible to specify many properties for each selector, and indeed we are able to specify several selectors to have the same properties. For example, the following block is taken from the **garland** stylesheet, **style.css**, and is used to provide all the header text within the theme with a similar look-and-feel by giving them all the same properties:

```
h1, h2, h3, h4, h5, h6 {
  margin: 0;
  padding: 0;
  font-weight: normal;
  font-family: Helvetica, Arial, sans-serif;
}
```

In this instance, multiple selectors have been specified in a comma delimited list, with each selector given four properties to control the **margin, padding, font-weight,** and **font-family** of the header tags.

It is important to realize that tags can be referenced using either the **class** attribute, or the **id** attribute, or both. For example, the following HTML:

```
<p class="signature" id="unique-signature"></p>
```

...makes it possible for this tag to be referenced both as part of a class of tags all with the same property, or specifically by its unique **id** attribute. The distinction between the two is important because **class** gives broad sweeping powers to make changes to all tags within that class, and **id** gives fine-grained control over a tag with the unique id.

This introduction to CSS has been very brief, and there are plenty of excellent resources available. If you would like to learn more about CSS (and it is highly recommended), then visit:

- **CSS Discuss**: `http://css-discuss.incutio.com/`
- **HTML Dog**: `http://www.htmldog.com/`

We are ready to begin looking at...

Themes

The use of themes makes Drupal exceptionally flexible when it comes to working with the site's interface. Because the functionality of the site is by and large decoupled from the presentation of the site, it is quite easy to chop and change the look, without having to worry about affecting the functionality. This is obviously a very useful feature because it frees you up to experiment knowing that if worst comes to worst, you can reset the default settings and start from scratch.

You can think of a theme as a *template for your site* that can be modified in order to achieve virtually any design criteria. Of course, different themes have wildly varying attributes; so it is important to find the theme that most closely resembles what you are looking for in order to reduce the amount of work needed to match it to your envisaged design.

Also, different themes are implemented differently. Some themes use fixed layouts with tables, while others use div tags and CSS—you should play around with a variety of themes in order to familiarize yourself with a few different ways of creating a web page. We only have space to cover one here, but the lessons learned are easily transferred to other templates with a bit of time and practice.

Before we go ahead and look at an actual example, it is important to get an overview of how themes are put together in general.

Theme Anatomy

Some of you might have been wondering what on earth a theme engine is, and how both themes and theme engines relate to a Drupal site. The following two definitions should clear up a few things:

- **Theme**: A file or set of files that defines and controls the features of Drupal's web pages (ranging from what functionality to include within a page, to how individual page elements will be presented) using PHP, HTML, CSS and images.

- **Theme engine**: Provides PHP-based functionality to create your own unique theme, which in turn, gives excellent control over the all aspects of a Drupal site.

Drupal ships with the PHPTemplate engine that is utilized by most themes. Not all theme engines are pure PHP-based. For example, there is a Smarty theme engine available in Drupal for use by people who are familiar with Smarty templates.

Looking at how theme files are set up within Drupal hints at the overall process and structure of that theme. Bear in mind that there are several ways to create a working theme, and not all themes make use of template files, but in the case of the Drupal's default theme setup, we have the following:

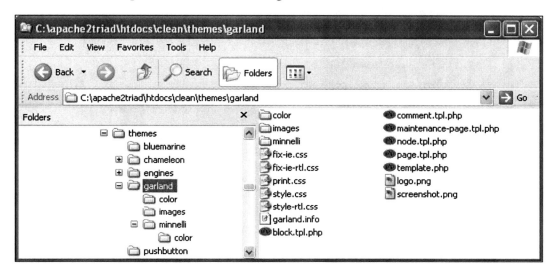

The left-hand column shows the folders contained within the **themes** directory. There are a number of standard themes, accompanied by the **engines** folder that houses a **phptemplate.engine** file, to handle the integration of templates into Drupal's theming system.

Looking at the files present in the **garland** folder, notice that there are a number of PHPTemplate files suffixed by **.tpl.php**. These files make use of HTML and PHP code to modify Drupal's appearance—the default versions of these files, which are the ones that would be used in the event a theme had not implemented its own, can be found in the relevant **modules** directory. For example, the default **comment.tpl. php** file is found in **modules/comment**, and the default **page.tpl.php** file is located, along with others, in the **modules/system** folder.

Each template file focuses on its specific page element or page, with the noted exception of **template.php** that is used to override non-standard theme functions—i.e. not block, box, comment, node or page.

The theme folder also houses the stylesheets along with images, and in the case of the default theme, colors. What's interesting is the addition of the mandatory **.info** file (**.info** files were present in Drupal 5 modules, but are only mandatory in themes for Drupal 6) that contains information about the theme to allow Drupal to find and set a host of different parameters.

Here are a few examples of the type of information that the **.info** file holds:

- **Name** — A human readable theme name
- **Description** — A description of the theme
- **Core** — The major version of Drupal that the theme is compatible with
- **Regions** — The block regions available to the theme
- **Features** — Enables or disables features available in the theme — for example, slogan or mission statement
- **Stylesheets** — Stipulate which stylesheets are to be used by the theme
- **Scripts** — Specify which scripts to include
- **PHP** — Define a minimum version of PHP for which the theme will work

To see how **.info** files can be put to work, look closely at the **Minnelli** theme folder. Notice that this is in fact a *sub-theme* that contains only a few images and CSS files.

 A sub-theme shares its parents' code, but modifies parts of it to produce a new look, new functionality or both.

Drupal allows us to create new sub-themes by creating a new folder within the parent theme (in this case, **Garland**), and providing, amongst other things, new CSS. This is not the only way to create a subtheme — a subtheme does not *have* to be in a subdirectory of its parent theme, rather it can specify the **base theme** directive in its **.info** file, in order to extend the functionality of the specified base, or parent, theme.

As an exercise, access the **Minnelli .info** file and confirm that it has been used to specify the **Minnelli** stylesheet.

So far we have only looked at templated themes, but Drupal ships with a couple of CSS driven themes that do not rely on the PHPTemplate engine, or any other, at all. Look at the **chameleon** theme folder:

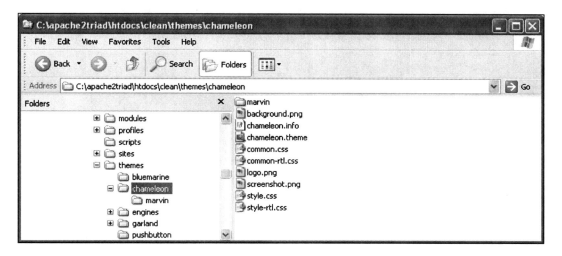

Notice that while it still has the mandatory **.info** file, a few images, and stylesheets, it contains no **.tpl.php** files. Instead of the template system, it uses the **chameleon.theme** file that implements its own versions of Drupal's themeable functions to determine the theme's layout. In this case, the *Marvin* theme is a nice example of how *all* themes can have sub-themes in the same way as the template-driven theme we saw earlier.

 It should be noted that engine-less themes are not quite as easy to work with as engine-based themes, because any customization must be done in PHP rather than in template files.

In a nutshell, Drupal provides a range of default themeable functions that expose Drupal's underlying data, such as content and information about that content. Themes can pick and choose which snippets of rendered content they want to override—the most popular method being through the use of PHP template files in conjunction with style sheets and a **.info** file. Themes and sub-themes are easily created and modified provided that you have some knowledge of CSS and HTML—PHP helps if you want to do something more complicated.

That concludes our brief tour of how themes are put together in Drupal. Even if you are not yet ready to create your own theme, it should be clear that this system makes building a new theme fairly easy, provided one knows a bit about PHP. Here's the process:

- Create a new **themes** folder in the **sites/default** directory and add your new theme directory in there—call it whatever you want, except for a theme name that is already in use.

- Copy the default template files (or files from any other theme you want to modify) across to the new theme directory, along with any other files that are applicable (such as CSS files).

- Modify the layout (this is where your PHP and HTML skills come in handy) and add some flavor with your own stylesheet.

- Rewrite the **.info** file to reflect the attributes and requirements of the new theme.

Now, when it is time for you to begin doing a bit of theme development, bear in mind that there are many types of browser, and not all of them are created equal. What this means is that a page that is rendered nicely on one browser might look bad, or worse, not even function properly on another. For this reason, you should:

[Test your site using several different browsers!]

The Drupal help site has this to say about browsers:

> *It is recommended you use the Firefox browser with developer toolbar and the 'view formatted source' extensions.*

You can obtain a copy of the Firefox browser at `http://www.mozilla.com/firefox/` if you wish to use something other than Internet Explorer. Firefox can also be extended with Firebug, which is an extremely useful tool for client-side web debugging.

For the purposes of this book, we are going to limit ourselves to the selection of a base theme that we will modify to provide us with the demo site's new interface. This means that, for now, you don't have to concern yourself with the intricacies of PHP.

Choosing a Base Theme

As discussed, Drupal ships with a few default themes, and there are quite a few more available in the **Downloads** section of the Drupal site.

Some themes require the use of a theme engine other than PHPTemplate, in which case, you will need to also download and install it before attempting to use that theme.

Looking at how Drupal presents its core **Themes** page under **Site building** in Drupal, we can see the following:

Screenshot	Name	Version	Enabled	Default	Operations
	Bluemarine Table-based multi-column theme with a marine and ash color scheme.	6.0	☐	○	
	Chameleon Minimalist tabled theme with light colors.	6.0	☐	○	
	Garland Tableless, recolorable, multi-column, fluid width theme (default).	6.0	☑	◉	configure
	Marvin Boxy tabled theme in all grays.	6.0	☐	○	
	Minnelli Tableless, recolorable, multi-column, fixed width	6.0	☐	○	

You might be wondering why it is possible to enable as many themes as are available, yet select only one as the default. The reason is that by enabling more than one option, several options are available for users (assuming they have sufficient permissions) to select by editing their **Theme configuration** preferences on the **Edit** tab of the **My account** page as shown here:

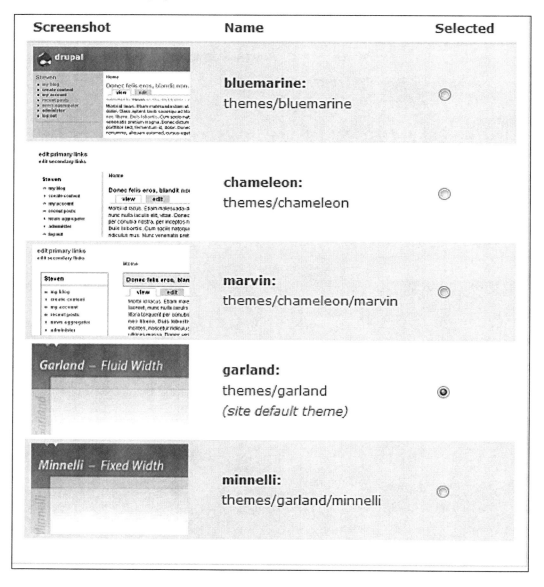

Screenshot	Name	Selected
	bluemarine: themes/bluemarine	○
	chameleon: themes/chameleon	○
	marvin: themes/chameleon/marvin	○
	garland: themes/garland *(site default theme)*	●
	minnelli: themes/garland/minnelli	○

In this case, **minnelli, garland, marvin , chameleon**, and **bluemarine** have all been enabled, with **garland** selected as the default. Users can then select (by themselves) their preference for how they wish to view the site.

 Be aware that some themes might not implement functionality that is important. Ensure you test each theme thoroughly before allowing users to select it.

Enabling the **pushbutton** theme, and setting it as the default, causes the site, which has been presented in the standard **garland** theme up until now, to look something like this:

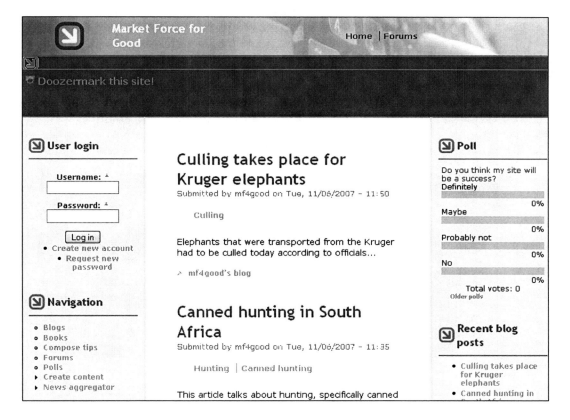

This is a fairly vast change from the previous look; however, you should be able to spot the fact that the generic layout hasn't changed much—there are still three columns, there is a heading section containing the site name and logo, there is a navigation section and various boxes, and so forth. What *has* changed are the fonts, colors, and a few images—notice in particular that there is now a background image in the heading section of this theme.

 Take the time to view each and every theme that is available by default in order to get a feel for what is on offer.

That is not the end of the story, because the Drupal site also has a whole bunch of themes for us to explore, so let's head on over to the themes page at `http://drupal.org/project/themes` and select the relevant version tab to bring up the themes that are available for your installation of Drupal.

You have already seen how to download and install other modules, and the process for installing themes is no different—download and extract the contents of the desired theme to the themes folder in **sites/default** or **sites/all**. For example, the **Barlow** theme was downloaded and extracted, and provides us with a new option in the list of themes (some downloads will provide a number of sub-themes too):

Saving these changes causes the site to look like this:

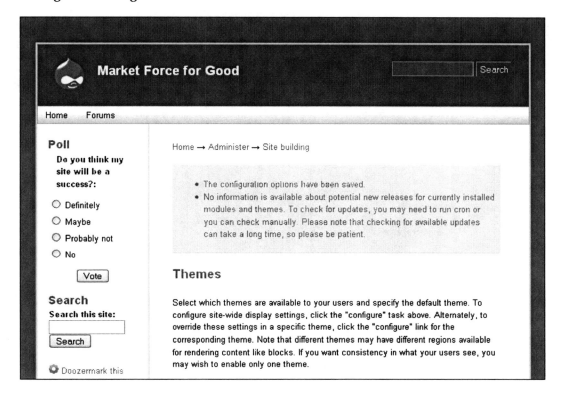

There are now a bunch of default themes to choose from as well as a couple of contributed ones to look over. There are a few things to contend with, before moving to the next phase. As you might expect, we can configure the theme by clicking on the **configure** link on the **themes** page, so let's take a look at that here.

Configuring Themes

Clicking on the **Configure** tab at the top of the **Themes** page, brings up the global theme options that will influence each theme regardless of which one is being used—useful if you always want certain features enabled (it's also easy enough to navigate between global and theme-specific settings using the tabs given at the top of the **configure** page).

We will concentrate on the **global settings** page here, as this is fairly representative of all the theme configuration pages—so you won't have any problems working on each one individually. Remember that it is possible to override these settings by working on the **Configure** page of a specific theme.

Along with a selection of page elements to be hidden or displayed, Drupal provides the ability to specify which content types require post information to be shown. Now, we have already seen that there are certain types of pages for which we don't need to display this information—for example, the *About us* page should be presented as is without informing users precisely who created it:

```
┌─Toggle display──────────────────┐  ┌─Display post information on──────────┐
│                                 │  │                                      │
│ Enable or disable the display of│  │ Enable or disable the submitted by   │
│ certain page elements.          │  │ Username on date text when           │
│                                 │  │ displaying posts of the following type.│
│ ☐ Logo                          │  │                                      │
│                                 │  │ ☑ Blog entry                         │
│ ☐ Site name                     │  │                                      │
│                                 │  │ ☐ Book page                          │
│ ☐ Site slogan                   │  │                                      │
│                                 │  │ ☑ Forum topic                        │
│ ☐ Mission statement             │  │                                      │
│                                 │  │ ☐ Page                               │
│ ☐ User pictures in posts        │  │                                      │
│                                 │  │ ☐ Poll                               │
│ ☐ User pictures in comments     │  │                                      │
│                                 │  │ ☐ Story                              │
│ ☐ Search box                    │  │                                      │
│                                 │  │                                      │
│ ☐ Shortcut icon                 │  │                                      │
│                                 │  │                                      │
│ ☐ Primary links                 │  │                                      │
│                                 │  │                                      │
│ ☐ Secondary links               │  │                                      │
└─────────────────────────────────┘  └──────────────────────────────────────┘
```

The reason for the settings, as shown in this screenshot, is that it is important to identify a blog posting with the person who posted it, and likewise for forum topics. However, when it comes to things like polls, pages, book pages, or stories, it is less important to do so—often because these sorts of things will be handled by site administrators, anyway.

Think about what makes sense for your site and apply the settings that reflect *your specific needs*. For example, it may well be important to identify who has contributed certain book pages so that the authors can be contacted in case there is a need to query or modify content on the book page (especially because books are generally collaborative efforts).

The following section allows you to either use the default logo supplied with the theme, or alternatively, specify a path to another logo or upload a new logo to the site:

Logo image settings

If toggled on, the following logo will be displayed.

☐ Use the default logo
Check here if you want the theme to use the logo supplied with it.

Path to custom logo:

[   ]

The path to the file you would like to use as your logo file instead of the default logo.

Upload logo image:

C:\mypics\mf4goodlogo.png   [Browse...]

If you don't have direct file access to the server, use this field to upload your logo.

In the case of the demo site, we will be making use of a background image to display the logo and name, so this option can be unchecked. If you have a site logo, or plan to have one, then upload it here.

The final section works with favicons (an icon that will be displayed in the site's address bar and in any bookmarks). Once again, what you use here is really up to you.

Icons can be a bit of a pain to create. Internet Explorer looks for icons in **.ICO** format, whereas FireFox will happily include **.PNG** files. There are a couple of online icon creation websites that can make or convert favicons—http://www.html-kit.com/favicon/ is one such example.

 Ensure that whatever you set here is not unintentionally overridden in the individual theme's **configure** page.

Drupal provides a **Reset to defaults** button that will allow you to go back to the theme defaults in the event things go awry during testing, so don't be afraid to get your hands dirty to begin with.

Customizing Themes

Up until now, any settings or changes made have been fairly generic. Things are about to change as we begin to implement some more radical modifications that will require amendments to the stylesheet in order to get things just right. In the case of the demo site, I have chosen to work with the **Barlow** theme, as this most closely resembles the look that is envisaged.

 If you haven't already, now is the time to find a fairly good code editor, as you will be looking at code files of one sort or another from here on out.

Opening up the `barlow` folder, notice that there are a few `.tpl.php` files, namely:

* `block.tpl.php`
* `box.tpl.php`
* `comment.tpl.php`
* `comment-wrapper.tpl.php`
* `node.tpl.php`
* `page.tpl.php`
* `template.php`

...that are responsible for the layout of their namesakes. For example, a snippet of the code in `page.tpl.php` looks like this:

```
<div id="main">
   <?php if ($breadcrumb && !$is_front){ ?>
     <div id="breadcrumb"><?php print $breadcrumb ?></div>

   <?php } ?>
   <?php if ($messages != ""){ ?>
     <div id="message"><?php print $messages ?></div>
   <?php } ?>
   <?php if ($mission != ""){ ?>
     <div id="mission"><span><?php print $mission ?></span></div>
   <?php } ?>
   <?php if ($title != ""){ ?>
      <h2 id="title"><?php print $title ?></h2>
   <?php } ?>
   <?php if ($help != ""){ ?>
       <p id="help"><?php print $help ?></p>
   <?php } ?>
   <?php if ($tabs != ""){ ?>
```

```
            <?php print $tabs ?>
        <?php } ?>
        <div class="content">
        <?php print $before_content ?>
        <?php print $content ?>
        </div>
    </div>
```

This file uses HTML to create page areas (within the **<div>** tags) to present content. It uses a series of PHP `if` statements to check whether or not, for example, to display things like the mission statement. The PHP code is embedded within HTML tags that have certain attributes associated with them—like `id="mission"` or `id="message"`. Don't worry about how these PHP variables are populated; we don't want to alter the way in which the site functions, we are simply looking at how it is laid out.

Notice that the `class` and `id` attributes are set for different sections of the HTML page. Recall that we can classify a `class` or `id` of content to be of a certain type, and then using the relevant selector, specify how it should be laid out within the stylesheet. This is a good example of using **id** to control a unique, individual section of the page (in this case, amongst others, the breadcrumb and mission statement), and class being used to control parts of the page that should appear uniformly, such as the content.

To prove this for yourself, open up the `style.css` file in the `barlow` theme and search for the snippet of code that reads:

```
#header {
  background: #193547;
  border: 1px solid #aaa;
  border-bottom: none;
}
```

Change this to:

```
#header {
  background: #FF0000;
  border: 1px solid #aaa;
  border-bottom: none;
}
```

Save these changes, and refresh the view of your Drupal site in your browser. The content should change so that your pages look something like this (in case it's not obvious in print, the header section has become red):

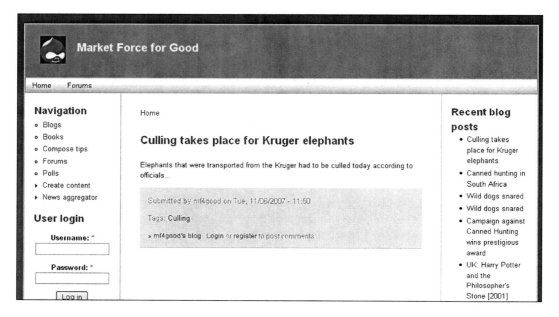

A single change to the `header` tag in the stylesheet has changed the background color of the site's header section throughout each and every page of the entire site. This is quite a powerful and useful property of stylesheets, and is precisely why everyone uses them so much. You can change this back to the original setting or leave it as is—it makes no difference at the moment because it will no doubt change once you have decided on a color scheme.

Now that you know how to implement a change and view the effects of this change, you are ready to continue with modifying the stylesheet to reflect the site's intended look. In the sections that follow, we will discuss several different types of modifications, without grinding through each and every one in excruciating detail.

Once you have the hang of making changes in one area, it is easy to apply that knowledge somewhere else; so you should find the coverage here sufficient to get up and running with confidence.

One of the first tasks required for the demo site is to create and upload an image that will serve as the logo and title in the header section of the site.

Images

Images and background images can be tricky to work with because they are a fixed width, unlike web pages that can be resized. It can look quite awful if an image stops short of the page size or is in the wrong place, so we need to work out on how to make our images blend into the site; so that viewers working on different screens don't end up getting odd results.

As it so happens, the particular theme chosen demonstrates this point quite nicely because it can have either one or two sidebars and changes its width accordingly. If you know that you are going to always have one or the other, then you can go ahead and create images tailored for those dimensions—if not, you will have to think about how to cater for the changes.

In the case of the demo site, I wanted a fairly hard-hitting, graphically-rich page title that sticks in the mind without being overly colorful or loud. In this case, the site's name/logo is actually part of the image, so I have done away with the standard site name and logo in the theme settings:

In order to present this on the site, however, we need to do a bit of work. Adding this as the site's logo is a simple matter of uploading it in the theme's **Configure** page, as shown here:

Logo image settings

If toggled on, the following logo will be displayed.

☐ Use the default logo
Check here if you want the theme to use the logo supplied with it.

Path to custom logo:

```
                                                              
```
The path to the file you would like to use as your logo file instead of the default logo.

Upload logo image:

| C:\mypics\mf4goodlogo.png | Browse... |

If you don't have direct file access to the server, use this field to upload your logo.

...and ensuring that the **Logo** option is enabled for this particular theme. As you have access to the file system, you could also copy the image directly to the `files` folder, and then reference it from the **Path to custom logo** text box directly above the **Logo image settings** box:

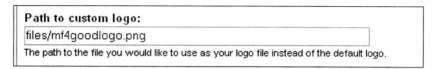

You could also save the new logo image over the old original one, and it will display as expected, but lose the old one irretrievably.

If you are having problems with viewing this image, then it is most likely that the **File system** settings under **Site configuration** are at fault. Check these to ensure that files are being saved to the correct place, and that you are then attempting to access them from the same place.

With that done, we can now take a look at the site to see the effect this has had:

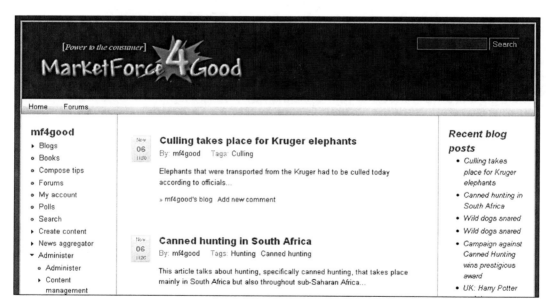

It's worth remembering that life is made a lot easier by creating images on transparent backgrounds. This saves time and effort in the event you decide to change color schemes because the image will allow the background color to show through—we'll see a demonstration of this with the site logo, in just a moment, when we change the basic color scheme for this demo.

Notice that this logo is not affected by whether or not the width of the page caters for one or two sidebars, because it simply blends in with the background color.

Images can also be used to change the look and feel of certain aspects of the site. Often, rounded images are used to break up the sharp, angular look and feel of standard websites, and we shall make use of a couple to delimit blocks in the left and right sidebars.

To display additional images within each block, there is some work that needs to be done to the template files before any changes will be visible. So, open up **block.tpl. php** and modify it as follows:

```
<div class="block-top"></div>
<div class="block block-<? print $block->module?>" id="block-<?php
print $block->module . "-" . $block->delta ?>">
<div class="block-center">
<?php if ($block->subject) { ?>
<h2 class="title"><span><?php print $block->subject ?></span></h2>
<?php } ?>
   <div class="content"><?php print $block->content ?></div>
</div>
</div>
<div class="block-bottom"></div>
```

The bolded code here adds a new top and bottom section to each block, and wraps the content within another **div** tag. The top and bottom sections will house the rounded outline images that will divide up the content in the sidebars into clearly defined blocks. The images we will use are set height and width as shown here:

We now need to use the stylesheet to tell the browser to display these images in the top and bottom div tags, so open up the **style.css** file and add the following in:

```
.sidebar a:hover,
.sidebar a:focus {
  border-bottom: 1px solid #999;
}
.block-top{
  background: url('blocktop.png') no-repeat bottom center;
  height: 15px;
  padding: 5px;
}
 .block-bottom{
  background: url('blockbottom.png') no-repeat top center;
  height: 15px;
}
```

```
  .block-center{
      border-left: 0px;
  }
/*
*   Footer
*/
#footer {
  color: #999;
  border-top: 1px solid #ccc;
  background: #fff url(bg1.png) bottom left repeat-x;
}
```

In this case, I have named the images **blocktop.png** and **blockbottom.png**, and stipulated that the image should not be repeated. Further, they should be displayed in the center of the **div**, either at the bottom or the top of the region, depending on whether or not we are in the **block-bottom** or **block-top** area.

 Add all theme-related images to the actual `theme` folder — don't simply upload them to the standard `files` folder.

With these changes saved (and the images saved to the relevant theme folder), we can now look at what effect these have had on the site:

Now, each block has its own top and bottom bracket that helps separate and define its content. You can continue adding borders by modifying the **block_center** class in the **style.css** stylesheet, but I think it looks quite nice as it is. Before we move on, you may have noticed that the borders for the sidebars have been removed here. Can you guess how this was achieved?

There are a number of sidebar settings in the stylesheet and removing the border is a case of changing the **1px** width to **0px**, as shown here:

```
.sidebar {
  background: #fff;
}
#sidebar-right {
  border-left: 0px solid #ccc;
}
#sidebar-left {
  border-right: 0px solid #ccc;
}
```

We aren't quite finished with images yet, because they can be used in any number of different areas of the site. For now though, we will move on to discuss other parts of the theme, using images where appropriate. You should spend some time practicing not only adding images, but actually designing them properly in order to give your site a professional look-and-feel.

Remember, above all, the site needs to be intuitive and easy to use, so don't get too carried away making wild graphics that are going to slow everything down or make it confusing. People should be visiting your site for its content, anyway.

Colors

With a few new images in place, the site is starting to look quite nice. However, it is still fairly similar to the base theme that we chose because the color scheme is much the same. The main background colors (the area around the actual content) are produced using an image for the top half of the page that fades from a dark to a lighter shade of blue and merges at the bottom of the image with the background color.

All of this is controlled from the **body** tag in the stylesheet:

```
body {
  color: black;
  background: #3b617f url(bg.png) repeat-x;
}
```

From this, you can see that the image **bg.png** is repeated along the x-axis and that the background color is set to **#3b617f**. Let's provide a new image and background color to give the site a new look:

```
body {
  color: black;
  background: #fff url(bgnew.png) repeat-x;
}
```

bgnew.png, in this case, is a textured image that fades to white (or **#fff**) towards the bottom:

Looking at the site, we now have:

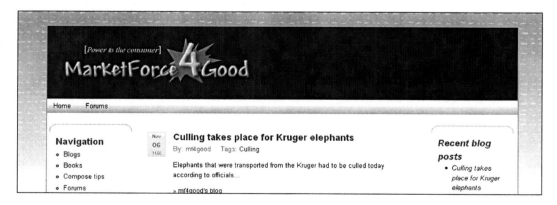

So far so good, but there is a lot more we can do with colors. All the text on the site can be controlled from the stylesheet, and you should think about what color, for example, hyperlinks are to be presented in. This theme bundles all the various types of hyperlinks along with some headings into the same group:

```
a, a:link, a:active, a:visited,
h1, h2, h3, h4, h5, h6 {
  color: #3b617f;
}
```

If you wanted to give the heading styles their own color, you would simply remove them from the current list and set them separately:

```
a, a:link, a:active, a:visited,
{
  color: #3b617f;
}


h1, h2, h3, h4, h5, h6  {
  color: #BF2323;
}
```

Now, headings that are not also hyperlinks are displayed in their own color. Headings that are hyperlinks are dealt with separately by the stylesheet, and are therefore, not displayed in the new color. Look for the section that reads:

```
h1 a, h1 a:link, h1 a:visited, h1 a:hover, h1 a:active,
h2 a, h2 a:link, h2 a:visited, h2 a:hover, h2 a:active,
h3 a, h3 a:link, h3 a:visited, h3 a:hover, h3 a:active,
h4 a, h4 a:link, h4 a:visited, h4 a:hover, h4 a:active,
h5 a, h5 a:link, h5 a:visited, h5 a:hover, h5 a:active,
h6 a, h6 a:link, h6 a:visited, h6 a:hover, h6 a:active {
  color: #3b617f;
  border: none
}
```

...if you would like to modify these. You can now, in the same way, practice your hand at color coordinating the rest of the site by going through the stylesheet and making changes to taste. Remember, when making adjustments you really need to test changes quite regularly to ensure that there are no nasty surprises (like text being the same color as the background).

Before we look at the next item on the agenda, bear in mind that you can also control the alignment of text, its size and font, and much, much more. It really is worth looking over some of the CSS resources mentioned earlier on in this chapter to get a good idea of what is possible.

Page Modifications

It's entirely possible that the actual layout of the page is not to your liking. In this case, there are two options open to you when it comes to effecting change—the stylesheets or the template files. The stylesheet can be used for a limited number of changes; for example, broadening (or narrowing if required) the sidebars to a fixed width in pixels, by altering the appropriate block in the **layout.css** stylesheet:

```
.one-sidebar #wrapper {
  width: 780px;
}
.two-sidebars #wrapper {
  width: 970px;
}
#header #logo, #branding, #main, .sidebar {
  float: left;
}
#search, #header-additional {
  float: right;
}
#menu, #content, #footer {
  clear: both;
}
#main {
  width: 500px;
  padding: 2em 35px 1.5em 35px;
}
.sidebar {
  width: 200px;
}
```

Of crucial importance here, is that one remembers to alter the width of the page overall to cater for the increased width of the sidebars (either that or decrease the content section). If this is not done, it could have undesired consequences for the layout of the site.

With two sidebars, the site is now nearly 1000px in width, and traditionally, a site should be designed at 800px in width. It is my opinion (and some will disagree) that this is becoming less important as more and more people purchase better quality monitors with higher resolutions, so I would be quite happy with a screen of this width.

But what if you needed some more drastic alterations to the site? If it is a more complex structural change you require, then it's time to go to the **.tpl.php** files—the actual file will depend on the type of change you need to make.

Let's say, for example, that you wanted to add an extra row to each page in order to insert some advertising in the hope that some revenue can be generated from the site. In order to do this, we need to look at the `page.tpl.php` file, because this is where the layout of each page is controlled. Depending on how adventurous you are, you could add some conditional PHP code in order to display the column with its advertising only at specific times. For our purposes, it is enough to simply add the new row.

Let's say we want the new row to appear above the content but below the heading—perhaps this could also be used for quick alerts or announcements or even scrolling news. If this is the case, we need to find the spot in the code where the main content is added and insert a new region immediately above. Look for this snippet of code in the `page.tpl.php` file:

```
    </div>
<div id="content">
<?php if ($left != ''){ ?>
  <div id="sidebar-left" class="sidebar">
  <?php print $left; ?>
  </div>
<?php } ?>
<div id="main">
<?php if ($breadcrumb && !$is_front){ ?>
  <div id="breadcrumb"><?php print $breadcrumb ?></div>
<?php } ?>
```

This `div` area is responsible for containing the main content of the site—specifically, it houses the left and right sidebars as well as the main body of content. To insert a new row, we can do something like this:

```
    </div>
<div id="content">
    <div class="newcontent">
      This is where the new content will appear!
    </div>
<?php if ($left != ''){ ?>
  <div id="sidebar-left" class="sidebar">
  <?php print $left; ?>
  </div>
<?php } ?>
<div id="main">
<?php if ($breadcrumb && !$is_front){ ?>
  <div id="breadcrumb"><?php print $breadcrumb ?></div>
<?php } ?>
```

Taking a look at the site now shows the new message as expected:

What you actually add within this new section of each page is entirely up to you! In Chapter 9, on advanced topics, we look at how to add some neat Web 2.0 features that you might want to consider. Before you do:

 It is extremely important that whatever changes are made to a site are tested on more than one browser!

Testing your layout goes deeper than simply checking if everything is in the correct place. It is important that you ensure the CSS and HTML is valid and correct, and resources to achieve this are available online—try http://validator.w3.org/.

If any problems are reported, then it is up to you to ensure that the site complies as closely as possible, because errors can damage not only how people browse your web pages, but also how search engines index and rate the site.

Summary

From learning about what considerations must be taken into account when planning a website's look-and-feel, to making changes to the code, this chapter has provided a firm grounding in the fundamentals of working with Drupal interfaces.

One of the most important aspects of customizing a site's look is understanding how Drupal is set up, in order to leverage the power of themes. As we saw, themes provide a kind of template from which you can work to create your own unique site. This saves a lot of time and effort because we no longer need to work from scratch. We also briefly touched on the possibility of generating themes from theme engines, and hopefully, you will soon feel confident enough to begin looking at this in more detail.

With respect to building your site's interface, experience is very important. There are three main technologies that you need to spend some time working with: HTML, CSS, and PHP. In this chapter, we looked at CSS in some detail before setting about modifying the stylesheet supplied with our chosen base theme. Whatever base theme you choose, the tasks that lie ahead will be similar in nature to the ones discussed in this chapter, and hopefully, you will find that CSS is a most powerful and useful tool in this regard.

The knowledge gained from working with images and HTML, as well as the application of the design considerations discussed, will help not only with your Drupal site, but with any other web-based application that you end up working with. Gaining an appreciation for the various different types of design, as well as having to work with images and code, will allow you to create more ambitious graphical user interfaces in the future.

9
Advanced Features and Modifications

We are going to start out by looking at a grab-bag of modules that showcase some of the more advanced or interesting features in Drupal, in order to give you the opportunity to add that *special something*.

Remember though, that if this chapter does not quite cover exactly what you are after, you are not totally out of luck. The chances are, someone else in the community has had to do something similar before, so making inquiries in the Drupal forums should yield some fruit. If at some point, you do manage to create something utterly fantastic, please give back to the community by sharing your work with others.

This chapter will look at the following topics:

- OpenID
- Actions and Triggers
- Language Support
- Performance and Throttling

With that said, it is often important to be able to make your own additions to a site in order to get it just right. Accordingly, we will also look at some interesting embellishments using script that is freely available on the Internet or ships with Drupal. Incorporating JavaScript and other small, working units of code (commonly known as snippets) is a great way to enhance your site without having to learn everything about programming first.

Accordingly, we will go on to demonstrate:

- How to add effects with jQuery
- Implementing a scrolling news ticker using 3rd party scripts

One final thing to remember before we begin, is that you *must, must, must* make backups of the whole site, including the database, from time to time (preferably before adding a new feature). The topic of making backups is discussed in the following chapter—I mention this just in case you feel it is time to make a backup of what you have now before making changes.

OpenID

One of the biggest obstacles you will need to overcome when promoting and running a website is trying to convince people to actually make regular use of it. Adopting yet another new site is, for your run-of-the-mill Internet user, actually quite a chore, and people will do surprisingly little in terms of spending time registering or finding their way around a new domain. Ultimately, providing content that is valuable to them is the best way to keep users loyal to you, but there are a number of other things one can do to make adoption of your site easier.

At present, a new user to your site might read something that interests them, and decide to post a comment about it. Assuming you are not going to allow anonymous users to post comments (I suggest finding a good anti-spam module if you do), they will need to register on the site first. This means they need to go to the registration page, enter their details (by now most people are sick of doing this on every site they go to), wait for the confirmation email, set their new password, and so on.

While it might not seem like too much work to you—after all, it only takes a minute or two—it can put a lot of people off because they only want to post their comments, and not have to create and remember a whole new set of login details. OpenID circumvents this by allowing people to sign in with their OpenID information that is stored with their OpenID operator of choice.

Please take a few moments to visit `http://openid.net/` and read about what OpenID is, and how it came about. In short:

 OpenID eliminates the need for multiple usernames across different websites by providing a single digital identity in the form of a URL.

What this means is that if someone has an OpenID account, and they visit your site, they can log in straight away using their OpenID, despite having never visited you before. Of course, individual sites may still require them to enter some additional information before a new account is registered. One reason for this is that often a URL is not a suitable login name for websites (including Drupal), so they request one to be entered before setting up the OpenID account.

To enable OpenID support, head on over to the **Modules** section under **Site building** and check the appropriate module before clicking **Save configuration** and logging out. Look at the login block on your Webpage, there is an additional option to log in using OpenID:

The **OpenID** module utilizes some nice Web 2.0 features to immediately convert the login form to OpenID standard, without having to refresh the page once the link is clicked:

Naturally, this needs to be tested, so if you don't have one already, head on over to `http://openid.net/get/` and pick a provider. For example, I opened a myOpenID account and created the OpenID login: `http://davidmercer.myopenid.com/`. Using this as my OpenID login on the Drupal webpage, and clicking **Log in** redirects to the following authentication page (assuming you are not already logged into your OpenID account):

After **Sign In**, the following page is presented that allows you to make a decision regarding the request for authentication from the site you are logging into:

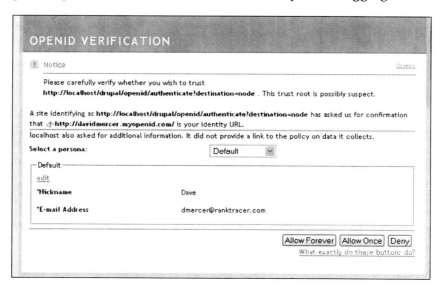

Notice that this page is telling us it has had a request from a website (in this case, my localhost development machine) to confirm whether or not the OpenID in question (**http://davidmercer.myopenid.com/**) is valid and whether or not it should provide some requested info—in this case, a **Nickname** and **E-mail address**.

This particular OpenID provider allows users to select any one of a number of personas in order to provide that persona's details for the requesting site. Using these details, one can allow requests from this URL to *always be authenticated* with the details provided, in which case, this OpenID on this particular URL never has to provide a password. Alternatively, it is possible to select a single login, so that this page is brought up each time, or **Deny** the request completely.

Clicking **Allow Once** or **Allow Forever** brings up the following:

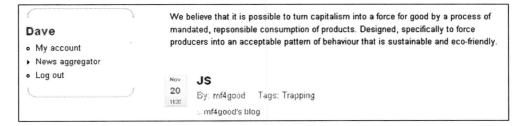

We're back on the site and logged in as **Dave** (recall this nickname was supplied with the persona by myOpenID). If you want to confirm that the account has been correctly set up with the email address as well, click on **My account** and select the **Edit** tab:

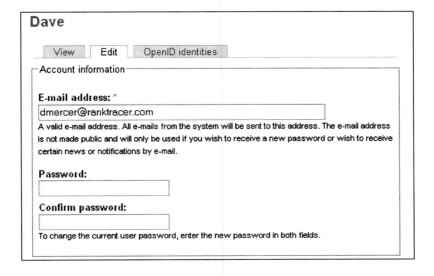

Now, any and all correspondence between this user, **Dave**, and the website will occur using the **dmercer@ranktracer.com** email address. Note that there is little point in setting a new **Password** because it is easier to log in with the OpenID-especially if it is set to always authenticate for this site. If for some reason you really wanted to log in with the nickname (**Dave**) and a password instead of using OpenID, go ahead and set the password as normal and save to complete the account set up process begun by OpenID on your behalf.

The **OpenID** module also provides a new tab in the **My account** section for users, so click on this to bring up the following page that provides users with a list of OpenIDs used and the ability to add or remove them.:

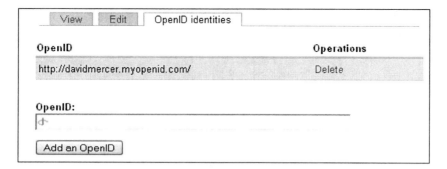

In closing, OpenID is undergoing rapid adoption all over the Web and there are a number of really big websites that now support the standard. As time goes by, it will be more and more important for a site to implement this feature, and ultimately, in doing so, lower the "price of admission" to your community.

Actions and Triggers

Quite often, it happens that for specific events it is useful to have Drupal automatically perform a specified task or action. An action, in the Drupal sense, is one of a number of tasks that the system can perform and these usually relate to performing actions on content, emailing people or acting upon user accounts. There are a number of default actions that are available as well as a few more advanced actions that can be set up by anyone with sufficient permissions.

To configure said actions, navigate to **Actions** in **Site configuration** in the **Administer** main menu:

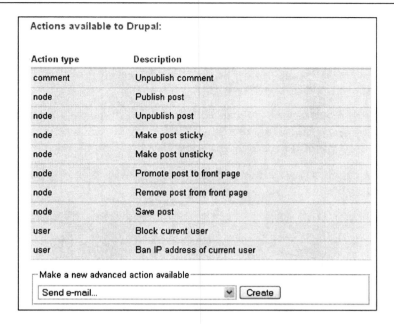

Default actions cannot be modified, so we will ignore these for the moment and focus on creating a **new advanced action**. Let's set up a new **Send e-mail** action by selecting it from the drop-down list, and then clicking **Create**, as shown in the previous screenshot. This brings up the following page that can be set according to how this specific action will be used:

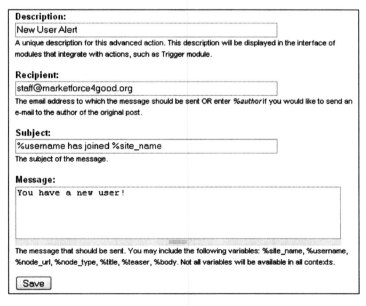

It should be clear that the intention of this email is to notify the staff/administration of any new site members. The **Description** field is important in this respect because it is how you will distinguish this action from any number of other ones you may create in the future. Make the description as accurate, meaningful, and concise as possible to avoid any potential confusion.

Notice too that there are several placeholder variables that can be inserted into both the **Recipient, Subject,** and **Message fields**. In this instance, two have been used to inform the email recipient of the new username and the site that generated the email.

Clicking **Save** adds this new action to the list where it can be modified or deleted, accordingly:

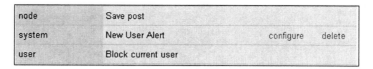

Great! We have set the action, but this in itself does absolutely nothing! An action cannot do anything unless there is a specific system event that can be triggered to set it off. These system events are, perspicaciously enough, called *triggers* and Drupal can listen out for any number of triggers, and perform any actions that are associated with it—this is how actions and triggers work together.

Triggers are not enabled by default, so head on over to the **Modules** section under **Site building** and enable **Triggers**. With triggers enabled, there will now be a new **Triggers** menu item towards or at the bottom of **Site building**. Clicking on this brings up the following page:

Triggers are divided up into five different categories, each providing a range of triggers to which actions can be attached. Assigning a trigger is a case of selecting an action to apply from the drop-down list of the relevant trigger, and clicking **Assign**.

To continue with our example, select the **Users** tab and in the **Trigger: After a user account has been created** box, select the **New User Alert** action before clicking **Assign**. The newly assigned action will show up in the relevant trigger box, like so:

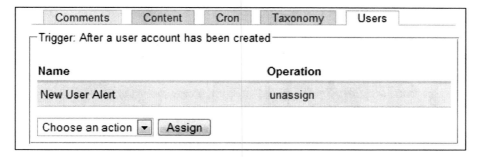

In the same way, a large number of actions can be automated depending on the system event (or trigger) that fires. To test this out, log off and register a new account—you will find that **New User Alert** is dutifully sent out once the account has been registered:

Language Support

As of Drupal 6, support for Internationalization (i18n) and Localization (l10n) have gone into overdrive. Given that there is a huge demand for content in languages other than English, Drupal's developers are ensuring that multi-lingual support is more powerful and efficient.

Not only have language related modules been revamped and included in the core, but new contribs for dealing with localization issues and translations have been created and more are still coming. Multi-lingual support can now be considered to be an integral part of Drupal, and as we saw in Chapter 2, it plays a role right from installation.

Localization

Native support for localization is contained within the **Locale** module that can be enabled as always in the **Modules** section. Once this is done, a couple of additional menu items are available for us to explore.

One of the most useful components of Drupal's support is the ability to translate all the standard language in a site (such as block headings, buttons and so on) by downloading a translation pack from the Drupal site. To see how this is done, head over to the newly added **Languages** link under **Site configuration**, where you will be presented with a list of all the current languages available on the site—by default this is English. Select the **Add language** tab to bring up the following page that allows us to add pretty much any language one can imagine. (Note that it is possible to create your own custom language in the event that your desired tongue is not available from the fairly authoritative list provided):

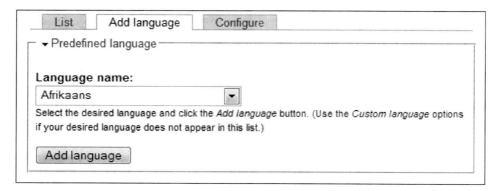

Pick a language from the drop-down list and click **Add language**. This adds the selection to the main list:

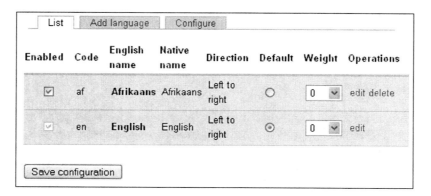

This in itself is not that useful because at the moment, there is no Afrikaans on the site—only English. What is required is a language pack that can be downloaded from the Drupal site at `http://drupal.org/project/translations`. Locate the desired language pack, and then download and unzip the file to your file system.

Once that is done, go to **Site building** and select the new **Translate interface** link to bring up a list of the available languages on the site (in this case, English and Afrikaans). Select the **Import** tab and then specify the extracted **.po** file from the translation download:

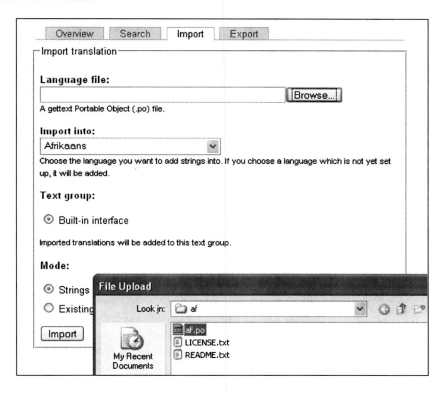

Go ahead and click **Import**, once you are happy that the correct language pack is being imported into the new language. Once this is done, the initial page will display the amount of translations that have been performed for the new language:

Overview	Search	Import	Export

Language	Built-in interface
Afrikaans	1846/1850 (99.78%)
English (built-in)	n/a

In this case, 1846 of our 1850 strings have been translated into Afrikaans, representing about 99% of the overall interface language. To see the effect this has on the site, you can set the new language as the site default by going back to the **Languages** section in **Site configuration** and making the appropriate changes:

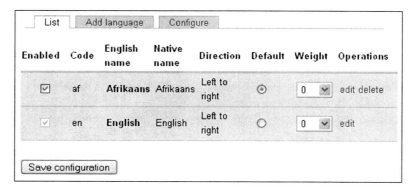

The default language is the one that displays to anonymous users, although registered users can specify their language of choice in the **Language setting** section of their account page, as shown here:

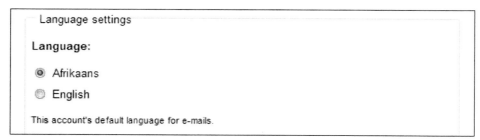

Viewing the site after the translation has taken effect confirms that the changes have been made (note the block headings and button language):

This shows the dialog for deleting a content posting in Afrikaans, but notice that the navigation menu is still presented in English. Obviously, it is preferable to provide a completely Afrikaans interface, so more work still needs to be done before we can consider the translation complete (as indeed, Drupal indicated by telling us only 99% of interface strings were translated).

> Translation packs may not always translate 100% of the interface strings available for a number of reasons. For example, you may have enabled an unusual module that the creators of the translation pack have not used and therefore not translated.

One way to do this, is to go to the **Search** tab of the **Translate Interface** page in **Site building** and search for each string you would like to translate, then provide Drupal with the translation. (Remember to go back to English if you find that easier to work in). For example, translating **Administer** into its Afrikaans equivalent would require us to search for it:

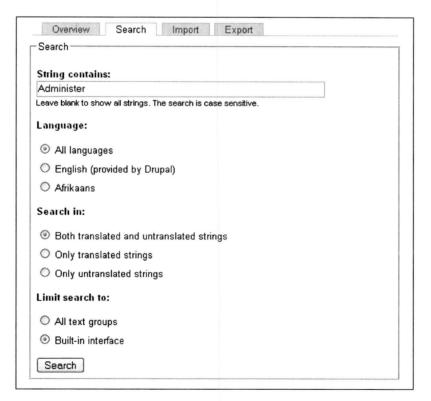

Then select which occurrences to modify:

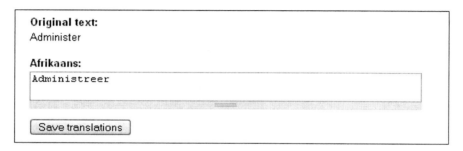

Text group	String	Languages	Operations
Built-in interface	Administer /drupal/admin/settings/language	af	edit delete
Built-in interface	Administer the FlashVideo module. /drupal/admin	af	edit delete

In this instance, we want to change the navigation menu item, so the first option is the one we want to edit, and provide a translation as follows:

Original text:
Administer

Afrikaans:
Administreer

[Save translations]

With this change made, the translated string will appear in the navigation menu whenever the site is viewed by an administrator in Afrikaans.

 Note that a string will not be available in the search until after the page containing it has been viewed because Drupal indexes strings on a page view basis — you have to view the page with the string you want to translate first.

There is, however, a far more sophisticated method that is better to use for larger numbers of translations, and this functionality is provided by the **Localization client** module, downloadable from the Drupal site in the **Modules** section.

Installing and enabling this module (which depends on the **Locale** module) presents the administrator with a new interface for translations. In order for the interface to appear, you need to have whatever language you want to translate enabled — because there is nothing to translate if you have the default set to English.

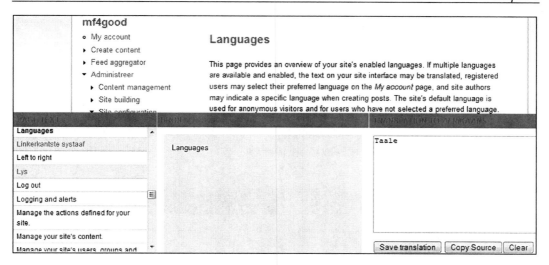

It is important to realize that the localization client interface (everything below the solid blue line in the previous screenshot) initially appears minimized along the bottom of your screen:

TRANSLATE TEXT

The **TRANSLATE TEXT** link must first be clicked before the form expands and you can make use of its features.

The client is divided up into three sections. The first provides a list of all un-translated strings, the second, displays the specific string chosen for translation, and finally, a form for entering the translation for each selected source string.

Incidentally, the **Copy source** and **Clear** buttons allow you to quickly duplicate the source string or clear the text area. The first implements the translation once you have entered it.

In the screenshot before last, the string **Languages** was selected as the source to translate and the (hopefully) correct translation, **Taale**, entered into the space provided. Notice that the selected source is shown in bold in the left-hand list. Upon saving this change, the background color of the modified source goes green to indicate that it has been translated, and in this way, you can keep track of what does and doesn't have a translation.

Refreshing the page once the translation has been saved, shows that everything has gone to plan:

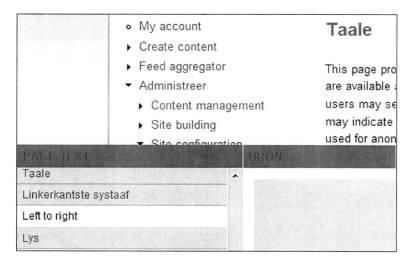

In this way, one can create a fairly complete interface translation, as well as a translation of the Drupal interface and, if you get a set of translations fairly complete, or make improvements to a language file, then the community, in general, would certainly appreciate if you used the **export** link to share your translation files with everyone.

Once you have exported a file in .po format by selecting the language to export and clicking the **Export** tab of the **Translate interface** page under **Site building**, you can then set about getting it up on the Drupal site (take a look under the **Contribute** tab on the Drupal site for more information).

Before we finish with this section, it is important to note that the administrator has some control over how and who is exposed to which language on the site. By default, registered users can select their language of choice from the list of available sites, but this is not always convenient because many sites (like the United Nations for example) would like to present information in a given language without the user having to first register.

In this instance, it is possible to direct Drupal to implement language changes based on other criteria such as the file path or domain of the site. These features are contained under the **Configure** tab of the **Languages** page under **Site configuration**:

| List | Add language | Configure | |

Language negotiation:

◉ None.

◯ Path prefix only.

◯ Path prefix with language fallback.

◯ Domain name only.

Select the mechanism used to determine your site's presentation language. **Modifying this setting may break all incoming URLs and should be used with caution in a production environment.**

[Save settings]

Let's assume that you have a website that should be presented in English and Afrikaans, and that users can select an option on the landing page that redirects them to the appropriate subdomain. It is generally easier to select a subdomain name, or pathname that reflects the language used there so that the site is intuitive. By default, all languages are given their international language designation—i.e. en for English, de for German, and so on.

So, for argument's sake, let's say we have created subdomains, **af.mf4good.org** and **en.mf4good.org**. We can now select the final option in the list (**Domain name only**) and click **Save settings** to force Drupal to examine domain names before applying the language settings. At present, however, nothing will work because we have not yet specified what the language domain is for each language.

To do so, visit the list of languages available on the **Languages** page, and click **edit** next to one of them. This will bring up a page of settings, as shown here for Afrikaans:

Language code:
af

Language name in English: *
Afrikaans

Name of the language in English. Will be available for translation in all languages.

Native language name: *
Afrikaans

Name of the language in the language being added.

Path prefix:

Language code or other custom string for pattern matching within the path. With language negotiation set to *Path prefix only* or *Path prefix with language fallback*, this site is presented in this language when the Path prefix value matches an element in the path. For the default language, this value may be left blank. **Modifying this value will break existing URLs and should be used with caution in a production environment.** *Example: Specifying "deutsch" as the path prefix for German results in URLs in the form "www.example.com/deutsch/node".*

Language domain:
http://af.mf4good.org

Language-specific URL, with protocol. With language negotiation set to *Domain name only*, the site is presented in this language when the URL accessing the site references this domain. For the default language, this value may be left blank. **This value must include a protocol as part of the string.** *Example: Specifying "http://example.de" or "http://de.example.com" as language domains for German results in URLs in the forms "http://example.de/node" and "http://de.example.com/node", respectively.*

Direction: *

◉ Left to right

◌ Right to left

Direction that text in this language is presented.

[Save language]

By and large, the only setting you should need to change in here is the **Language domain** (although **Path prefix** must be blank if you are setting **Language domain** and vice versa), and in this case, we have specified the domain **http://af.mf4good.org**. Once this is saved, Drupal will dutifully check the domain of any web page visited and apply Afrikaans as the interface language in the event that the page belongs to the **af.mf4good.org** domain.

In the same way, languages can be applied to path settings such as **www.mf4good. org/af/** using the **Path prefix only** or **Path prefix with language fallback** options in the **Configure** tab. Remember though that changing from one option to another changes the actual path to links etc, so it is possible to end up with broken links when moving from one to another.

Path prefix with language fallback is a very powerful feature. It can analyze the language settings of the user's browser, and automatically supply the same language if it is available.

It's important to realize that having more than one language available to choose from means there is a block called the **Language switcher** available for use in the **Blocks** section of **Site building**. Setting this block to display somewhere on your page provides users with a choice of languages whenever they visit the site:

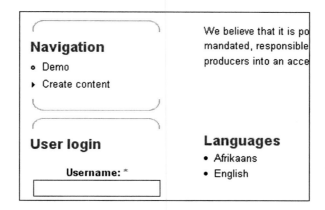

Assuming you have selected **Path prefix only, Afrikaans** changes not only the language displayed by Drupal, but also the file path of that page, inserting the language code, **af**, so that the Afrikaans homepage is displayed at **http://mf4good. org/af**, and not **http://mf4good.org**, as it would be if you simply selected Afrikaans as the default language and left the **Language negotiation** (under the **Configure** tab of **Languages**) as **None**.

Getting used to this large array of possibilities takes a bit of practice, and you should keep a close eye on developments within the Drupal community as there are some exciting improvements sketched out for Drupal 6 and beyond.

Content Translation

You're no doubt wondering why we have moved from discussing translations in *Localization* to a section entitled *Content Translation*! The reason is that up to now we have been utilizing the facilities provided by the **Locale** and **Localization client** modules that concern themselves predominantly with translating strings in Drupal's interface. We haven't looked at how Drupal allows us to handle multi-lingual support for content that is posted to the site.

Having all the strings on a site translated to the intended audience's language is not much good if that audience can only read and write content in English—especially if that language is right to left or does not use the latin-based alphabet. To cater for this, Drupal ships with the **Content translation** module that can be enabled under **Modules** in **Site building**, so go ahead and enable that now.

Content translation provides users with the ability to select the language of their post as well as translate others. This privilege is automatically given to you, the site administrator, but head over to the **Permissions** section of **User management** and enable it for any roles that should also be allowed to work with translations. For example, the authenticated user:

Permission	anonymous user	authenticated user
taxonomy module		
administer taxonomy	☐	☐
translation module		
translate content	☐	☑

The next thing to do is to add whatever languages you intend the site to be fluent in. At the time of writing, the best example of how powerful Drupal's content translation features are, can be elucidated using the Hebrew language because this highlights Drupal's enhanced right to left language support.

Go ahead and add this language to your site by clicking on the **Add language** tab in **Languages**, under **Site configuration**, selecting **Hebrew** from the drop-down list and clicking **Add language**. You should now have Hebrew added to the list of available languages on the site:

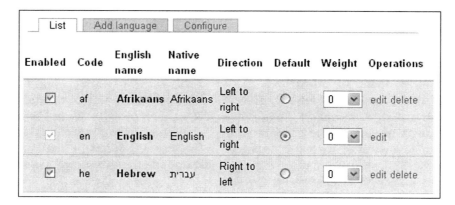

At this point, you can import the Hebrew **.po** translation file for Hebrew into this language using the **Translate interface** page under **Site building** once it is downloaded from the Drupal site, but this is only necessary if you intend to actually provide your site in Hebrew. This section only really needs to demonstrate how user-posted content translations are handled because we have already seen how to handle the interface translations with the Afrikaans demonstration earlier in the chapter. In this case, it's enough to have the language available on the site without having to translate the interface too.

Having already determined which users have the right to translate content, it is now the turn of the content types themselves to be modified. Head over to **Content types** under **Content management** and click on edit for the **Blog entry** type. Scroll down the page and open up the **Workflow settings** section:

There is now a **Multilingual support** section available (recall that it was not there the first time we looked at this section) that provides three options:

- **Disabled** – no translations will be possible for this content type
- **Enabled** – posters can select which language they are posting content in
- **Enabled, with translation** – posters can select which language they are posting content in, and this content can subsequently be translated to other enabled languages

Save this new setting, **Enabled, with translation**, and then go to **Create content** and post a new blog entry. Notice that there is now an option to specify the language in which this post is written (Drupal can't enforce or check the content posted to ensure it matches the chosen language—by selecting a language here you are only classifying it as belonging to a specific language):

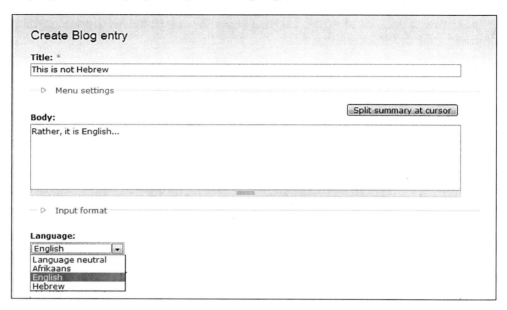

Type in some text, select **English** and then click on **Save**. You should notice nothing out of the usual with the exception of an additional **Translate** link towards the top right-hand side of the screen (This would not be available had we not selected **Enable, with translation**):

To add a translation into one of the other enabled languages, click on **Translate**, and then select a language to provide a translation for by selecting the appropriate **add translation** link:

Language	Title	Status	Operations
Afrikaans	n/a	Not translated	add translation
English (source)	This is not Hebrew	Published	edit
Hebrew	n/a	Not translated	add translation

This will bring up the translation page for the selected language in order for you to post the translation—once that is done, click **Save**. My Hebrew is not great, so the translation leaves everything to be desired—in fact, I left it in English entirely. However, look closely at the translated page and towards the bottom you will notice a language link:

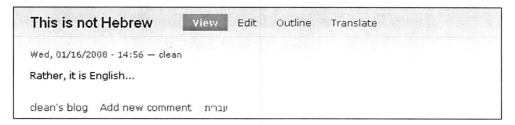

Blog entry *This is not Hebrew* has been created.

Wed, 01/16/2008 - 15:07 — clean

Rather, it is English...

clean's blog   English

Clicking on this displays the alternative translation, in this case English, but retains a link for the other language (and any other language for which there is a translation of the post):

This is not Hebrew   View   Edit   Outline   Translate

Wed, 01/16/2008 - 14:56 — clean

Rather, it is English...

clean's blog   Add new comment   עברית

Notice the Hebrew link at the bottom of this screenshot. This demonstrates how each translation is dutifully targeted to its specific language, and how Drupal links the translations using the language name at the bottom of the screen for easy access by users.

At present however, the Hebrew version is being displayed from left to right, which is a problem because those who are fluent in Hebrew would rather have it presented correctly. The reason we are not yet able to view Hebrew correctly, is because I reset my installation to not perform any language negotiations when changing themes.

Quickly, it is important to note:

> Not all themes behave in the same manner with respect to Drupal's language support! It may be useful to revert to the default **Garland** theme, when learning about translations (along with any other important or complex concepts and customizations).

In order to change this, go back to the **Configure** tab on the **Languages** page under **Site configuration** to bring up the following:

Language negotiation:

○ None.

○ Path prefix only.

◉ Path prefix with language fallback.

○ Domain name only.

Select the mechanism used to determine your site's presentation language. **Modifying this setting may break all incoming URLs and should be used with caution in a production environment.**

Click on **Save** settings, and then go back and take a look at the English version of the last blog post—it should appear normally. Now, click on the Hebrew link at the bottom of the page to show the Hebrew translation that was also created—you should see something like this (depending on how good your translation is):

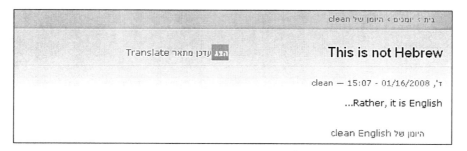

Ok, so my translation is non-existent, but the real point of going to the trouble of using Hebrew instead of Afrikaans (which I could have translated a bit better) is demonstrated nicely by this screenshot that demonstrates how powerful Drupal 6's language support really is. By tagging the content as a Hebrew translation and enabling language fallback, Drupal can now present both content and interface in the likeliest language of choice for any user—after all, it's a fairly good bet that if a user is reading Hebrew content, then they want it presented right to left along with the rest of the page.

Clicking **English** takes us back to the English version of the page as well as the English interface, and left to right layout as expected. Notice that Drupal automatically switches between the default English URL, without the language prefix, and the language prefixed URL whenever another language post is clicked on—in this case, `http://localhost/drupal/he`.

Using the language modules and contribs discussed here, it should be possible to create a fairly powerful multilingual site that can cater for posts in any number of languages, and allow for translations by any users with sufficient permissions and linguistic skills.

However, it is important to realize that Drupal's language support, while impressive, is not yet complete—for example, there is no native support for taxonomy term translations. As time goes by, more and more contribs will become available to plug any gaps, so if you find that there are certain things that cannot be achieved right now, remember to watch out for any new modules that might do the trick.

Performance

Every once in a while someone makes a site that becomes wildly popular. Having loads of people visiting all at once can put some serious strain on the server's resources and cause all sorts of problems as the congestion builds. Even if a site is not exceedingly popular, it is possible that it may come under a **denial of service** attack from somewhere.

Before even thinking about setting up the throttling mechanism on a site, it is important to know what resources are at your disposal:

 Ensuring that there are facilities in place to handle a *large amount of traffic*, will go some way in ensuring that your site scales well.

If you are unsure about what resources are available on your site, check with the hosting service and find out what they are providing. It's important to know the limitations of the hardware and network resources, but don't fall into the trap of believing this *is the* most important thing to know.

It's a time honored tradition in the corporate world to throw extra resources at computing problems — buying the latest, fastest servers to help speed up slow applications, upgrading network hardware to allow data to travel more freely, and so on. Invariably though, poorly designed software, or software that is poorly tuned for performance always finds a way to utilize all the resources one can throw at it, and still want more.

More often than not, it is better to look at *why* software is chewing resources and see what can be done to either stop it or at least alleviate the problem, so that the software utilizes its resources wisely. Drupal already has several strategies in place to help you, the site administrator, decide how and when to use resource intensive modules, and how to maximize the site's efficiency.

Caching

The first one we discuss here comes in the **Performance** section under **Site Configuration**. This page provides several options to improve the performance of your site and as nothing in this world is really for free, you need to understand that by and large obtaining a performance boost comes at the expense of something else. As a result, you need to have a good understanding of how the site is going to run when it comes time to work on this page.

Let's take a look at the first option:

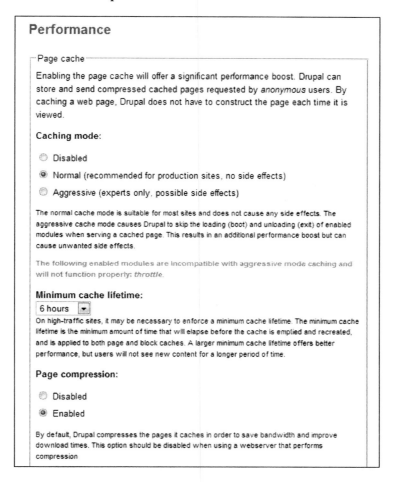

As you know, Drupal uses PHP to build web pages that are returned to a user's browser. Most of the time, these pages are unchanged between requests, and Drupal is working to build the same page before sending it off to the various users who requested it. It makes sense then to tell Drupal that if it has created a web page once, it should store a copy of this page and serve that copy instead of going to the trouble of recreating it.

The process of storing copies of web pages in order to reduce the amount of effort required to repeatedly create a page is known as *caching*.

The trade-off when using page caching is that any changes to a page are only shown to users once that cached version has expired and been replaced. This makes caching a suitable method for boosting performance whenever content is not updated very often, or when it is not important to have new content presented immediately.

The previous screenshot showed page caching, enabled with a minimum cache lifetime of 6 hours. You will need to decide how long you think it is suitable to go before any updates made to a page must be shown—the longer you leave a cached page for, the less work Drupal has to do, but the longer it will take for new content to show on the site.

Remember too that caching can have effects on, or be affected by, other modules. Most notably, the **Throttle** module that is discussed later in this section cannot be used in conjunction with aggressive caching. In the event that caching is desirable for most, but not all, pages then it is worth checking out the **Cache Exclude** module that can disable page caching for certain, specified pages.

 It is important to only enable caching on a live site, and not the development machine, because changes to a page show up only when the cache expires—causing confusion if you are expecting something else during testing.

Aggressive caching is not really necessary in the vast majority of cases and can cause problems with a variety of modules because it skips their boot and exit functions (which is how it provides that extra performance boost). Enabling it may well lead to some ugly warnings to this effect from Drupal: make sure you do some research about its effects before attempting to use it.

The next section of the page deals with block caching, and this can offer performance benefits for authenticated users because page caching is *only ever* enabled for anonymous users. The reason for this is that authenticated users have a lot of customized content that needs to be displayed—along with any changes or posts—without having to wait 6 hours at a time.

Blocks are constructed independently from the page as a whole, and often require expensive database requests or other operations in order to provide the information they contain. Enabling block caching as shown here:

```
┌─ Block cache ──────────────────────────────────────────────────────────┐
│                                                                        │
│   Enabling the block cache can offer a performance increase for all users by │
│   preventing blocks from being reconstructed on every page load. If page cache is │
│   also enabled, this performance increase will mainly affect authenticated users. │
│                                                                        │
│   Block cache:                                                         │
│                                                                        │
│   ○  Disabled                                                          │
│                                                                        │
│   ◉  Enabled (recommended)                                             │
│                                                                        │
│   Note that block caching is inactive when modules defining content access restrictions are enabled. │
│                                                                        │
└────────────────────────────────────────────────────────────────────────┘
```

...means that blocks no longer have to query the database (or whatever else it is they are doing) each time a page refreshes. Rather, they simply serve up the cached version and save on all that work.

The next section, entitled **Bandwidth optimizations**, deals with how to best transfer data from your server across the Internet to the users' browsers. The way in which data is transferred plays a role in the optimal way to do things, and the most important things to remember are:

- Keep files small
- Keep the number of files down

- As shown in the following screenshot, Drupal can aggregate and compress disparate CSS and JavaScript files in order to reduce the size and number of requests made to a server. Obviously, this has a huge number of benefits, especially if you are charged for bandwidth usage:

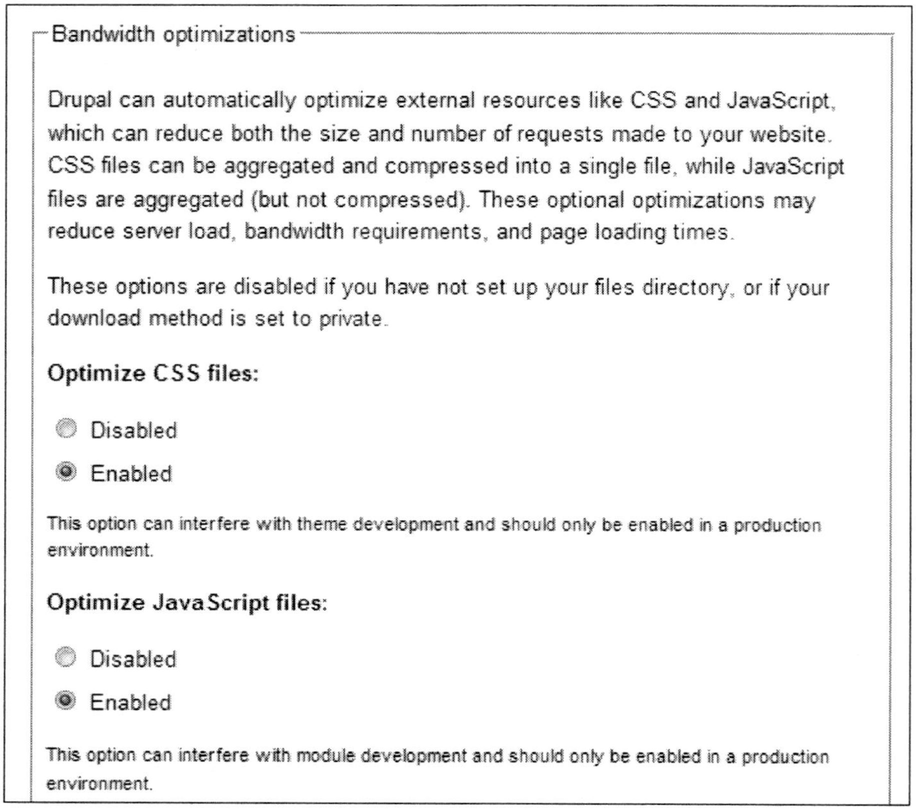

Bandwidth optimizations

Drupal can automatically optimize external resources like CSS and JavaScript, which can reduce both the size and number of requests made to your website. CSS files can be aggregated and compressed into a single file, while JavaScript files are aggregated (but not compressed). These optional optimizations may reduce server load, bandwidth requirements, and page loading times.

These options are disabled if you have not set up your files directory, or if your download method is set to private.

Optimize CSS files:

◯ Disabled

◉ Enabled

This option can interfere with theme development and should only be enabled in a production environment.

Optimize JavaScript files:

◯ Disabled

◉ Enabled

This option can interfere with module development and should only be enabled in a production environment.

The final option is useful when making modifications to a site because it helps to ensure that changes are definitely displayed and not held up while the site cache is still in operation:

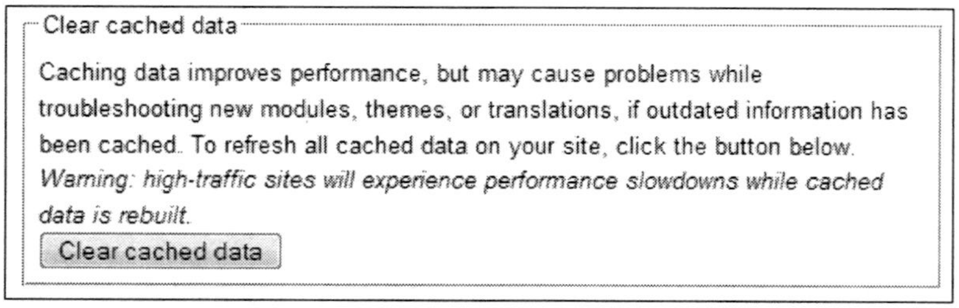

Clear cached data

Caching data improves performance, but may cause problems while troubleshooting new modules, themes, or translations, if outdated information has been cached. To refresh all cached data on your site, click the button below. *Warning: high-traffic sites will experience performance slowdowns while cached data is rebuilt.*

[Clear cached data]

Having the ability to clear the cache in order to view precisely how pages are being built is useful, but comes at a price. Remember that if you have a large site with much content then Drupal will have to do a lot of work to rebuild its cache and it is possible that users may notice a slowdown during this time.

Throttling

With that, it's time to look at another method for keeping Drupal running smoothly, even under heavy loads. Anticipating the need for some sort of congestion control, a good way to deal with surges in traffic or bandwidth usage is to enable the throttling mechanism that ships with Drupal, in the form of the aforementioned **Throttle** module.

Go ahead and enable it in the **Modules** section of the administration tool under **Site building**. Once that is done, configure how the module acts on the site in general by navigating to the **Throttle** page under **Site configuration**. This displays the following:

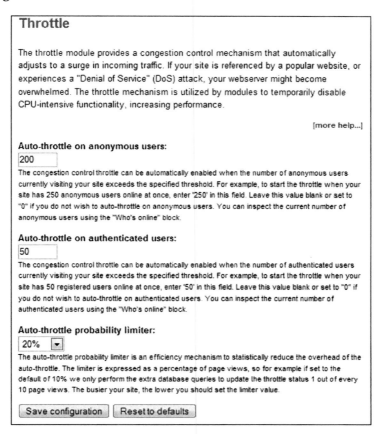

Throttling deals with congestion from the point of view of controlling how many people use the site. In this case, Drupal is instructed to engage the auto-throttle on anonymous users provided there are **200** or more online, and the same for authenticated users provided there are more than **50** of them online.

The final option deals with actually limiting the amount of work the throttle mechanism has to do, so that it does not become a resource hog. If, each time there is a page request, Drupal looks to see if it should engage the throttle mechanism, the process of doing this can start to become a burden on the server—setting the throttle to a smaller percentage of page views means that it is not working so hard to see whether or not to throttle CPU intensive recourses.

> The **Throttle** module itself doesn't impede other modules—it merely determines when throttle mode is on.

But what if you know that it is a specific module or block that is consuming more than its fair share of resources? In this case, enable the auto-throttle for that specific module or block in either the **Modules** or **Blocks** sections, respectively:

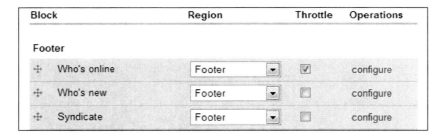

Block	Region	Throttle	Operations
Footer			
⊹ Who's online	Footer ▼	☑	configure
⊹ Who's new	Footer ▼	☐	configure
⊹ Syndicate	Footer ▼	☐	configure

In this screenshot, the throttle has been enabled for the **Who's online** module. This is a perfect example of a block that starts aggressively hogging resources when there are a lot of people suddenly visiting your site (obviously, it has to work quite hard to keep up with who's who). Now, you might think that as the site is new, it is unlikely that any of this really matters for a year or so, but bear the following in mind:

> A single mention or good review on one of the big websites, like Digg or Slashdot, can mean thousands of visitors pouring into your site in a matter of hours. Naturally, the first thing that happens in this situation is that the server crashes because you don't have everything in place to handle the congestion. Everyone then wonders why your site had such a good review in the first place, when it is never up and running.

But what does throttling blocks ultimately mean? If a server is under strain, and a block is set to be automatically throttled, it will be temporarily disabled and not contribute to the load on the server.

You can take a look at log messages to determine what the throttle module is up to at any given time. For example, I set the throttle mechanism to engage after only one user visited the site. The following log message was then created:

Details	
Type	throttle
Date	Wednesday, November 21, 2007 - 11:54
User	mf4good
Location	http://localhost/drupal/node?destination=node
Referrer	http://localhost/drupal/
Message	Throttle: *2 guests accessing site; throttle enabled.*
Severity	notice
Hostname	127.0.0.1
Operations	

It's not much, but at least it makes it clear when the throttle is on. Once the load has dropped sufficiently, a corresponding message will be sent stating that the throttle can be disengaged and things can return to normal.

Finally, it is important that you gain some idea about the performance of your site and what you can do to ensure it is good. Take a look at `http://drupal.org/node/2601` to learn about how to:

- Reduce the load on servers by preventing access to certain parts of the site for web crawlers of various kinds, using the `robot.txt` file.
- Learn about Apache performance, and PHP and MySQL tuning.

Any knowledge you gain now can be put to good use preemptively to guard against poor performance that may discourage users in the future—you never know when popularity will come knocking.

Dynamic JavaScript Features

One of the nice things about working with PHP-based applications like Drupal is that not only are they open source, but they can be combined with pretty much any other technology you can get your hands on. There is a huge online programming community, and many people make their neat little scripts available for the likes of you and me to include into our own sites. Not all are free, but many are, and many more are very cheap; so it is always worthwhile looking around at some of the scripting sites to see what you can pick up.

Here a few sites that you should consider looking over:

- `http://www.phpbuilder.com`
- `http://www.hotscripts.com`
- `http://www.php.resourceindex.com`
- `http://drupal.org/node/257` — *Customization and Theming*

Many of you may be shying away at this point because you are not keen to get involved with hardcore programming. Don't worry! With the exception of jQuery, the scripts are, by and large, autonomous and complete, so all that is required of us, is a few cut and pastes in the right place, perhaps the odd tweak here and there, and away we go.

Talking of scripts, this section will focus predominantly on using JavaScript to enhance web pages. For those not in the know:

 JavaScript is a client side language (i.e. it is run on the browser and not on the server) for creating rich and dynamic web pages.

It is important to be aware that you should always look at any and all licensing issues whenever you make use of other people's scripts. Many are made available for free for non-commercial uses, but you are required to purchase a license otherwise. As you get more confident with scripting, however, you should find that it is possible to build fairly powerful features by using your own code or tying together snippets of freely available code.

Drupal comes with built-in JavaScript libraries, so let's take a quick look at jQuery and how it can be used to add a few basic effects before we move on to cover some third-party JavaScript applications.

jQuery

jQuery, `http://jquery.com/`, is a library of JavaScript functions that make developing AJAX and other JavaScript features quick and easy. With the trend for rich, dynamic, and responsive web pages (Web 2.0) becoming more and more pervasive, it is important that Drupal keeps up with the times. Accordingly, jQuery has been built into the Drupal core, and you can find the main library files in the **misc** folder of your installation.

Before we can go ahead and start adding dynamic and powerful features, we need to know a little bit about how jQuery works, so let's take a crash course. I should warn you that this section really is a crash course — to become proficient in utilizing jQuery you will need to practice. Consider purchasing *Learning jQuery: Better Interaction Design and Web Development with Simple JavaScript Techniques* by Chaffer and Swedberg (ISBN 978-1-847192-50-9), Packt Publishing.

jQuery Basics

Let's begin with a brief but insightful overview of jQuery. How jQuery works can be split into two main parts, summed up as:

 Find elements; do something with them.

If some of the code in the coming section appears quite complex, bear the previous statement in mind and it should all become quite clear.

Under normal circumstances, the standard procedure to include a JavaScript library into a Drupal 6 site is to reference it from the theme's **.info** file. This is demonstrated in the following section, *jQuery in Action*, so we will concentrate on how the code itself works in this section before adding it in the next.

Because different parts of a web page can be loaded up at different times, we need to wrap any jQuery statements inside the `ready()` function to cause the jQuery JavaScript to be executed only once the page is fully loaded — this prevents the jQuery application from breaking, in the event it is run before everything (specifically, its target page element) is present:

```
$(document).ready(function(){
  // Your code here
});
```

Let's take a look at a simple jQuery statement to highlight the general syntax we use:

```
Clicking on this will <a href="#">trigger an alert</a>
<script type="text/javascript">
$(document).ready(function(){
    $("a").click(function() {
      alert("Hello world!");
    });
});
</script>
```

The first line is straightforward HTML, with a single hyperlink created using the **<a>** tag. Next, we have the JavaScript wrapped in both the **<script>** tags and then the **ready()** function. The statement:

```
$("a").click(function() {
    alert("Hello world!");
});
```

...tells jQuery that it must find all the **<a>** tags on the page, and when someone clicks on the link, it should execute the function (containing the **Hello World** alert).

Looking at it more generically, the statement **$()** is actually an alias for a jQuery object. It can be created using a number of CSS style selectors. A selector can be the name of a tag as used in this instance, it can be the class name of a tag (i.e. **<a class="classname">**), and even the id of a tag. So, if for example, you had an **<input>** tag, it would be easy to apply effects to this tag by creating a new object like so:

```
$("input")
```

Bear in mind though, that applying effects to a tag like this means that you might get some unexpected results, because jQuery will apply whatever effects you specify to *the entire set of tags that match the selector throughout the page*. If you want to limit the scope of the effects to a single piece of HTML, you would use the ID selector (note the leading #):

```
$("#uniqueid")
```

...and this would act on the unique tag that has the matching ID. For example:

```
Clicking on this will <a href="#" id="uniqueid">trigger an alert</a>
```

This jQuery object has a number of predefined methods that can be used to provide all sorts of functionality and effects. The one we used in the previous example was **click()**, to bind a specified function to the mouse click event but there are many more. To look over a list of what's available, go to http://docs.jquery.com/Events.

We aren't limited to applying random functions like the **alert()** used in the last example. jQuery has a whole lot of effects. For example, if you wanted a link to disappear after being clicked once, you could make use of the **hide()** method provided by jQuery to remove it:

```
$("a").click(function() {
    $(this).hide("slow");
});
```

Again, there are a large number of effects that can be achieved and you should refer to http://docs.jquery.com/Effects for a complete list.

Now, one of the most powerful features of jQuery is its methods actually return the jQuery object itself. This means that you can apply one method after the other in a process known as **chaining**. To get a nice combination of effects, simply add one after the other in a line:

```
...

.new{
background: #eded11;
font-weight: bold;
font-size: 20px;
align: left;
}

...

$('#uid').click(function() {
        $(this).addClass("new").fadeTo("slow", 0.2);
});
```

Here, we have chained together two methods, namely **addClass** (**addClass** applies a class definition, specified as **new**, to an element) and **fadeTo**, to slowly reduce the opacity of the tag to 0.2 times normal (i.e. 20%).

Let's take a look at how all this turns out on an actual web page.

jQuery in Action

As much as we are demonstrating jQuery in action, this section also shows off **.info** in action. Open up your current theme's folder and add a new file, entitled **jquery_test.css** with the class definition that will be used in the example:

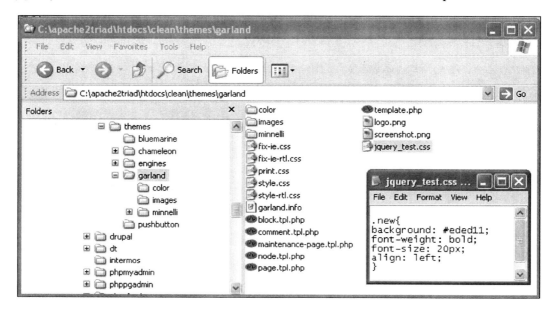

Next, create a new JavaScript file, entitled **jquery_test.js**, to house the jQuery call and add it to the same folder:

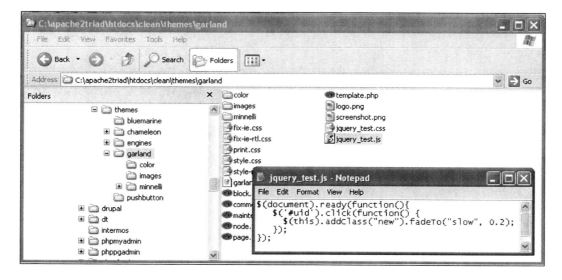

Next, edit the theme's **.info** file to ensure that the theme can locate the new css and
JavaScript files to include theme. For example:

```
; $Id: garland.info,v 1.5 2007/07/01 23:27:32 goba Exp $
name = Garland
description = Tableless, recolorable, multi-column, fluid width theme
(default).
version = VERSION
core = 6.x
engine = phptemplate
stylesheets[all][] = style.css
stylesheets[print][] = print.css

stylesheets[all][] = jquery_test.css
scripts[] = jquery_test.js

; Information added by drupal.org packaging script on 2008-02-13
version = "6.0"
project = "drupal"
datestamp = "1202913006"
```

Save the changes and then create a page with some HTML, against which the jQuery
can act:

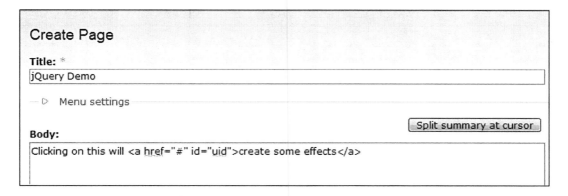

Take special note that the **id** attribute shown here, matches the identified specified
in the jQuery statement—**uid**. In order for the new **.info** settings to take effect,
the theme in question should be reloaded—ensure this is done before trying
anything out.

The page initially looks quite ordinary because no effects are applied until the link is clicked. In this case, we have:

jQuery Demo

Clicking on this will create some effects

Once the link is clicked, however, things change somewhat:

jQuery Demo

Clicking on this will

create some effects

Notice that the style information has been applied, and that the text is now quite faded—just as we expected from the chained methods applied to the tag.

That wraps up this brief overview of the exciting world of jQuery. There is much, much more for you to learn and one of the best places to start is with the entire API overview found at http://docs.jquery.com/API. This will give an excellent overview of what is available and what can be achieved—there are plenty of jquery tutorials and demonstrations that can be found around this site too.

Scrolling News Ticker

News tickers can be a nice feature for sites that attempt to provide up-to-date information (such as breaking news). If you need to present several bits of information at once, then a dynamic news ticker could be just the thing. With a bit of work, you can even integrate the news ticker with an RSS feed to present breaking news from other sites without having to do any work in creating content yourself.

We'll keep it simple and create a scrolling news ticker across the top of each page on the site. The ticker will show information stored in a .txt file on the site, but you can use still use this ticker to add links to sponsors, or even add image links. There is quite a lot of scope for change; so we will look at how to get everything up and running—what you create with the ticker is up to your imagination.

Obtaining the Ticker

The first task is of course to actually find a workable ticker script. In this case, a free ticker script was downloaded (after a brief search on Google) from **mioplanet** at http://www.mioplanet.com/rsc/newsticker_javascript.htm. The conditions of use presented on this page are fairly simple, so make sure you understand the terms before downloading and using anything.

Assuming you are happy to continue, download the JavaScript source-code file, entitled webticker_lib.js, and save it to the theme folder you are currently developing in:

 If you are going to use a few widgets like this, it may be better to create a widgets folder within your theme, in order to keep everything neat and tidy and easy to locate.

Next, open up the .info file (this example will utilize the **Barlow** theme because we made space for this feature earlier on when discussing themes) and add a reference to the ticker JavaScript file:

```
stylesheets[all][] = typography.css
stylesheets[all][] = layout.css
stylesheets[all][] = style.css

scripts[] = webticker_lib.js

regions[left] = Left sidebar
regions[right] = Right sidebar
regions[before_content] = Before content

; Information added by drupal.org packaging script on 2007-12-20

. . .
```

Save this and then reload the theme.

Next, the actual code required to add the ticker to a web page is given on the mioplanet page, so copy and paste this directly into the **page.tpl.php** file in the space created (recall we added an additional section to the template page earlier in Chapter 8):

```
...
<div id="menu">
   <?php if ($primary_links){ ?>
     <?php print theme('links', $primary_links, array('class' => 'links
primary_menu')) ?>
   <?php } ?>
```

```
    <?php if (count($secondary_links)){ ?>
      <?php print theme('links', $secondary_links, array('class' =>
'links secondary_menu')) ?>
    <?php } ?>
    </div>
</div>
<div id="content">
    <div class="newcontent">
        <DIV ID="TICKER" STYLE="overflow:hidden; width:100%"
onmouseover="TICKER_PAUSED=true" onmouseout="TICKER_PAUSED=false">
    <? include_once('ticker.txt'); ?>
        </DIV>
    </div>
<?php if ($left != ''){ ?>
    <div id="sidebar-left" class="sidebar">
    <?php print $left; ?>
    </div>
<?php } ?>
    ...
```

As you can see, this places the script at the top of the content in its own **<div>** tag with **class="newcontent"**.

> It is necessary to wrap the content of the `webticker_lib.js` file within the jQuery `$(document).ready(function(){`
>
> ...
>
> `});`
> statement to prevent the ticker script being run before the page elements are in place. When you do this, ensure that you leave the `TICKER_tick` function outside of the jQuery statement, otherwise this will also lead to problems.

In addition, the new code references a `ticker.txt` file that needs to be created and saved in the theme folder before attempting to use the script. If you would rather test whether the ticker is working correctly before dealing with additional code, then replace:

```
 <? include "ticker.txt"?>
```

with:

```
Hi! You should see me scrolling across your page. Make sure this text
is longer than the width of your scroller or else it may not scroll at
all.
```

and view the site in your browser.

You should see the message scrolling across your page. If that works, replace the text message with the PHP `include` statement, and let's move on.

Adding the Content

For our humble purposes, all we really need to do is feed the JavaScript file we have just installed on our site a list of lines to print out to the screen. You can add in pretty much anything you want here; however, ensure that you test everything thoroughly before releasing it to the public.

Before adding lines of information to `ticker.txt`, bear in mind that you should try to create a standard format for each news item, so that the work in creating new elements is minimized. In this case, each line is delimited by a single vertical bar, except the start and end of the first and last element that have two in order to keep everything even.

The following snippet shows the current contents of the `ticker.txt` file on the demo site:

```
|| <a href="http://www.mioplanet.com/rsc/newsticker_javascript.htm"
target="_blank"><strong>Scrolling News Ticker</strong></a> by <a
href="http://www.mioplanet.com"
target="_blank"><strong>mioplanet</strong></a> |
| This book was brought to you by <a href="http://www.packtpub.com"
target="_blank"><strong>Packt Publishing</strong></a> |
| It was written by <em>David Mercer</em> who has worked on a number
of books for Packt and also contributes to <a href="https://www.
ranktracer.com">RankTracer</a> and <a href="http://www.linkdoozer.
com">LinkDoozer</a>. For more info please find him at his LinkDoozer
homepage... ||
```

...and this is what the result is (bear in mind that the text would be moving from right to left across the screen):

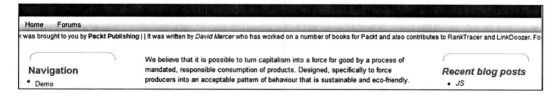

You might even want to try and experiment with adding images or even a special style. In this way, title icons or logos can be added to each item.

The main problem with this script as it stands is that it requires you to manually enter each item, which will no doubt become a pain several times a day for the next ten years. There are several ways around this:

- Create a script to pull information from a database.
- Pull information from an RSS feed.
- Only enter content that changes infrequently — such as links to sponsors.
- Get someone else to do it for you.

While we won't continue on this topic here; it would be great experience for you to attempt any one or more of the previous list of options with the exception of the third, which is covered by default.

Remember to be very, very careful not to introduce errors or security problems when using code from someone else — either in or outside the Drupal community. Ensure that you understand what the code is doing and that it is tested thoroughly before going live with it.

Summary

This chapter focused on two quite different aspects of a Drupal website. The first dealt with functionality and explored a couple of the more advanced features and modules available, while the second looked at how to utilize JavaScript to enhance and modernize your Drupal site.

The use of OpenID to homogenize the login process for your site, as well as implementing actions and triggers to automate tasks, should both encourage new community members to join and make managing the site easier.

Drupal 6 has vastly improved multi-lingual support, and this chapter has provided a firm grounding on how to set up a truly international website to cater for a variety of different users around the world. In addition, the process of understanding and dealing with the stresses and strains that your site will be subject to, once it becomes well used, was discussed and the caching and throttling mechanisms built into Drupal were introduced to take care of these.

All in all, your website should now be pretty much complete, or, if there is something you want to add that was not explicitly discussed here, you should now have enough general experience to go ahead and make some bold changes. Gaining the confidence to create an advanced website is simply about taking the time to learn your way around things, and this chapter has given you the platform from which to start.

The following chapter looks at administrative tasks associated with maintaining a live website, and doesn't relate to the development of your site as directly as these first nine have. Because of this, I would like to take the time to congratulate you on completing your website now, as well as assure you that all the hard development work is done.

If you would like to get your site up and running as soon as possible, feel free to skip the next chapter and go directly to the Appendix, which outlines how to properly deploy a new site to its home on the Web. You can always come back to Chapter 10 and learn how to maintain and administer everything once it is up and running.

10
Managing Your Website

By now, the vast majority of the development for the new site is complete! You should also feel confident that, from a development perspective, you can respond to whatever demands the site throws at you and operate Drupal with proficiency. Like all things in the computing world, however, it is never sufficient to build something and then leave it to run by itself. There is always work to be done to ensure that everything runs smoothly.

Often, there are certain jobs that need to be performed every now and then that are not specifically related to Drupal, but are intrinsic to working with websites in general. These tasks can vary greatly in nature, but all those discussed here will be useful at some stage during the life of your website, even if you don't need them right now.

One of the problems with presenting a chapter like this is that we can't possibly hope to cover each and every nuance of the huge array of different platforms on which Drupal can be run. Internet Service Providers (ISPs) offer wildly varying packages that are either totally bereft of any type of helpful functionality, or packed full with all the latest gadgets.

As a result, we will look at functionality that is in common use, and that in the event you do not have access to the same software, will clearly demonstrate the tasks you need to perform. Hopefully, you can still successfully operate with the software you do have access to. For example, by using the Apache2Triad package, we already have certain technologies that we can make use of on the development machine, such as phpMyAdmin.

 It may be helpful to read through this chapter before selecting a hosting package (assuming you haven't already) in order to get a feel for the type of functionality that may prove to be useful.

There are also a few other web-related activities inherent to Drupal that we should take the time to look over quickly. As a result, this chapter will talk about:

- Backups
- Cron and scheduled tasks
- Website activities—including paths, xml sitemaps, and user maintenance
- Search engine optimization and website promotion
- Upgrades

Armed with the information presented in this the final chapter, you will be a well-equipped Drupal website administrator. Ultimately, the experience gained from running a live website, in itself, should prove to be far more valuable than this humble book. Hopefully, you will find the entire experience richly rewarding, and share your hard-won knowledge with the rest of the community in the future.

We're on the home stretch, so let's get on with it.

Backups

There are plenty of reasons to make backups of both the file system and database. As mentioned, several times throughout the course of the book, always back up anything that is at risk of being damaged, whenever you modify code, add a new module, or even implement upgrades. It sounds like a real pain to do this because the vast majority of the time, nothing goes wrong with the application. Sooner or later though, for some unfathomable reason, if you don't make backups you *will* get stung in precisely the most painful spot.

Most especially, corrupting or breaking a database, which in turn leads to a loss of precious data, can be a real pain in the back end of your application! So, while it is fairly easy to back up the files on the file system by making copies of the directories in question, or indeed copying the entire `drupal` folder (whatever you have named it), it is of paramount importance that you learn how to back up the database too, because this is not as trivial.

Before continuing, it is important to have a *strategy* for backing up files, folders, and data. It is good idea to back up the entire site at fairly regular intervals, as well as backing up the database more frequently. These backups should be clearly marked, so that you know when they were made, making it easy to determine the correct one to use in the event of some sort of disaster. You might also consider holding these backups away from the main file system, perhaps on a CD or remote backup server, so that you don't have to rely on your host's disaster-recovery policy—you have your own.

Most hosts provide software such as cPanel to help administer your site. A standard cPanel administration page looks like this:

General account information:	
Hosting package	default
Dedicated Ip Address	204.15.10.108
Subdomains	0 / unlimited
Parked Domains	0 / 0
Addon Domains	0 / 0
MySQL Databases	1 / 1
Disk Space Usage	0.00 Megabytes
MySQL Disk Space	1.23 Megabytes
Disk space available	Unlimited Megabytes
Bandwidth (this month)	239.17 Megabytes
Email Accounts	7 / 10
Email Forwarders	9
Auto-responders	0
Mailing Lists	0 / unlimited
Email Filters	0
Ftp Accounts	0 / 0

General server information:

Operating system	Linux
Service Status	Click to View
Kernel version	2.6.9-023stab044.11-smp
Machine Type	i686
Apache version	1.3.36 (Unix)
PERL version	5.8.8
Path to PERL	/usr/bin/perl
Path to sendmail	/usr/sbin/sendmail

Mail | Webmail | Change Password | Parked Domains | Addon Domains

FTP Manager | File Manager | Disk Space Usage | Backups | Password Protect Directories

Error pages | Subdomain | MySQL® Databases | SSH/Shell Access | Redirects

FrontPage® Extensions | Web/FTP Stats | Raw Access Logs | Raw Log Manager | Error log

Subdomain Stats | Chatroom | PhpMyChat | Bulletin Board | CGI Center

Scripts Library | Agora Shopping Cart | Cron jobs | Network Tools | MIME Types

Apache Handlers | Manage OpenPGP Keys | HotLink Protection | Index Manager | IP Deny Manager

Notice that one of the options (second row, second from the right) provides backup facilities. Clicking on this link, brings up the following page that can be used to back up not only the database, but all the files along with any other important bits of information about your file system:

Backups

Backup Not Enabled

Full Backup

Generate/Download a Full Backup
Full backups can only be used for moving your account
to another server or keeping a local copy of your account

Home Directory

Download a home directory Backup

Restore a Home Directory Backup
[   ] Browse... Upload

Download a MySQL Database Backup

horatio

Restore a MySQL Database
[   ] Browse... Upload

Download Email Domain Forwarder or Filter Backup

Aliases   Filters
ranktracer.com ranktracer.com

Restore an Email Domain Forwarder/Filter
[   ] Browse... Upload

[Go Back]

The backups are generated and stored on the host machine to download or use whenever you wish. Remember that it is prudent to transfer a full site backup over a secure connection in case the transfer is eavesdropped. In addition to this standard facility, hosters often provide a regular backup service to a remote server; although, this service will often be subject to charges.

More often than not, it is the data in the database that needs to be regularly backed up instead of the whole site, and there are two ways of backing up a database (or any part of it) that we will consider here. One way is to make use of phpMyAdmin, which comes as part of the Apache2Triad package, and hopefully with any hosting package you use. Let's start with that.

phpMyAdmin

phpMyAdmin is an exceptionally popular and commonplace tool for interacting with MySQL via the Web. Instead of having to learn how to use the MySQL command-line client, phpMyAdmin provides us with a graphical interface that makes viewing and maintaining databases, tables, and content a lot easier. Issuing commands is also made easier with the interface for many of the most commonplace data-related tasks.

The following steps can be followed in order to create a backup with phpMyAdmin:

1. Log into phpMyAdmin and select the relevant Drupal database. (The username and password required is for the pertinent database user and not necessarily a system user.)

2. Click on the **Export** tab along the top of the page, and set up the options, as shown here:

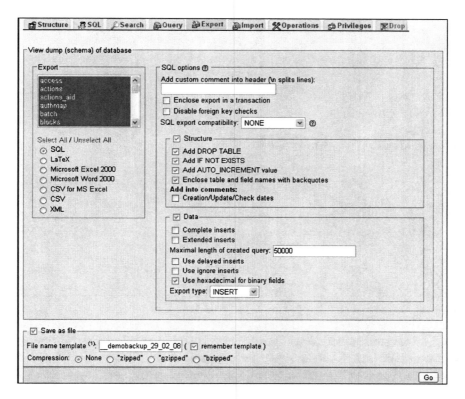

In the screenshot, all the tables were selected for backup, all the **Structure** checkboxes were selected in order to prevent us having to manually drop a corrupted database, and a useful name (automatically contains the database name once the backup file is generated) was provided—appending the date as shown is a good idea as it will help you to keep track of which backup is which.

Notice too that the option **Save as file** has been selected. This will create the backup in the form of a file rather than display the output to the screen. It is suggested that you always use this option for full database backups because the backup file can get large and cause all sorts of problems if printed to the screen.

3. Click **Go** once you are satisfied with your options, and this will then create a SQL file (although there are other formats to choose from such as LaTeX or XML) from which you can recreate the database if needed.

Once the backup file has been created and saved, it is a simply matter of causing MySQL to run the contents in order to recreate the database. To do this, click on the **Import** tab at the top of the page, and enter the name of the .sql file that should be run, as shown here:

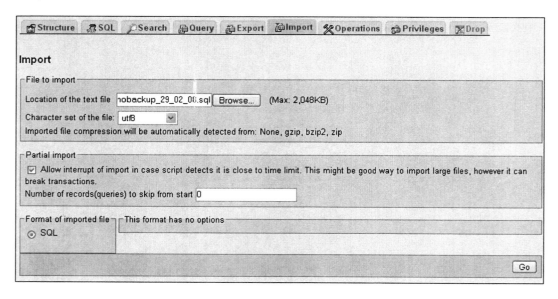

That makes life fairly simple, but it isn't the only way. If you have gotten used to using the command line, or simply prefer it, then the **mysql** command line utility can run the contents of a SQL file against the database using a command like this:

```
C:\ mysql -uroot -p mf4good < C:/backups/mf4good_13_01_08.sql
```

This command supplies a username (root), specifies the name of the database against which the file should be run (mf4good) and then indicates the file to be used (mf4good_13_01_08.sql). In this instance, no password has been specified but mysql will prompt for it before performing any task, whenever it is required.

Another way of creating backups is by using the mysqldump utility from the command line.

The mysqldump Utility

It is probably worthwhile spending some time using this because it provides greater flexibility should you ever need to perform anything out of the ordinary. I will confess, though, that for most database-related tasks phpMyAdmin will perform admirably. In the event that no access to phpMyAdmin is provided on the hosted site, or if it is unavailable for whatever reason, then the following section will come in most handy.

To create a backup, type in something like the following at the command line (remember to use **–uuser –p** if required):

```
C:\ mysqldump -uroot -p mf4good > mf4good_13_01_08.sql
```

This will create a backup file called `mf4good_13_01_08.sql` in the current directory. Ensure that this has worked by viewing the contents of the file that will contain reams and reams of SQL statements. There are plenty of different options used to get a variety of different types of backup file. Type in:

```
C:\ mysqldump -help
```

...in order to obtain a list of what's available. `mysqldump` is a powerful and flexible tool, and knowing how it works will benefit you in the long run if you are going to attempt some more advanced backup options.

 Drupal uses the utf8 character set so, in particular, setting the **default-character-set** option to **utf8** when using **mysqldump** can help to avoid problems.

To reiterate, it is good practice to back up the database on a regular basis, regardless of whether or not there is a specific reason. Doing so will protect you from a total loss of data in the event that some sort of disaster destroys the database or loses its information.

Cron and Scheduled Tasks

In order to keep the site running smoothly, and keep it up-to-date, there are a variety of chores that need to be performed on a regular basis. For example, we saw earlier in the book that the **Aggregator** module needed to be run on a regular basis so that it can update all its feeds. The Drupal developers are well aware that different modules all have different tasks to perform on a regular basis, so they created `cron.php` to manage the process.

Keeping modules up-to-speed is a case of setting the **crontab** (on Linux) or **scheduled task** (on Windows) to execute the `cron.php` script that is housed in the main folder of the Drupal installation. The **cron.php** script triggers outstanding scheduled tasks for modules that require regular updating, clearing out, or whatever.

Let's take a look at how to control the crontab, followed by setting up a scheduled task for the Windows users among us.

The Crontab

It is recommended that you learn how to manually make use of the crontab, despite there being a number of modules available to help out. Effort now will no doubt come in handy someday when your Drupal site is not immediately available to do it for you.

All the variables set in the crontab are numeric constants, with the exception of the asterisk character, which is a wildcard that allows any value. The ranges permitted for each field are as follows:

- Minutes: 0-59
- Hours: 0-23
- Day of month: 1-31
- Month: 1-12
- Weekday: 0-7 (Sunday is either 0 or 7)

You can include multiple values for each entry by separating each value with a comma. The command you wish to issue can be any command line command, and can be used to execute web pages, like the `cron.php` script.

Assuming you have access to a command line facility on your host server (and assuming it is a Linux server), editing the crontab can be done with the following command:

```
$> crontab -e
```

With the file open, give each individual command its own line, and separate each field with a space. For example, the line:

```
0 0 * * * /usr/bin/lynx - source http://www.marketforce4good.org/
cron.php
```

...causes the cron script to be run at the stroke of midnight, each day—this command is repeated at the bottom of the **Standard Cron Manager** screenshot that follows shortly. Compare the two lines if you are not entirely sure how this works, because the graphic interface elucidates the syntax better.

You can also use the -1 option with the `crontab` command to show the contents of the crontab file for the invoking user—useful if you want to find out what is already there without opening up the file for editing.

If manually working on the crontab doesn't sound too appealing, many hosting companies provide an interface such as the following one that allows you to modify the crontab without directly editing it:

Standard Cron Manager

This is a web interface to the crontab program. For example, * * * * * would mean every min and 0 0 * * * would mean at midnight.

Please enter an email address where the cron output will be sent: `cronjobs@marketforce`

Minute	Hour	Day	Month	Weekday	Command	
31	4	4	*	*	php /home/wwwlink/cron/im_cron_tagcloud_mon	Delete
23	3	*	*	*	php /home/wwwlink/cron/im_cron_tagcloud.php	Delete
15	2	*	*	*	php /home/wwwlink/cron/im_cron_sitecloud.php	Delete
3	1	*	*	*	php /home/wwwlink/cron/cron_sites.php	Delete
0	0	*	*	*	/usr/bin/lynx –source http://www.marketforce4g	

[Commit Changes] [Reset Changes]

[Go Back]

In the final entry, you can see (more or less) that the `cron.php` script is set to run at midnight every day using the command:

```
/usr/bin/lynx -source http://www.marketforce4good.org/cron.php
```

...whereas, for example, the first task is set to run on the 4th day of every month at 04:31. Notice too that, unlike the other files, the php command is not used to execute the **cron.php** script—this is because the `cron.php` file needs to be accessed as a web page so that certain environment variables are properly set.

In this case, we have used the lynx utility (a command line web browser) to access the script, but it may be that lynx is not available on your platform. In this case, try using the following:

```
/usr/bin/wget -O -q http://www.marketforce4good.org/cron.php
```

Set `cron.php` to run at regular intervals to ensure that your site is kept as up-to-date as possible! Hourly is recommended—more if it is specifically required.

If you have trouble with both of these methods, then check out `http://drupal.org/cron` for more info.

Windows Scheduled Tasks

On the off chance you are using a Windows-based server, or simply wish to enable scheduled tasks on your Windows PC while developing, you can make use of the **Scheduled Task** wizard. The following instructions, taken from the Drupal site, explain exactly how this is done:

1. Go to **Start | Programs | Accessories | System Tools | Scheduled Tasks**.

2. Double-click **Add Scheduled Task**.

3. The **Scheduled Task** wizard will appear. Click **Next**.

4. Select the program to run. Choose your **browser** from the list (for example, Internet Explorer or Firefox). Click **Next**.

5. Give the task a **Name**, such as **Drupal Cron Job**, and choose the **Frequency** with which to perform the task (for example, **Daily**). Click **Next**.

6. Choose specific **date and time options** (this step will vary, depending on the option selected in the previous step). When finished, click **Next**.

7. Enter your **password** if prompted. Change the **username** if required (for example, if you'd like the task to run under a user with few privileges for security reasons). Click **Next**.

8. On the final page, select the checkbox **Open advanced properties for this task when I click Finish** and click **Finish**.

9. Go to the task's setting page either by checking the checkbox at the end of the last step, or by double-clicking on the task.

10. In the **Run** box, after the text that is there now (for example, **C:\ PROGRA~1\MOZILL~1\firefox.exe**), enter a space and then type the address of your website's `cron.php` page in double quotation marks (for example, **C:\PROGRA~1\MOZILL~1\firefox.exe "http://localhost/drupal/ cron.php"**)

11. To set a frequency higher than **Daily** (for example, **Hourly**), click the **Schedule** tab, and then click **Advanced**. Here you can set options such as **Repeat** task, every **1 hour** for **23 hours**. Click **OK** when finished.

12. Change the **start time** on the task to **one minute from the current time**. This will allow you to test the task and make sure that it is working.

13. When all settings have been configured to your liking, click **Apply** and **OK** (note that you may be prompted for your password).

If you are unable to set a cron job to run on the host site once it is live, then set your Windows scheduled task to access the `cron.php` script directly from your home PC instead, using the instructions just listed. This means that the cron script is executed whenever your PC is online and able to access web pages.

This last point highlights how easy Drupal has made things when it comes to performing necessary tasks on a regular basis. All that's required is a browser application of some sort to access the `cron.php` script, and any tasks that need to be run by the various Drupal modules will be taken care of. You can access this script from your own browser (there are links for manually executing the cron script in **Status report** under **Reports**), or set your own PC to do it whenever you start it up, or any number of other things.

Website Activities

Once the site is developed and running on the live servers, you will find that your ISP probably offers a fair number of toys to play around with. Some of these can be very useful for the budding website administrator. But what could we need, now that the entire site has been built?

There are plenty of different tasks that still lie ahead. For example, are you sure that malicious people out there can't hotlink to your site and chew bandwidth? What is hotlinking? What is bandwidth? These questions constitute only a very small part of the types of concerns that must take focus once development is completed.

While the subject of this book is to *build a site*, this task is only one side of the coin. As we saw earlier in the section on **Backups**, hosters often provide a standard administration interface such as cPanel or Plesk, and it is recommended that you spend some time finding out what is available for use and how to use it. Knowing what is available is important because it means you are better able to plan *how* you work.

Another important thing to note here is that most hosting services will offer a full array of statistics for your website. Things like where people have come from, how many accessed the site, which pages are being accessed, and so on. Drupal comes with modules that do pretty much the same thing, so check to see whether the site's native statistics are sufficient or whether you need to consider installing a new module—adding *Google Analytics* might also be useful.

Since it is possible you have an entirely different set of options available on your hosted site, we won't discuss this any further here, but there are still a couple of other matters that warrant attention.

Path and Pathauto

By default, Drupal labels pages by number—for example, `http://www.mf4good.org/node/25`. This is not particularly descriptive to either humans or search engines, so the *Path* module ships with the Drupal core as a way to provide meaningful aliases for content. Providing relevant aliases (in other words, a descriptive keyword that occurs in the content) can be a real benefit when it comes time for Google to rank your pages.

Head over to the **Modules** section and enable **Path**. This will create a new **URL aliases** page under **Site building** that contains a **List** tab and an **Add alias** tab. Initially, there will be no aliases present, so the **List** tab is not too interesting. The **Add alias** tab looks like this:

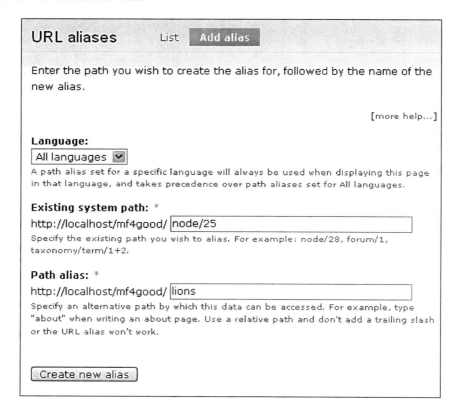

In this instance, node 25 contains information about lions and the alias provided, **lions**, is clearly a good one both in terms of being descriptive of the content and in terms of being a relevant keyword because the term **lions** appears in the content of this post several times (take my word for it).

Notice too that aliases can be applied to pretty much any type of page there is — including forums and taxonomy term pages. If, for example, you want to show a page that contains all the posts tagged with **conservation** and **wildlife** (for argument's sake, say these are taxonomy terms 2 and 7) but provide it with a user-friendly name (perhaps because it will be a prominent page accessed from the navigation), you would specify **taxonomy/term/2+7** as the existing path and provide a suitable alias, perhaps **wildlife-conservation**. It is far easier for users to find a page called **wildlife-conservation** than try to remember the taxonomy values of each of the terms.

Take heed of the fact that selecting a **Language** means that the alias provided will apply only to that language's content. In other words, aliases should be provided for each individual language or left as is to apply to all of them at once.

It is also important to note that while it is possible to give the same node multiple aliases, for example, assigning **node/25** the alias **lions** and **kingofthejungle**, this should be avoided because search engines take a dim view of this practice and may drop page rankings accordingly. The reason being that malicious webmasters could write a single page and copy it a million times to slightly different URLs — to give the impression that they are important producers of content for that topic, when in fact they are not.

Click **Create new alias** to add the new path to the **List** page:

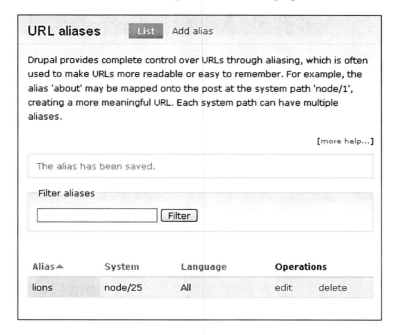

The interface here should be quite intuitive for you now — aliases are listed at the bottom of the page with the option to **edit** or **delete** each one. A **Filter** box is also provided to reduce the number of visible aliases to only those that you are interested in — entering **lions** in the **Filter** box returns this one result, while entering **tigers** returns an empty set.

> It should be noted that aliases don't have to be single words — multiple words and relative paths are often more intuitive. It's very useful to be able to use aliases like **cats/lions** rather than just **lions**, for instance. Also, **king-of-the-jungle** is better than **kingofthejungle** for both readers and Google.

Ideally, all content should be provided with a path alias right from the start. In this case, using the **Add alias** tab is not required because a new option to specify the node alias is now provided to content posters (assuming they have sufficient privileges) whenever they post something:

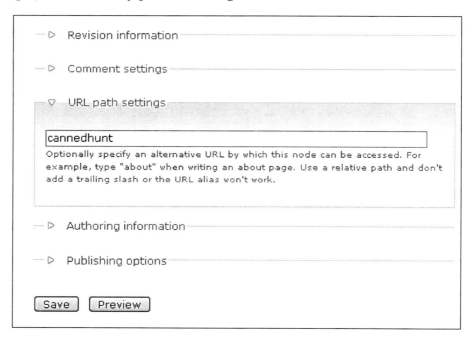

Now, whenever new content is posted, the node is automatically referenced by the path alias provided (notice the URL of the page shown):

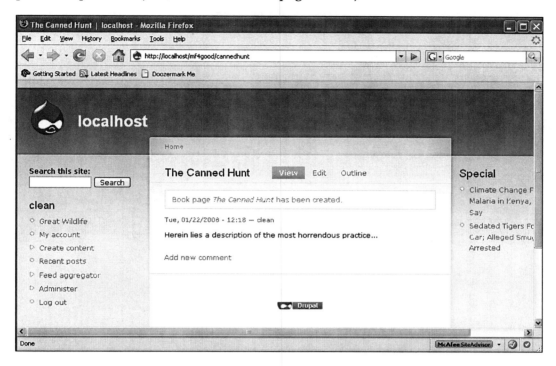

Naturally, this alias is automatically added to the **URL aliases List** page and can be edited or removed as normal.

While this does the trick for the moment, it may be better to consider automating the process with the **Pathauto** module. **Pathauto**, utilizing a host of preset parameters, automatically provides a relevant path alias for any content posted to the site.

To see it in action, download the **Token** module (required by **Pathauto**) along with **Pathauto**. Install and enable the **Token** module and then do the same for **Pathauto**. With **Pathauto** enabled, you will need to visit the **Pathauto** settings page under **Site configuration** in order to work with the vast array of settings available:

The screenshot, in this case, shows the **Node path settings** section and from here you can decide on the format of the **Default path pattern**, along with patterns for all different types of content. By default, the pattern **content/[title-raw]** is provided, but clicking on the **Replacement patterns** link displays a large array of alternative options. As an exercise, try out a few of the given patterns and post some new content to get a feel for how the patterns affect the paths.

For the most part, the default settings are sensible. Posting a blog with nothing altered shows that the alias has been generated from the title (**Aliased Blogging**), like so:

Pathauto doesn't force you to automatically generate an alias—users still have the power to specify their own ones, if necessary, by scrolling down the content creation page and unchecking the **Pathauto** option, and entering a new alias in the **URL path settings** section:

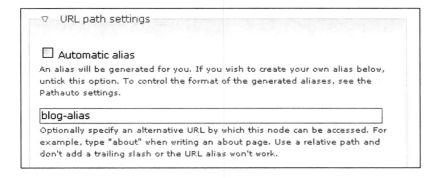

Without boring you too much with the vast array of settings to consider, most of which are the same thing repeated for each different content type, it's worth looking at the two generic sections:

- **General settings** – Use this section to specify generic properties of path aliases. Settings such as maximum and minimum alias lengths, word separator character, update actions, and strings to remove are all provided here.

- **Punctuation settings** – Instruct **Pathauto** to handle any non-alphanumeric characters in a number of ways. By default, characters such as braces, brackets, and quotes are all removed but they can be replaced by a separator or left as is—it is strongly advised that you simply leave the default settings as is.

It is also possible to generate automatic path aliases for content that has already been created. In order to do this, go to the pertinent content type and select the **Bulk generate** option before clicking **Save configuration**:

> ☑ Bulk generate aliases for nodes that are not aliased
> Generate aliases for all existing nodes which do not already have aliases.

Pathauto will go ahead and create the aliases (based on your settings) and inform you of how many have been created. It is easy to view and edit them from the **URL aliases** page in **Site building**.

Pathauto provides an additional **Delete aliases** tab on the **URL aliases** page that presents a number of options for removing aliases. As an exercise, delete all the aliases created by **Pathauto**, leaving any manually created aliases intact—note that the number of aliases in each section is given at the end of each alias type descripton. The options shown on this page should not present you with any trouble, so let's move onto the next thing.

Uninstalling Modules

It's worth mentioning that not all modules are created equal and some make database modifications that can hang around on the system long after the files from the **modules** folder are erased. In order to keep things neat and tidy, the following few steps should be kept in mind when removing a module from your site.

By way of example, let's look at the process of uninstalling CCK:

1. Back up your database and module files—it's quite possible you realize that you can't live without CCK and want it back the way it was.
2. Disable the various interdependent modules in order. The following screenshot shows the bulk of CCK modules being disabled with those modules that are still required remaining enabled—until Drupal allows us to disable them:

Enabled	Throttle	Name	Version	Description
☑	☐	**Content**	HEAD	Allows administrators to define new content types. Required by: Content Copy (enabled), Fieldgroup (enabled), Node Reference (enabled), Number (enabled), Option Widgets (enabled), Text (enabled), User Reference (enabled)
☐	☐	**Content Copy**	HEAD	Enables ability to import/export field definitions. Depends on: Content (enabled)
☐	☐	**Fieldgroup**	HEAD	Create field groups for CCK fields. Depends on: Content (enabled)
☐	☐	**Node Reference**	HEAD	Defines a field type for referencing one node from another. Depends on: Content (enabled), Text (enabled), Option Widgets (enabled)
☐	☐	**Number**	HEAD	Defines numeric field types. Depends on: Content (enabled)
☑	☐	**Option Widgets**	HEAD	Defines selection, check box and radio button widgets for text and numeric fields. Depends on: Content (enabled) Required by: Node Reference (enabled), User Reference (enabled)
☑	☐	**Text**	HEAD	Defines simple text field types. Depends on: Content (enabled) Required by: Node Reference (enabled), User Reference (enabled)
☐	☐	**User Reference**	HEAD	Defines a field type for referencing a user from a node. Depends on: Content (enabled), Text (enabled), Option Widgets (enabled)

3. Once all the modules in the package have been disabled, click on the **Uninstall** tab at the top of the **Modules** page and select those modules you wish to remove from the database and click **Uninstall**:

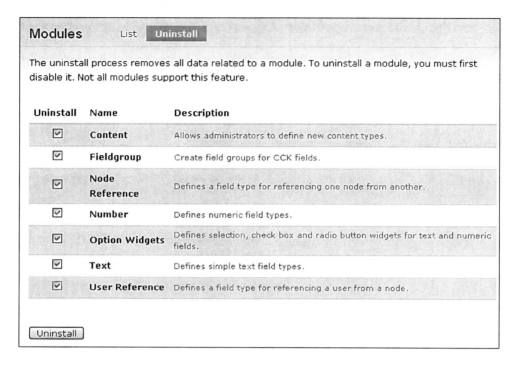

4. Drupal will warn that all the data held in this module's tables will be permanently lost—assuming you are happy with this, click **Uninstall**:

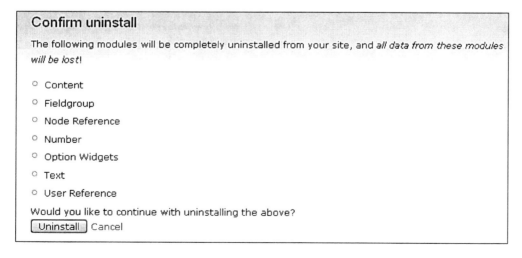

5. Once the database clean-up is complete, remove the module files from the **modules** folder.

It is generally a good idea to completely uninstall all evidence of a module rather than leaves bits and pieces of data and files lying around. Most of the time, changes a module makes to the database should not harm the site if left in place. However, it is always better to be safe than sorry by removing unused modules completely because you never know if they can cause hassles further down the line.

Maintaining Users

It is quite likely that while some people register with the full intention of making regular use of your site, they will move on and their account remains hanging around without actually doing anything. It might be prudent to add a user maintenance module early on to keep track of how and whether site users are active, so that you can remove those who don't meet certain criteria.

At the time of writing, no user maintenance modules were available for demonstration, but hopefully, something like the **Inactive User** module will be upgraded in due course and can be downloaded and installed, as discussed earlier in the book.

Search Engine Optimization and Website Promotion

One of the most common goals for a website is to appear high up on the big search engine rankings. As you should know, having a good ranking increases the chances of potential users finding your site among the mass of other sites. So what can be done to rank as highly as possible without actually having to pay anyone?

There is no straight answer to this, unfortunately, and many people will give just as many different answers. However, there is a core set of tasks you can take up that should help—they might vary in importance, but it is probably worth performing all of them:

Optimization	Explanation
Write web-enhanced copy	Admittedly, you cannot control the content of other people's comments and pages, but this would still apply to any and all standard pages you write—such as the *Introduction* page, *About us*, or *FAQ*, or even your own personal blog.
	Make the content of these pages clear and concise (so that people can read them quickly), and ensure that you use any keywords that you would like to see showing up in searches where appropriate.
Use meaningful path names	It certainly helps to have everything named meaningfully, not least because search engines do look at file names. Instead of naming a page 19, give it something appropriate like `expert-opinion`.
	Path and **Pathauto**, discussed earlier, help in this regard.
Use meaningful anchor text	IMPORTANT: Search engines, in particular Google, place a large amount of emphasis on the anchor text used in links. Make sure all your links have meaningful text associated with them. For example, you could rewrite the following sentence:
	`Donate to the Wildlife community <a href ="<yourlink>">here</a>.`
	to:
	`Donate to the <a href ="<yourlink>">Wildlife community</a> here.`
	The reason for this is that the word **here** is not particularly meaningful to a search engine, even though humans can easily make the connection. For the sake of your rankings, simply move the link to the key phrase **Wildlife community** to place more emphasis on it for the search engine.

Optimization	Explanation
Manage links	A high level of importance is placed on the perceived popularity of a website. Search engines can judge the popularity of a website by looking at how many incoming and mutual links there are to the site, and how popular the sites that link to it themselves are. For this reason, you should ensure that you link to only sites that you feel are suitable partners—don't be fooled by offers to buy millions of incoming links because these generally use poor quality sites that are not rated highly. This can actually damage your perceived popularity by Google. Effectively, you should search for as many relevant link pages as possible, or actually speak to the relevant sites to determine whether you can provide mutual links. The more links you have from popular sites, the better your ranking will be. You can also try to get one-way links to your site—these are also rated highly by search engines.

Write meaningful `alt` tags for images	Search engines don't see pictures like humans do, so there is nothing you can do about images… or is there? Instead of naming images `02_03.jpg`, consider giving them names like `cruel_hunter.jpg`. Don't stop there either. Instead of adding an image like this:
	
	`<img src="cruel_hunter.jpg"/>`
	
	...write it like this:
	
	`<img src="cruel_hunter.jpg" alt="Hunter making his kill" />`

Submit to search engines and online directories	Make sure your site is listed wherever possible. Most hosting packages provide an automated SE-submission facility, which will automatically forward your site to search engines for indexing.
Read up on and contribute to lists, forums, and online tutorials	There is a lot of helpful information out there. Do some research and come up with an SEO policy that is right for you.

The **XML Sitemap** module that automatically generates a sitemap according to the `sitemaps.org` specification should really have been mentioned in the second to last entry of this table—**Submit to search engines and online directories**. However, given its importance for the major search engines, I would prefer to mention it like this:

Submitting a site map is highly recommended (by Google amongst others) for controlling and improving the efficiency of how your site is indexed by major search engines—a must for Drupal SEO.

The **XML Sitemap** module generates a sitemap automatically upon installation, so it is left as an exercise to download and install this module. There are a number of additional features that are provided along with the sitemap creation, so take a moment to look around this before submitting your sitemap to the search engines.

Possibly the single most important thing you can do to promote a website (and this is not specifically related to SEO) is to get other people talking about it. You need to create a buzz by getting well known bloggers or subject experts to talk about it (and link to you in the process). Even if it means talking about them, cajoling and stroking their egos—most popular bloggers are keenly aware of the value that their links or reviews hold for other sites.

Bloggers are not the be all and end all either—there are plenty of review sites that specifically look to write reviews about up-and-coming, exciting websites. Finding and engaging with them is a worthwhile endeavor.

Social media sites are also a good place to go—mentioning your blog on Digg or saving it to LinkDoozer exposes your pages to a whole new target audience.

Online networks can also be invaluable and you should consider joining sites like LinkedIn in order to meet other people with similar business interests who may be willing to join in strategic partnerships with you.

Writing articles and submitting them to directories or news sites can also have an impact on your traffic. Creating a newsletter or RSS feed also serves to create a more tangible link with the users who do visit your site, and RSS feeds in particular can have quite far reaching effects if they are picked up by a variety of aggregators.

Upgrades

From time to time it becomes necessary to upgrade your installation of Drupal in order to keep your site up-to-speed and trouble free. As of Drupal 6, the **Update Status** module ships as part of the core and is an extremely useful tool for keeping up-to-date because it notifies you any time it detects a possible or required Drupal update. Actually, this goes for each contribution too—modules and themes are also under constant development (well, many of them) and the **Available updates** page under reports will notify you of any and all outstanding and important changes:

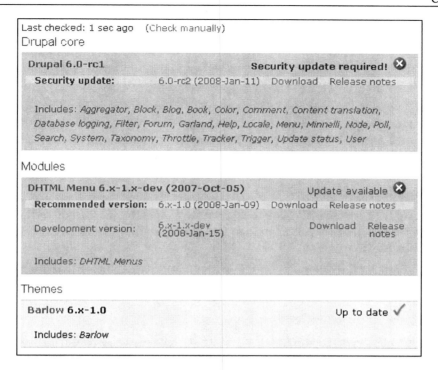

Last checked: 1 sec ago   (Check manually)
Drupal core

Drupal 6.0-rc1   **Security update required!** ⊗
  Security update: 6.0-rc2 (2008-Jan-11)   Download   Release notes

  Includes: *Aggregator, Block, Blog, Book, Color, Comment, Content translation,*
  Database logging, Filter, Forum, Garland, Help, Locale, Menu, Minnelli, Node, Poll,
  Search, System, Taxonomy, Throttle, Tracker, Trigger, Update status, User

Modules

DHTML Menu 6.x-1.x-dev (2007-Oct-05)   Update available ⊗
  Recommended version: 6.x-1.0 (2008-Jan-09) Download   Release notes

  Development version: 6.x-1.x-dev   Download   Release
                         (2008-Jan-15)   notes

  Includes: *DHTML Menus*

Themes

Barlow 6.x-1.0   Up to date ✓

  Includes: *Barlow*

Every now and then, for example, a security issue may be identified and it is important to upgrade in order to avoid falling prey to malicious hacking—in this case, the report will tell you in no uncertain terms, **Security update required**.

All software, proprietary or open source, have weaknesses. Weaknesses are something you are not able to escape. What counts is how they are dealt with once they are found. In the case of Drupal, there is an entire community of people watching for bugs, reporting them, fixing them, and then offering the solutions to all users.

Upgrading Drupal

Should it be necessary, it is important you know what to do in order to result in a painless upgrade. With Drupal, the process is fairly simple, but before we look at it, I should warn you:

 If you are using a theme other than the default, it is possible that your site may suffer some unusual effects. It may be best to revert to the default theme before performing an upgrade.

Let's continue:

1. Make a backup of your current database so that all the information added by users, as well as any configuration changes you have implemented, are saved.

2. Back up the old files to somewhere else on your filesystem, especially those that have important changes and settings like your stylesheet, **altered themes,** or the configuration file contained in the sites/default/directory.

3. If you are upgrading on a live site, log in as the site administrator (user number 1) and put the system into **Maintenance** mode in the **Site maintenance** section.

4. Unpack all the new files – keeping any site specific files intact in the **sites** directory (otherwise, you lose all the information built up in the **themes** and **modules** directories).

5. Navigate to the Drupal homepage and run the update.php script by accessing it from the browser. For example, the demo site's update page would be http://localhost/mf4good/update.php. This will bring up a page of notes as follows:

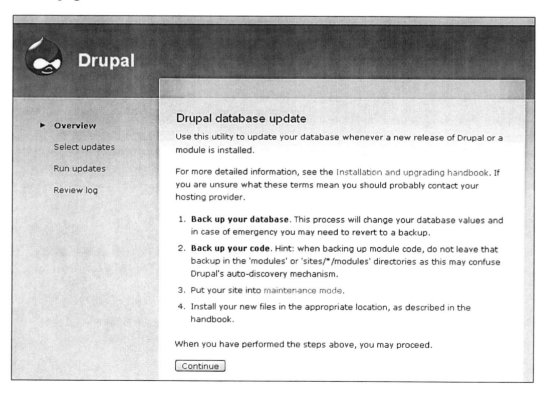

6. Read through these notes before clicking the **Continue** button to ensure you perform all the tasks that may be required.

7. Following on, a list of the possible updates that can be implemented will be displayed:

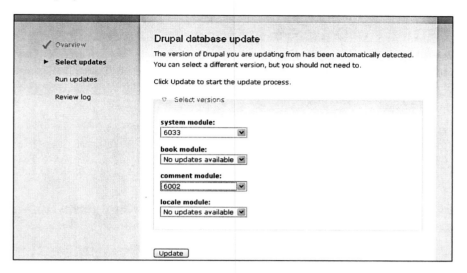

8. Click **Update** – there should rarely be a reason for making changes to the updates selected. If everything goes well, you should see a list of updates that were performed, along with the status of those operations; something like this:

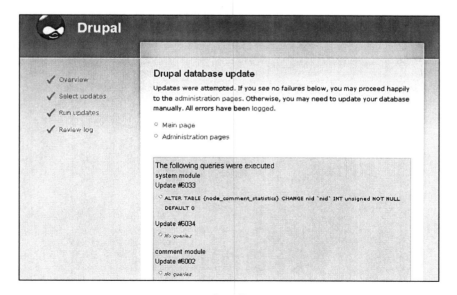

From this, you can see that there were a few alterations to the current database to bring it in line with the newer version. More importantly, no errors were reported so we can now take the site out of maintenance mode and continue on as normal. That is, until the next time...

Upgrading Modules

With time, modules also need to undergo upgrades and, as mentioned earlier, Drupal will inform you whenever a module is outdated or an upgrade is required for security purposes. These warnings will be displayed at the top of the page and look something like this:

There are updates available for one or more of your modules or themes. To ensure the proper functioning of your site, you should update as soon as possible. See the available updates page for more information.

Clicking on the **available updates** link that leads to **Available updates** page in the **Reports** section demonstrates that all is not well at the moment:

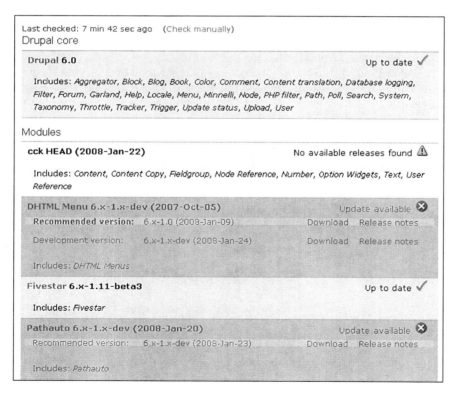

In this case, both **DHTML Menu** and **Pathauto** are outdated, so we will need to follow the standard procedure for safely upgrading each of these modules (it's fairly similar to backing up the site as a whole):

1. Make a backup of your current database (sometimes a module may not need to make any changes to the database—but, better safe than sorry) so that all the information added by users as well as any configuration changes you have implemented are saved.

2. Select the best upgrade option (in the **DHTML Menu** case this would be the **6.x-1.0** version—that is recommended). Remember to favor official releases over development releases because these will (hopefully) be more stable.

3. Unpack all the new files into the **modules** directory under **sites/default** (or wherever you have saved the other contribs).

4. Read through the INSTALL.txt and README.txt files that come with the module to see if there are any special notes or issues with the new contrib..

5. Run the update.php script to execute any required updates to the system. If all goes well, you be presented with a far prettier **Available updates** page:

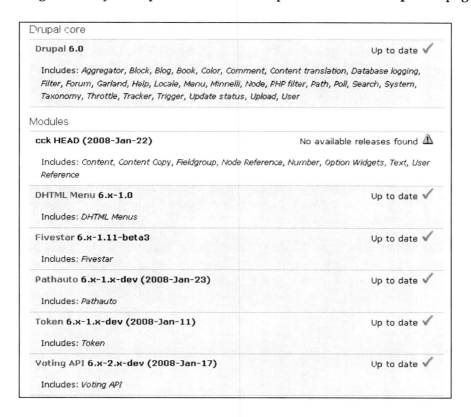

Remember that any errors that occur during the update process should be logged, and you can review them in the **Reports** section at the **Recent log entries** page.

There is another valuable source of information you should look at, whenever you need to make an upgrade, namely the Drupal site itself: `http://drupal.org/upgrade/`. This page contains useful notes and version-specific issues and instructions that could come in handy.

Summary

This chapter has rounded off the picture painted by the rest of the book by taking a look at some of the most important website-related chores that you will have to undertake. Knowing how to make backups at the click of a button will be an invaluable tool in the coming weeks and months as you develop and maintain a fledgling site or two.

Ensuring the cron script is run on a regular basis is also part and parcel of maintaining a healthy Drupal system and you saw how to access and edit the crontab manually or by using the host's GUI.

Implementing a user and search engine friendly site is one of the most important things you can do to get your new site noticed. **Path** and **Pathauto** can help to make URLs easier to read and parse for humans and bots alike. Submitting a site map will also go a long way in ensuring that the major search engines index your content correctly and efficiently.

Finally, keeping your site up to date with the latest core distribution and modules is extremely important for a variety of reasons. The process for both was outlined, and with a bit of practice, you should find that everything goes like clockwork.

With the end of this chapter, we come to the end of the book. For those of you who now need to upload your new site, your live domain, the appendix contains further instructions on deployment.

Congratulations on finishing the book, and I wish you all the best in your future endeavors on the Web. Please remember to take the time to give back to the Drupal community so that it can continue to flourish and help others.

A
Deployment

By the end of this appendix, your site will be live, and only a few minor deployment issues remain. Actually, that's not quite true! I should make it clear that there's nothing particularly complex about deployment; it's just that you need to keep on top of a lot of different issues. Making silly errors at this stage can have dramatic effects on the final product because we are dealing mainly with configuration issues when we deploy a fully developed application. Of course, making errors is not the end of the world, because we are going to test everything very thoroughly.

At first glance, deploying a site like Drupal has got to be pretty easy — it's just a case of copying the `drupal` folder over to the new server, right? There are a number of concerns that go hand-in-hand with ensuring everything goes smoothly during the transfer. For example, the database will also have to be rebuilt exactly as it is on the development machine — I'm sure that because most of you have spent some time configuring everything and populating tables, you'll be anxious to not have to do everything all over again. Apart from this, there are the connection parameters and some security issues to think about.

Specifically, the appendix looks at how to:

- Get everything ready for deployment
- Transfer the files to their new home
- Set up the site, including the database
- Test everything thoroughly

Chin up, we're nearly at the end; and it hasn't been all that bad, has it?

Getting Ready to Deploy

First thing's first — are you completely happy with the site as it is? While it is not a huge problem to make modifications after deployment, there is no point in making things difficult by having to recode some pages or make design changes later, when you can get them done now.

Here is a checklist to use in order to ensure that, from a user's point of view, the site works nicely:

Site Checklist

Use at least two different browsers.	One browser may implement some features that others do not—you might find that something you rely on heavily works on your browser of choice but not on others.	[ ]
Resize your browsers for a variety of pages.	This helps to determine whether you have HTML elements that have not been set correctly. For example, some section may use the full page width, while others expand only to a certain limit.	[ ]
Access pages from slow as well as fast connections.	You might find that certain pages load very slowly over a dial-up connection. This might mean you need to rethink image and page sizes.	[ ]
Check all links—text and image.	Often, links break during deployment because of differing file paths and so forth. You should: • Check all links and buttons on each page. • Check all links in blocks. • Check that large as well as small images display appropriately. • Check that any ads link correctly.	[ ]
Check each page's look.	Important, because not all browsers can render certain style sheet settings.	[ ]
Use each page.	This is vital for ensuring that users can: • Register accounts • Manage their accounts • Add content depending on permissions • Correctly access content depending on their roles • Make use of all the site's facilities	[ ]
	Ensure that: • The search engine works correctly • Contact emails can be sent properly • Privacy and conditions of use are shown along with any important copyright information.	
Try to break the site (as a restricted user, of course).	Just as important as ensuring everything works properly (if not more important), is ensuring that nothing can be broken at will.	[ ]

If you can perform everything listed in this checklist with several browsers, with no problems, then you can be reasonably certain that the site will hold up when it goes live. If everything is in order, then we can begin with the preparation process. Preparation comes in three stages. In no particular order, we need to ensure that we have a nice, clean, working version of the site, a nice, clean working copy of the database, and finally, a nice, clean file system ready for the files on the host site. Let's take a look at how this is done.

Make Sure the Host is Ready

Intuitively enough, you have to make sure you have an adequate host. By this, I mean you have a host on which you can *create a MySQL database*, and that allows *access to a file system*, and whatever other goodies you think are needed. To make life easy, it is important to have an FTP account available to transfer files across to the host file system. More often than not, you should be able to log onto the FTP account with your administrator's username and password automatically.

To test this out, try and navigate to the following URL:

```
ftp://ftp.your_domain_name.com
```

If you are prompted for a password or are shown the contents of the home directory, then congratulations, there is an FTP account available. If you don't have one, then consider getting one from your ISP, or finding out from them how they upload files. Incidentally, instead of being prompted for a username and password every time, you might want to send them in the URL, like so:

```
ftp://username:password@hostname/
```

If you're worried about security (by this, I mean: you *are* worried about security), then it's best to leave out the password and simply pass the username, because otherwise this can cause security problems if URLs are logged in a non-secure place. Remember that this information is already being passed in an unencrypted format. If you wish to do everything securely, speak to your host about how to secure file transfers.

If you don't have access to an FTP account, then don't panic. Read the section entitled *Transfer the Files* a little later on in this Appendix — it will still be easy to move your files to the host site. However, no FTP account may be an indication of a poor service, so be careful to ensure that everything else required is available.

Now that there is somewhere to upload the Drupal files to, and something to do it with, you need to create a database. The process for creating a new database and user account varies widely from host to host, so we won't discuss every possibility here.

Take a look at the administrative interface and see if there is a section for creating and controlling MySQL databases (hopefully, phpMyAdmin is available). For example, the demo site's host has the following **Manage Mysql** link in the **Databases** section that provides an interface used to create databases. It also provides phpMyAdmin in order to administer those databases:

Clicking on the **Manage MySQL** link brings up the following page. Once the database is created, make note of its name—often hosts will append something to the name you choose, as shown here in the demo site's database creation interface:

This database has been called **wwwlink_mf4good**, where **mf4good** is the name I chose for the live database, and **wwwlink_** is the part that was added. Before we continue, it is important to note that this database needs a valid user, so ensure that it has one as shown here:

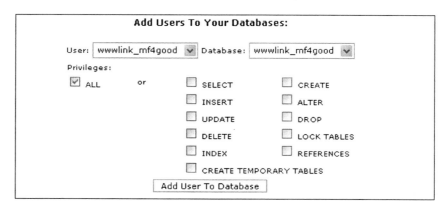

In this case, the **wwwlink_mf4good** database now has the user **wwwlink_mf4good** (it's not necessary to specify the same name, any one will do), and with that, the host site is pretty much ready to receive the new Drupal website. Take note:

 Drupal needs almost all privileges available to a database user. Ensure that you grant **ALL** privileges here, otherwise there may be problems down the line.

Remember, these usernames, passwords, and database names are all important for the configuration of the site, so don't forget any of them.

If you get stuck, get help from the host's support team; that's what they are there for.

Get the Files Ready

Before transferring anything, make a master copy of the site. ZIP up and store the exact version of the `drupal` directory that you send across.

 At the moment, the target URL for the Drupal index page will be something like: `http://www.domain_name.com/drupal/`. If you want it to be `http://www.domain_name.com/`, then ZIP the files without the parent directory so that files are extracted directly to the `public_html` folder on the live site.

While we are on the subject, you may as well clean up the Drupal file system properly, so that you don't end up saving erroneous files.

Access your site from a browser and perform the following four important tasks:

1. *Disable all caching and clear all caches* — hopefully, these haven't been enabled during development anyway.

2. *Disable clean URLs* — in case the new server isn't set up correctly. You can enable it later.

3. *Set any logging options (such as database logging) to small values and run cron* — to clear out old log files that are no longer needed and cut down on transfer size.

4. *Remove redundant posts* — try not to transfer over a whole lot of stuff that will be deleted anyway.

Next, focus on the actual file system. If you're like me, then you probably create backups of all the modified files as you work. As far as Windows machines go, these are denoted by `.bak`, and placed in the same folder as the original file. Make a backup of your `drupal` folder before deleting anything, just to be safe. Then, remove all backup files from the `drupal` folders.

While it might seem a bit excessive to do this at the moment, there are a couple of good reasons for it. First, having any sort of unused files lying around on your host file system is poor security practice. Second, why clutter up a brand-new installation with files you don't need? Working on a lot of files over the course of the development phase, adding and removing functionality, and so on, adds a lot of unnecessary size to the upload if you don't trim away what isn't needed.

Now, open up the configuration file, `settings.php`, and remove the username and password. The current database name and password will change to the ones set when you created a new database on the host, but there is no point in transferring any type of sensitive information like this—especially because people often prefer to use the same username and password for a variety of things.

Once this is done, you have to wait until the next section to add one more file, and you can then make a master, zipped copy of your Drupal site—call it RTP (Release to Public) or something similar to distinguish it from other versions.

If you are working on a Linux box, you can **tar** and **gzip** your files instead—doing so will help with the upload time. If you are developing on Windows, then you might want to make sure that your host can unzip `.zip` files because they will more than likely be using a Linux server—there shouldn't be a problem, however. In the unlikely event that there is, the best thing to do is download and install a gzip utility for Windows at `http://www.gzip.org/`, which you can then use to ZIP up files in the `.gz` format.

Get the Database Ready

In order to deploy the database, there must be a backup of it. It is this backup file that is transferred across to the host site and used to create a new database there. As you already have all the information you need regarding backups (from Chapter 10), we need look at them no further here.

With the backup file of the entire Drupal added somewhere to the `drupal` folder (anywhere will do, so long as you can find it again), you are now ready to begin transferring files across to the host. Remove the `.sql` file from the site as soon as it has been used—hold it somewhere out of the document root in case you need to use it again.

Transfer the Files

You should now have a final, clean version of the site, with a copy of the database, all zipped up and ready to go. Assuming there are images and a fair bit of data held within the site, you can be sure that the size of the upload is quite substantial. For this reason, you need a reasonably high speed connection—dial-up connections can be slightly erratic over long periods of time, so it may even be worth using a friend's computer (or your office connection) to send the files to the host site via a broadband connection.

By far, the easiest method would be to use a native upload feature from the host's file manager over a quick connection. If this is available, simply use it to upload the archive file across to the host server. The demo site has this facility, as shown here:

File uploads are restricted to prevent account issues caused by exceeding your file system quota

Current available free-space: Unlimited MB
Maximum file size for upload: 0 MB
Required free space after upload: 5.00 MB (Default 5MB)

Please select files to upload to /home/wwwlink/public_html

cs\mf4good_RTM.tar.gz	Browse...		Browse...		Browse...
	Browse...		Browse...		Browse...
	Browse...		Browse...		Browse...
	Browse...		Browse...		Browse...

Overwrite existing files: ☐
Upload

Back to /home/wwwlink/public_html

Notice that the ZIP file is being uploaded to the public_html folder, because this is the document root from which all web pages on this server are served.

Alternatively, assuming your site has an FTP account enabled, either attempt to use FTP drag-and-drop, which is exactly the same as moving files around on your PC in Windows, or make use of an FTP utility.

When in doubt, simply get in touch with your host service and ask them for information about how to transfer files. The administrative interface and file manager for the vast majority of sites are easy to use, and you will have no problems uploading files. Because of this, we won't waste time discussing FTP utilities in detail. Simply ensure that, ultimately, the ZIP or gzip file ends up in the document root of your host's server.

Remember not to leave the ZIP folder lying around in the document root once it has been used.

Setting Up the Site

At this stage, there is a working database with a username and password, and the archive file has been uploaded to the host site. At last, we finally move from working on the development machine to working on the live site. First thing's first though; we need to...

Set Up the Files

Extract the archive file to the `public_html` folder—most likely your hosts will provide native ZIP functionality. (If there is no way to decompress files, then transfer files over without compression). Take note of the second option in the list shown here:

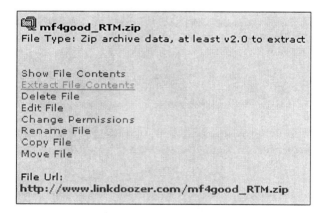

With these files extracted, there is now a replica of the files from the development machine on the host's site. Check this by browsing through the live site—you should find that if any attempt to browse one of the pages no longer results in a "page-not-found error", but some other type of error—most likely a MySQL error because we don't have a database connection yet.

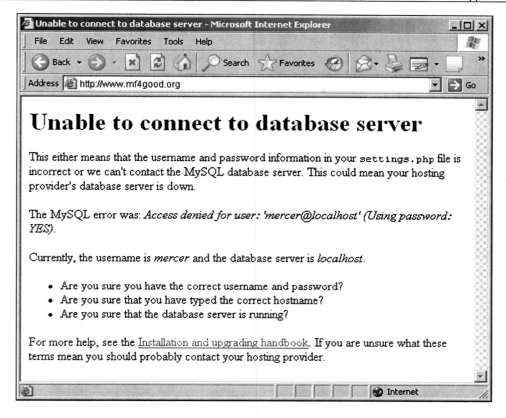

This is great news because it means that we are able to browse the files that are now on the live site with no problem. The fact that there is a Drupal error message here confirms that we are in fact browsing Drupal pages — note that the error message shown in the previous screenshot mentions a username that is not correct. This is here to demonstrate more clearly that we are browsing Drupal, but we have not yet entered the correct database or configuration settings.

Set Up the Database

If you have access to phpMyAdmin on the host site, then open it up and follow along:

1. In the left-hand panel on the phpMyAdmin homepage, click on the name of the database installed earlier. (Recall that for the demo site, this was entitled `wwwlink_mf4good`.)

2. In the new page that opens up, click on the **Import** tab along the top of the page.

3. Click **Browse** for the **Location of the text file** option.

4. Locate the database backup file to run against the database, and click **Go** as shown here:

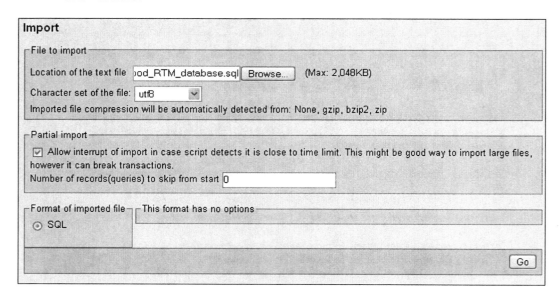

Assuming the file executes successfully, you can now take a look through phpMyAdmin to ensure that the database has got whatever tables are needed.

In the event that something goes wrong, ensure that the backup file was created with utf8 encoding and that the version of MySQL being used is sufficient for Drupal 6 (Discussed in the **Requirements** section of INSTALL.txt within the Drupal download).

If phpMyAdmin is not available, then install the database using the .sql file in whatever manner is appropriate for your particular site. Recall that the .sql file can be run from the command line if you have access to that—if not, it's time to get in touch with the support team and find out how they recommend populating the database.

Configure the Site

With the database in place, go back to the settings.php file in the sites/default/ folder on your live site and alter it according to the live system's setup—ensure that you add precisely the names and passwords required by your *live database* to $db_url.

File permissions on this file may prevent you from accessing it initially. Take note of the permission settings before altering them to allow you to edit its information. As soon as you are done, return the permission settings to their original state — to prevent others writing to the file.

Once the configuration settings are set appropriately, try browsing some pages. With a bit of luck, you will see everything more or less as it was on the development machine.

Access Problem?

Try to log into the administrator's account. I suspect that more than a few of you will come across a somewhat nasty surprise in that the browser will, no doubt, tell you that it cannot find the page you are looking for. If this is the case, it is more than likely because the .htaccess file was not successfully ported to the live site:

 You must ensure that Drupal's .htaccess *file is present on the live site!* .htaccess in the Drupal parent folder contains instructions and information vital to the healthy operation of the site. Ensure that you transfer it directly, or cut and paste its contents into the live site's .htaccess file.

When viewing the contents of the .htaccess file on the live site (most likely in the document root depending on how things are set up), you should see something like this:

```
#
# Apache/PHP/Drupal settings:
#

# Protect files and directories from prying eyes.
<FilesMatch "\.(engine|inc|info|install|module|profile|po|schema|sh|.*
sql|theme|tpl(\.php)?|xtmpl)$|^(code-style\.pl|Entries.*|Repository|Ro
ot|Tag|Template)$">
  Order allow,deny
</FilesMatch>

# Don't show directory listings for URLs which map to a directory.
Options -Indexes

# Follow symbolic links in this directory.
Options +FollowSymLinks

# Customized error messages.
```

```
ErrorDocument 404 /index.php

# Set the default handler.
DirectoryIndex index.php
. . .
```

If that is the case, then it should be possible to browse the live site as normal. Now that pages can be browsed, it's time to quickly re-enable any important settings that were disabled for deployment—such as caching, logging, and even clean URLS.

If you experience problems with the site once clean URLs are enabled, then it is possible that you can make some modifications to .htaccess in order to get things working. Please view the Drupal documentation at http://drupal.org/node/15365 for more information.

The only thing left on the list of things to do now is…

Testing

What is the goal of testing in this instance? Well, between now and the end of the appendix, we want to go from where we are (thinking everything is working) to *knowing* we have a fully functional, and most importantly, *live and operational* site. In order to get there, we need to ensure not only that everything works as expected from the customer's point of view, but also that the site is properly implemented and that we can administer it with no problems.

To give you an example of the type of thing that might rear its ugly head, take a look at the following error message I received the first time I tried to do a bit of administration on the live site:

- The directory *files* is not writable
- warning: mkdir(C:\apache2triad\temp): Permission denied in /home/contechj/public_html/includes/file.inc on line 91.
- The directory C:\apache2triad\temp does not exist.

Can you spot the problem straight away? Drupal is complaining that it cannot write to a files directory that should be contained within C:\apache2triad\temp. It's not surprising that this should be the case, because on the live site, *there is no* C:\apache2triad\temp directory. In fact, the only reason this fully qualified path is here is because I initially enabled the private download method (to a folder outside the document root), despite the fact that public access to files is suitable.

This means that we need to re-enter the settings that were made with the development machine in mind to reflect the specifics of the live system:

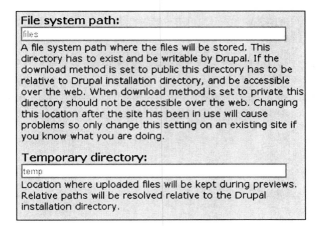

Assuming the requisite permissions are set so that Drupal can write and read in these folders, this particular problem is solved. (If you already have files on the site, then you might need to move them to the directory specified here.)

Now, all that's left is to test out everything else in the administration tool to ensure it works correctly, as well as redo the *Site Checklist* shown earlier in the Appendix to confirm that users will not encounter any problems when browsing. Often, users will find a way to encounter problems and providing a webmaster's email address is a good way to let them complain if they do. Open lines of communication between you and your users will help foster strong ties and improve the quality of your site.

Before we finally finish, there is one last thing that is yet to be done. Can you guess what it is? I'm sure you remembered to set the cron…

Summary

For a task as important as building a full-featured community-driven website, it is necessary to spend a lot of time considering your options, and developing and testing the new site. As it is not really feasible to do this sort of work on the live site, a development machine is required. The topic of deployment is therefore an important one in the overall scheme of things because it is deployment that links the development to the final, live product.

This chapter outlined a solid deployment process. It was also necessary to set up a new database on the host site, but this proved to be relatively easy because any good host makes the task fairly simple by providing a tool like phpMyAdmin to work with.

Hopefully, you came to realize that the deployment process itself is not particularly complex for a Drupal site, because the only real configuration work that needs to be done is modifying the `settings.php` file to reflect the new system's configuration. Having the complexity of the site's deployment reduced to configuring a single file is a real advantage for Drupal users.

While the actual deployment of the site is fairly simple, it was shown that there were quite a few issues to deal with, and not the least of them is testing. It is critical that a full suite of tests is carried out on any site before it goes live — losing valuable users to silly errors is the last thing that any competitive site needs.

That's it, we are all done. Thanks for joining me and I hope you enjoyed and continue to enjoy working with Drupal.

All the best.

Index

FTP used 349
FireFox browser **244**

G

GIF, image types 237
GIF image file format 237

H

htdocs folder 37
HTML
  about 222
  attributes 223, 224
  features 222
  tags 223, 224

I

input formats, content posting
  filter, types 216
  filtered HTML input format 216
  HTML corrector 216
  HTML filter 216, 218
  image files, displaying within posts 219
  line break converter 217
  PHP code input format 219, 221
  PHP evaluator 219, 221
  PHP filter 219
  spam link deterrent tool 218
  URL filter 217, 218

J

JPG, image types 237
JPG image file format 237
jQuery
  basics 301
  CSS style selector 302

L

language support
  content translation 285
  locale module 276
  localization 276
localization
  about 276
  language, adding 276

M

menus, Drupal
  adding 86
  configuring 85
  demo site 85
  navigation menu 85
  pimary links menu 85
  primary links menu, configuring 88-92
  secondary links menu 85
  secondary links menu, configuring 94, 95
  settings 86
modules, Drupal
  about 59
  adding 60, 61
  configuring 66, 67
  DHTML menu module 62
  e-Commerce module 63
  forum module, configuring 67-72
  forum module, demo site 68
  third party module 61
  upgrading 340, 341
  version issues 62
MySQL 33
mysqldump utility 319

N

news ticker,Drupal
  content, adding 309
  obtaining 307, 308
  scrolling 306
nodes 152

O

OpenID
  about 268
  modules 268
  OpenID login page 270
OpenID module 269, 272

P

path
  about 324
  new alias, creating 325
  URL aliases, adding 324

Thank you for buying
Building powerful and robust websites with Drupal 6

Packt Open Source Project Royalties

When we sell a book written on an Open Source project, we pay a royalty directly to that project. Therefore by purchasing Building powerful and robust websites with Drupal 6, Packt will have given some of the money received to the Drupal Project.

In the long term, we see ourselves and you — customers and readers of our books — as part of the Open Source ecosystem, providing sustainable revenue for the projects we publish on. Our aim at Packt is to establish publishing royalties as an essential part of the service and support a business model that sustains Open Source.

If you're working with an Open Source project that you would like us to publish on, and subsequently pay royalties to, please get in touch with us.

Writing for Packt

We welcome all inquiries from people who are interested in authoring. Book proposals should be sent to authors@packtpub.com. If your book idea is still at an early stage and you would like to discuss it first before writing a formal book proposal, contact us; one of our commissioning editors will get in touch with you.

We're not just looking for published authors; if you have strong technical skills but no writing experience, our experienced editors can help you develop a writing career, or simply get some additional reward for your expertise.

About Packt Publishing

Packt, pronounced 'packed', published its first book "Mastering phpMyAdmin for Effective MySQL Management" in April 2004 and subsequently continued to specialize in publishing highly focused books on specific technologies and solutions.

Our books and publications share the experiences of your fellow IT professionals in adapting and customizing today's systems, applications, and frameworks. Our solution-based books give you the knowledge and power to customize the software and technologies you're using to get the job done. Packt books are more specific and less general than the IT books you have seen in the past. Our unique business model allows us to bring you more focused information, giving you more of what you need to know, and less of what you don't.

Packt is a modern, yet unique publishing company, which focuses on producing quality, cutting-edge books for communities of developers, administrators, and newbies alike. For more information, please visit our website: www.PacktPub.com.

Drupal 5 Themes

ISBN: 978-1-847191-82-3   Paperback: 250 pages

Create a new theme for your Drupal website with a clean layout and powerful CSS styling

1. Learn to create new Drupal 5 Themes

2. No experience of Drupal 5 theming required

3. Set up and configure themes

4. Understand Drupal 5's themeable functions

Selling Online with Drupal e-Commerce

ISBN: 978-1-847194-06-0   Paperback: 264 pages

Walk through the creation of an online store with Drupal's e-Commerce module

1. Set up a basic Drupal system and plan your shop

2. Set up your shop, and take payments

3. Optimize your site for selling and better reporting

4. Manage and market your site

Please check **www.PacktPub.com** for information on our titles